THEY ARE COMING FOR YOUR CHILDREN

THE FIGHT WE MUST WIN!

DRENDA KEESEE

WHAT PEOPLE ARE SAYING ABOUT
THEY ARE COMING FOR YOUR CHILDREN: THE FIGHT WE MUST WIN!

They Are Coming For Your Children: The Fight We Must Win! by warrior mom Pastor Drenda Keesee, brings her heart of Deborah and a powerful presence of The Holy Spirit to expose and annihilate the enemy's most deadly strategy of creating deception in the hearts and minds of our children. Our children exposed to early life Adverse Childhood Events (ACEs) are more likely to have poor emotional and physical health as adults. This has an acute impact and a negative chronic impact on their overall health.

Children being exposed to highly stressful virtual environments creates total havoc. From a brain physiology standpoint, exposure to "mature content" at an early age (or any age for that matter) creates a post-traumatic stress disorder. Neurochemicals in the brain (Dopamine and others) increase and release the stress hormone cortisol, which can hijack one's sense of equilibrium and stability in their emotional and physical environment. This causes problems with memory and learning. Emotional resilience is also greatly diminished which leads to an inability to problem-solve and to maintain focus in new or challenging environments. MRI images taken from the brains of people with post-traumatic stress disorder (PTSD) have demonstrated a reduction in the volume of the hippocampus (major memory brain organ) along with neurophysiologic effects such as a weak verbal memory.

This creates, in our children, a sense of loss of awareness of self, learned values, and contextual understanding of the relevance of right and wrong when juxtaposed or compared to the world around them.

Drenda Keesee exposes this exploitation of our children and gives practical examples and direction from the Word of God and her experience as a Pastor of young and old people alike! This book is life-saving and accurate. Every person needs a copy of this book to be emboldened to take back the battlefield for our children's hearts and minds. Another job well done!

—Avery M. Jackson III MD, Neurosurgeon, Founder/
CEO Michigan Neurosurgical Institute PC, The God
Prescription LLC, The Bodyhealthcare PBO

Drenda Keesee's book, *They Are Coming For Your Children: The Fight We Must Win!* is the signs of the times book that you've been waiting for. With extensive research to back up her claims, this book is a wake-up call to fight like heaven to protect the children's innocence and help them know their God-given identity. It's a charge for God's people to get off the couch and on our knees to preserve our inalienable rights and change the nation for the sake of our children and the future of our world.

—Michele Bachmann, J.D., LL.M., Regent University
Dean of the Robertson School of Government R–
Minnesota, District 6 110th-113th (2007-2015)

The book of Judges tells us that Israel would not fight until Deborah arose to the battle. Drenda Keesee hears that call to battle once again for the children and shares the strategy on defeating the enemy's agenda to destroy our youngest generation. Her fact-laden book, "They Are Coming For Your Children," will compel you to go and save the children.

—Joni Lamb, Daystar Television Network

This book is a must-read for any parent, grandparent, or parent-to-be. Drenda Keesee is an anointed truth-teller. In this book, she exposes the depravity and utter darkness of this age in which we live, where the in-your-face immorality that saturates our current culture has a laser focus on our children. Drenda clearly pulls back the curtain to reveal how an insidious evil has sought to penetrate every aspect of our education system, our healthcare system, our ability to provide parental oversight and shelter, and even God's perfect design for sexual purity and gender identity—all systems meant to protect and shepherd our children—now being weaponized to destroy them emotionally and spiritually. She does not shrink back from waking us up and equipping us to stand firm and take back the ground that our children walk upon.

—Colleen Wilcox, Center for Christian
Virtue, Senior Development Officer,
Public Policy, Warrior Mom

Most of us used to think people were pretty moral at their core. Crazy things like child abductions and child trafficking were only in other countries and only in the most destitute environments. Now, parents and grandparents everywhere are in shock and disbelief as we see news reports from the border of prostitution and child slavery. But it isn't just at the border. It's in our middle and upper-class neighborhoods. It's happening right before our eyes, and we didn't even see it. And yes, even the church has become vulnerable, right under our noses. There seems to be no limit to the depravity of those who would harm our children.

Interviewing Tim Ballard and Jim Caviezel about *The Sound of Freedom* movie shocked me. Not just because child trafficking was happening here but because there were politicians, actors, corporations, and Hollywood studios that didn't want this even to hit the theaters. Well, the world showed up in a big way. Now this issue is front and center.

However, we cannot foolishly think our work is done because we went to see a movie. This battle is far from over, and we all have a lot of work to do. Drenda Keesee has valiantly picked up the fight in this book. Yes, it is shocking. So, take a deep breath, understand the battle, and get to work. Drenda does an excellent job laying out the roadmap we need to take, and then she equips us with the right spiritual and practical tools to fight the kingdom of darkness. Pray before you read this book and ask God to show you what you can do. Then, as you read this book, you'll see it's time to go fight like heaven!

—Gene Bailey, *FlashPoint* Host

Never has there been a time more urgent when we, as the body of Christ, must take our post and hold our ground. In her book, They Are Coming for Your Children, my friend Drenda Keesee galvanizes mothers and fathers to wage war on the home front —because now, it's personal!

—John Bevere, Best-selling Author and Minister
Co-founder of Messenger International & MessengerX

As a parent and now grandparent, I have known first hand the challenges we face when we dare speak up! Drenda Keesee, points out the concerns of raising kids in these evil times and gives parents the facts about what will happen to our children if we choose to not fight back on the enemy's agenda. The book is based on science, polls, studies, and above all, God's Word. Should we choose to be silent, the outcome is the loss of our children. *They Are Coming For Your Children* is filled with powerful information, and it is a practical manual on how to protect our children from being indoctrinated in this world's corrupt views. It is a fight we must fight together and win!

—Tina Konkin, Registered Professional Counselor,
Relationships Matter tinakonkin.com

I asked my husband, Gene Bailey, what he thought the number one thing going on right now was the most concerning to Jesus. Without hesitation, he said, "the children." Drenda knows and has the heart of the Father. In her newest book, *They Are Coming For Your Children: The Fight We Must Win!*, Drenda makes an intelligent analysis of all the current events that are aimed at the destruction of your children. She gives you yet another "deep dive" into the many plots and methods they use to attack our children and lineage. You might want to ask yourself, *why*? The obvious reason is that they are made in the image of God. The enemy loathes and wishes to destroy anything that looks like and sounds like our Creator. Drenda has nailed it in her book and points out that our culture has become hostile to anything remotely linked to God.

The challenge Drenda poses to you, is now that she has laid out the obvious evil agenda against the most innocent and weakest of our population, will you join the fight for them? Will you be like Deborah, Jael and Drenda– warriors for God? Will you do all you can with every available resource you have to fight for God's children, our children and grandchildren? There is absolutely no more looking the other way. You are either part of the problem or part of the solution. Which side do you fall on? Join Drenda and us in the battle of a lifetime with eternal consequences for our children and for God's children. This is truly a Fight that we MUST win!

—Teri Bailey, *Flashpoint* Army

If there is anyone I know who has the experience, maturity, insight, and wisdom to write this book, it is Drenda Keesee. *They Are Coming For Your Children* is a must for every parent. Although it is a hard-hitting subject, even unpopular and misunderstood today, Drenda is not afraid to expose it for what it is. Drenda is right to call it for what it is—a spiritual battle. Our enemy has the evil intent to destroy your kids through the lie of false sexuality of their identity. Our children and grandchildren are being wrecked by this evil agenda that is sweeping the world by storm. Romans, Chapter 1, lays it out very well, and we are living in those days. These days, like never before, children are exposed to and are vulnerable to the most hideous, harmful manipulation of a seduced society.

Today's fruit is pretty clear: We have produced a messed up generation, and it is not getting better but worse by the day. Drenda tells it as it is, no holds barred, to push back and turn the tide for your children's sake. As a modern-day Deborah, she has a passion, a godly conviction, a holy calling, and an anointing to stand up and speak out for the sake of this and the coming generations. Knowing her family personally, I can say without a doubt Drenda has the fruit of a hugely successful mum of 5 great adult kids, a beloved grandmother of 12, and a spiritual mom to hundreds. Let us not bury our heads in the sand, let us not be ignorant, let us join the good fight, read, and pass this book on.

–Pastor Peter Mortlock, Founding Pastor of City Impact Churches

Drenda Kessee has hit the ball out of the park once again with *They Are Coming For Your Children: The Fight We Must Win!* Her new book is truly a "home run" because victory over the current evil trends in our culture must begin in the home. So many parents are pressured and stressed, barely able to make ends meet and fulfill their basic responsibilities. In desperation, they entrust teachers, daycare workers, technology, and popular figures in the entertainment world with the oversight of their most precious gifts from God—their sons and daughters. Hoping these things will keep their children occupied and impart to them basic, helpful values, too often, quite the opposite happens—and the damage can last a lifetime. Certainly, there are plenty of exceptions to this rule, but negative examples abound.

A tsunami of corruption is cresting over our nation and our world. It is time for those who consider themselves just ordinary Christian parents to be awakened to an extraordinary, parental commitment—truly discipling the next generation. No one will be able to read this book without feeling that conviction and being stirred to move from reaction to action.

Woman of God, you are truly a "Deborah"—raising up an army of Nehemiah-like men who will rebuild the walls around their families and Proverbs 31 women who will model godliness and responsible-living to their offspring. There's an important aspect to this last example that is rarely celebrated. Most Bible readers know the prophesied outcome of the model woman, *"Her children rise up and call her blessed"* (Proverbs 31:28). But let's pause that sentence after the first four words—*"Her children rise up."* That's the most important thing a Proverbs 31 woman can accomplish—motivating her offspring to *"rise up"* to a biblical standard of living and a God-given purpose in their lives. The Jews influenced by Nehemiah responded in a similar way, saying, "*Let us rise up and build*"—and a new day of freedom from tyranny dawned for God's people (Nehemiah 2:18). So, let it come to pass in our day as well, "Let us all rise up, in Jesus name!"

–Mike Shreve, B.Th., D.D., evangelist, revivalist, publisher, founder of "The True Light Project" and "The Catholic Project," author of 17 books, including *65 Promises from God for Your Child* and *WHO AM I? Dynamic Declarations of Who You Are in Christ,* www.shreveministries.org / www.thetruelight.net

Drenda Keesee's compelling work, *They Are Coming for Your Children,* is a strong call to boldness for this fight we must win! The loud, so-obvious-but-almost-unbelievable evil agenda that is *coming for our children* is no longer hiding in the dark, but it's intensifying. This book is a powerful alarm, calling out evil, and stirring us to fight for the sake of every child, the future of our families, our freedom and life as we know it. This book will strengthen and encourage readers to rescue the next generation from being devoured. Drenda reminds us that we are well resourced with God's Strategy and Power over all the power of the enemy and we will win!

—Pastors Tom & Kathy Toney Founders, KUEST Student Leadership, Kuest. Org

THEY ARE COMING FOR YOUR CHILDREN
THE FIGHT WE MUST WIN!

Drenda has taken on the challenge of exposing the truth to the (Christian) World. With our involvement and prayers of protection, she is well able to take this fight to our nation and challenge many who are blind/complacent to wake up! This is the hour of our greatest battle. Drenda is declaring war! D-day is just ahead, and we are in training for the clash of the Titans!

As an intercessor for over 50 years, I have seen this hour coming. As we watch the world falling into great deception, the promise of our Savior's covenant stands as a banner of victory! With fervent and effectual prayer and great bravery, we will overcome, and the gates of hell will not prevail against God's Church, His victorious army!

As Drenda leads the charge, we must fall into battle positions, take up our weapons with bravery, and with faith in God's Word, we must shoot the arrows of scripture to annihilate this malignant aggression upon our children and the future of the world!

Drenda challenges us, as Deborahs and Jaels, to fight and win at all costs! We are called to drive a stake into the mastermind of the forces that are stealing our children! Like Queen Esther, we were born for such a time as this!

—Stephanie Lindsay, Handmaiden of the Lord, intercessor, friend.

There has never been a time like the one we are living in now, and I believe this book is to sound a wake-up call for all who care about the next generation. In the last days, the Bible says that God will raise up a remnant generation who will not bow to the idols of the land. I want my kids to be part of that remnant! As parents, we are called to raise our children with eternity in mind, teaching them the ways of the Lord, and acting as watchmen on the wall. It is so helpful to be aware of the plans of the enemy BEFORE he tries them on our children, and I am thankful that this book gives me inside information so I can protect the ones closest to my heart. After reading this, I have realized that now is not the time to sit back and hope for the best. It's a time to war in the spirit through prayer and to stand guard over the precious souls of this generation! It's a time for mothers and fathers and grandparents to rise and speak out. I'm so thankful that my mother, Drenda Keesee, who is a Deborah to this generation, has raised me with a focus on Jesus and a heart for His Kingdom. I truly would not be here today without her prayers, teaching, and mentorship. It changed my destiny, and I know it will impact your family's destiny, too!

—Amy Keesee Freudiger, pastor, worship leader, author of *The Truth About You: Overcoming the Seven Lies You Believe About Yourself, Healed Overnight* and *30-Day Healing Dare*

Wow! Drenda Keesee has done it again by exposing a silent enemy that has been lurking for years, preying on our most vulnerable—our children. With meticulous research and irrefutable evidence, Drenda exposes the malevolent individuals and organizations who operate and profit from the stolen identities of God's beloved. She shines a light on the disturbing tactics utilized by these villains, leaving no doubt that their intentions are nefarious. In *They Are Coming For Your Children: The Fight We Must Win!* Drenda courageously dives into the harrowing realities and unveils the sinister forces that seek to exploit our children. This book serves as a wake-up call, urging all to take immediate action to shield our children from these predators.

This book doesn't merely expose evil; it will empower you with the knowledge and tools necessary to protect our children. She warns that this is not just a fight for our children but a war for the future of everything we hold sacred and dear. *They Are Coming For Your Children: TheFight We Must Win!* should serve as an indispensable guide and clarion call to protect our children and preserve the values that form the bedrock of our faith and Godly society. Drenda Keesee leaves no room for ambivalence, demanding that we rise up and take a stand. Let this book be the catalyst that propels us into action—the future of our children and everything we cherish depends on it.

—Aaron Ward, Author, Retired Military
and Retired Law Enforcement

As a youth pastor of 12 years, I am positioned front and center in the daily fight for children and young adults. Anxiety, addiction, sexual grooming, suicide, and a whole host of other problems have risen at an astonishing rate and are beginning at earlier and earlier ages.

Drenda Keesee's *They Are Coming For Your Children: TheFight We Must Win!* is educational, practical, and empowering. I encourage all leaders, parents, and young people to read this insightful look into the behind-the-scenes of today's elites and the agendas they are propagating against the next generation. Drenda (who happens to be my mother-in-love) unpacks God's word with spiritual wisdom while exposing darkness and inspiring God's people in a way that only she can. This is a fight we WILL win thanks to Drenda and others like her sounding the alarm.

—Pastor Alecia Keesee, Faith Life Church,
Youth Pastor

As moms, we often focus on the purposes right in front of us—caring for our families, meeting needs at work, and serving at church. We might recognize, in a general sense, that the world is getting darker, but it is also easy to be lulled into a false sense of security—thinking those issues don't affect our neighborhoods, our children's schools, or our homes. Drenda's book, *They Are Coming For Your Children: The Fight We Must Win!,* is both a look into the dark roots of many cultural issues and a timely wake-up call to parents to protect their children from agendas contrary to God's word. As a children's ministry leader, I am especially grateful for Drenda's bold voice and encouragement to raise a generation of Deborahs who will not back down from this fight. Our children need us, and they are worth fighting for.

—Wendy Kirk, Children's Ministry
Coordinator, Faith Life Church

THEY ARE COMING FOR YOUR CHILDREN
THE FIGHT WE MUST WIN!

This book is truly a must read by my friend Drenda Keesee. It is a now and timely word for all of us. It is filled with truth and great insight into what is really taking place with your children and much more. Those who disregard history, will by default, repeat its mistakes. We will win this fight.

—Bernadette Smith, Eternal Word Church,
Co-Pastor Ethnic Vice chair, MIGOP

Drenda Keesee was made for such a time as this! *They Are Coming for Your Children* is a wake-up call to all parents, particularly mothers whom God has anointed to love, care for, and protect their children. In this book, Drenda asks, "Is [God] asking you to do something to help the innocent children who are being captivated by lies from the enemy himself to destroy their futures, their destinies, their God-called purposes?" After reading her book, my answer is a resounding yes! God has entrusted us, the Deoborahs of today, to be ferociously loyal and protective mothers to not only our own children but this entire generation. Children are being brainwashed, mutilated, sex-trafficked, and driven to suicide. Their futures and lives are literally at stake. *They Are Coming for Your Children* reveals what you need to know and how we, as "anointed mamas," can make a difference. As Drenda says, "With God's help, the gates of hell will not withstand us!"

—Amanda Prebble Lenhart, J.D.
Vice-President and Director of The Charles H.
Dater Foundation, Homeschooler and Mama Bear

As the survivors of The Abortion Holocaust, let us speak out with all boldness! Like Moses' mother, let us put our children in a basket to save them! Let us pitch it within and without, that the wickedness of the world does not leak in and fill their lungs with its water. Let us show the world how much we love our children and how far we will go to save them." This book shows the heart of a mother, the heart of a Deborah! May everyone that reads it catch the reality of it. May it spark within the mothers' of our great nation and of the whole world an inspiration to change these dark realities! God grant you strength!

—Prophet Robin D. Bullock

CONTENTS

INTRODUCTION

It is clear we are in a war for the future of everything we hold sacred and dear: our freedom, our justice system, the economy of free enterprise, and, most importantly, our children and grandchildren.

No society has ever existed that did not protect its children. So, when children become targets of moneymaking schemes by the greedy and perverse, that civilization is on the brink of destruction.

The satanic manipulations of youth for profit are the evil roots of a tree that can only be destroyed by the laying of an axe to those roots and eradicating the profiteers. Through fervent intercession of God's people and His divine intervention, we can win this. We are living in that time where God is moving heaven and Earth to bring the culprits of child pornography, child trafficking, abortion, and medical destruction and mutilation of children into daylight. Those who have hearts of gold must bring justice to these evildoers who have hidden behind government, education, and medicine.

This will only be accomplished if you and I raise our voices so loudly that we will not be silenced until they are held accountable and justice is served on a hefty plate.

You are being called to join this fight and destroy the works of darkness.

CHAPTER 1

WHO AM I, MAMA?

"God, raise up the wisdom of mothers! Give mothers the wisdom of Deborah, who was a mother in Israel. Let mothers again have the wisdom to tell their children what gender they are. And train them from the time they are infants to rise up and serve the Living God. Lord, speak to mothers and let them be champions in the earth today. With the wisdom of Deborah, let them show another generation the way.

Lord, raise up young prophets. Lord, raise up prophets of the generation to come to speak your Word and your truth, words of fire that cannot be overcome. Raise up Davids to be anointed by Samuels, and raise up Samuels to pour the oil.

Lord, show them that they can live in the richness of God and not serve in the night with rigor and toil.

Raise up a people, Lord, that will still stand and worship you and praise your name. Raise up a people who will turn a deaf ear to corruption and backbiting and live in a world of the blessing of rain.

Lord, I ask for the anointing of the mother to be upon a generation that needs mothered.

Lord God, raise it up. Let the wisdom fall like rain on the women of the day, the Deborahs, the Hannahs who are looking for children to raise. Let the wisdom of God fall like rain on the Deborahs, on the Hannahs. Like Mary, let them say: 'Be it done unto me according to your Word. Let it be done unto me.' Let their voices be heard with the anointing of Elizabeth, who conceived in her old age, to know that their relevance is still alive and well and can still say, 'Come on.'

Let it fall like rain, the wisdom of Deborah. Let it fall like rain, the wisdom of Deborah. Let it fall like rain and defeat the iron chariots carrying the enemy, who thought, 'I will destroy them all.' You just wait and see. Let it fall like rain, let it fall.

'It's the way of my voice on the desert wind,' says the Lord. 'There is a way. It's the way of the wind, the way of the wind. You can't tell where it started from or where it will end.

You can't tell where it's coming from or where it will end, but it's in the wind, in the wind. It's in the wind.'

You heard me speak of Deborah. And there was Barak, and I speak Barak in a mystery. Turn back, turn back, Barak, for the time of Deborah is upon you where a woman will get the glory.

The Lord is raising up mothers in America, mothers in America, to tell the old story. The wisdom of Deborah upon the moms, the wisdom of Deborah has come to tell their children what gender they are and to rescue them from afar.

Listen to the voice of the mama. Listen to her. She cries in the night. She has been fighting over the seed since Genesis 3:15, and she will win the fight!

'Oh, Mother, am I a boy or a girl? Oh, Mother, could you help me understand? So many voices in the wind, it's turning my

little head around. Oh, please, Mother; put my feet back on the ground. Oh, Mother, Mama! Can you tell me what I am? '

'Yes, my son, I can," I hear the mama say. 'You are a young man of God. You are a young woman of God. Do not be confused by what you see. Do not be confused by what they say! Mama knows. Mama knows, and I'll tell you what you are. And I will speak of your destiny. God has a plan for you, my son. God has a plan for you, my girl. You will fulfill your destiny.'

Don't come under a false flag. They unfurl and entrap you in letters you don't understand. No matter how many letters they spread across the land, the rainbow belongs to God, and it never belonged to a man.

My son, my girl (hallelujah). Hear the sounds of the wind. Do you hear them? The sound of a mystery.

'I'm raising up an army, an army that talks like me,' says the Lord, 'and that's the sound of the mystery.'

They were not counting on the anointing of Deborah to come at this time. They were not counting on mothers to speak up and open the eyes of their children that they made blind—to not even know when they look at their bodies what they are. They believe a lie, but the words of the anointed mama will open their blinded eyes.

'Take heed' says the Lord, 'all you mothers. Be glad and rejoice before the Lamb, for I have anointed you with the anointing of Deborah now."

So, speak out loud. Speak out loud. Speak to your children of their destinies. Speak to them of who they are and overcome this lie.

The Lord says this, 'This flag they fly is going to fall. It'll be trampled in the dirt. And you will hear them cry. 'How did righteousness get back in leadership?" they will say. It's from the anointing of Deborah that paved the way! 'How was he elected again? How did she make it up to that place of authority? We thought we had it sure. We thought we had it forever.'

The Lord says, 'Nay, you didn't count on the anointing of Deborah!'" [1]

There is no bond like that of a mother with her child. The first voice a child hears is her mother. The first face a baby sees is her mother. The fierce protection of a mother over her child is by design, God's design. Children look to the care of their mother. She is the first source of her baby's food supply and will suffer whatever it requires to protect her child. She is the hand that touches, soothes, nurtures, deeply shows love, and gives comfort to her child. And in the first months of life, she is the reason a baby lives. A child without the touch and caresses of a mother, though fed by machines, will die. [2]

I was in Los Angeles praying about an opportunity to purchase a hotel/retreat center that had been presented to us when I received a text from Mrs. Robin Bullock. She said her husband (also named Robin) had a word that he felt was for me. We had to make a decision whether to move on the property within the next few hours or it would go to another buyer. Already seeking the Lord, I jumped at the opportunity to hear from the Bullocks if God had a word for me.

At the beginning of this chapter, I shared the word Robin gave the day before on his public broadcast. He said the first person that God brought to mind was me. He began to share how God had shown him the men couldn't do it, that the women were going to have to do this. That God was awakening the spirit of wisdom, the spirit of Deborah.

My first book, *She Gets It!*, was my story of being a feminist, never going to marry or have children, and the divine intervention of God that radically changed my life forever. This life change resulted in a husband of over 40 years today, five children, plus twelve grandchildren and counting.

As Robin spoke to me about what he saw and heard, a conversation where children were asking their mothers to tell them who they were, I began to weep. I knew God was clearly charging me with championing the Deborahs and awakening them to save the children… to awaken the mothers, the grandmothers, the women who have nurtured but maybe never had their own children, women who still bear the mark of a Deborah. And these Deborahs would stir the Jaels to arise as well and defeat the enemy of our land.

Deborah has always been the character I most identified with in Scripture, and that first book included a charge of Deborah challenging women to return to their destiny from God. I know what God is asking of me. Is He asking you to do something to help the innocent children who are being captivated by lies from the enemy himself to destroy their futures, their destinies, their God-called purposes?

> **IS HE ASKING YOU TO DO SOMETHING TO HELP THE INNOCENT CHILDREN WHO ARE BEING CAPTIVATED BY LIES FROM THE ENEMY HIMSELF TO DESTROY THEIR FUTURES, THEIR DESTINIES, THEIR GOD-CALLED PURPOSES?**

If you aren't familiar with the story of Deborah, she was an anointed judge who decided matters among the people and was a prophetess of the Lord. She laments in the book of Judges that *"the highways were abandoned; travelers took to winding paths. Villagers in Israel would not fight; they held back until I, Deborah, arose, until I arose, a mother in Israel."* [3]

Deborah arose as a mother to the nation. Israel had turned from God and embraced wickedness; and because of their evil, they had fallen into captivity under King Jabin of the Caananites. Their lives were no longer safe, and they could not go into the cities or highways because violence and oppression had overwhelmed their land.

There came a day when God heard the cries of the people, and Deborah received a word for Barak, the captain of Israel:

> *The Lord, the God of Israel, commands you: "Go, take with you ten thousand men of Naphtali and Zebulun and lead them up to Mount Tabor. I will lead Sisera, the commander of Jabin's army, with his chariots and his troops to the Kishon River and give him into your hands."*

> *Barak said to her, "If you go with me, I will go; but if you don't go with me, I won't go."*

"Certainly I will go with you," said Deborah, "but because of the course you are taking, the honor will not be yours, for the Lord will deliver Sisera into the hands of a woman." So Deborah went with Barak to Kedesh.[4]

Deborah said to Barak, "Go! This is the day the Lord has given Sisera into your hands. Has not the Lord gone ahead of you?"[5]

Barak then pursued Sisera's troops, all of which *"fell by the sword; not a man was left."*[6]

Meanwhile, Sisera escaped to the tent of Jael, the wife of Heber the Kenite. Cunningly, Jael invited Sisera in, encouraging him to not be afraid. *"I'm thirsty,"* he said. *"Please give me some water."* She opened a skin of milk, gave him a drink, and covered him up.[7]

When Sisera went to sleep, Jael picked up a tent peg, *"went quietly to him"* and *"drove the peg through his temple into the ground,"* killing him. *"On that day God subdued Jabin king of Canaan before the Israelites. And the hand of the Israelites pressed harder and harder against Jabin king of Canaan until they destroyed him."*[8]

The people rejoiced in God and sang songs of victory, recalling all God had done and praising Him:

From the heavens the stars fought, from their courses they fought against Sisera. The river Kishon swept them away, the age-old river, the river Kishon. March on, my soul; be strong!

Then thundered the horses' hooves—galloping, galloping go his mighty steeds. "Curse Meroz," said the angel of the Lord.

"Curse its people bitterly, because they did not come to help the Lord, to help the Lord against the mighty. Most blessed of women be Jael, the wife of Heber the Kenite, most blessed of tent-dwelling women." [9]

As in the day of Deborah and Jael, our children are crying out for mothers to rescue them from the thief who would steal, kill, and destroy their identity and voices. Can you hear the sound of God's wind blowing and the spirit of Deborah, the wisdom of Deborah arising in the women of God, the mothers of the nation to save the innocent children?

AS IN THE DAY OF DEBORAH AND JAEL, OUR CHILDREN ARE CRYING OUT FOR MOTHERS TO RESCUE THEM FROM THE THIEF WHO WOULD STEAL, KILL, AND DESTROY THEIR IDENTITY AND VOICES.

CHAPTER 2

A TARGET ON YOUR KIDS

Darkness has declared hunting season on the innocent, and children are being barraged with darts of destruction. Retailers, sports, gaming, social media, hospitals, music, arts, celebrities, schools, politicians, and the financial sector's ESG (Environmental Social Governance) are all targeting kids in what seems to be a united effort to destroy their innocence. Their agendas destroy families and expose children to extreme violence, gender dysphoria, sexually explicit and pornographic material, medical misinformation, and addictive behaviors at younger and younger ages—resulting in the highest incidence of depression, suicide, gender confusion, and overall feelings of hopelessness ever among children.

> RETAILERS, SPORTS, GAMING, SOCIAL MEDIA, HOSPITALS, MUSIC, ARTS, CELEBRITIES, SCHOOLS, POLITICIANS, AND THE FINANCIAL SECTOR'S ESG (ENVIRONMENTAL SOCIAL GOVERNANCE) ARE ALL TARGETING KIDS IN WHAT SEEMS TO BE A UNITED EFFORT TO DESTROY THEIR INNOCENCE.

"Kids love social media and frighteningly, so do sexual predators. One in nine young people has been approached online by one of the estimated 500,000 of these dangerous criminals who are on these platforms daily." An estimated 1.6 million Americans at least 13 years old identify as transgender, according to a June 2022 estimate.[10]

About 5% of young adults in the U.S. say their gender is different from their biological God-given gender.[11] "The share of U.S. adults who are transgender is particularly high among adults younger than 25. In this age group, 3.1% are a trans man or a trans woman, compared with just 0.5% of those ages 25 to 29."[12] There are obviously far more factors influencing this explosive increase in younger adults experiencing gender dysphoria over the .0005 percent of children historically who experienced gender dysphoria. These children are clearly a targeted audience today as evidenced by the drastic rise in numbers of youth identifying as one of the plethora of sexual identities included in the LGBTQ "spectrum."

Changing identities or attractions may promise happiness in social media chats and well-designed marketing campaigns, but the numbers tell a different story. "Lesbian, gay and bisexual adults aged 18 to 25 are much more likely than their heterosexual peers to report mental, emotional and physical problems, according to a new poll. In the latest Gallup survey, 71% of non-heterosexual young adult respondents said they experienced anxiety 'a lot of the day yesterday' compared to 52% of straight respondents. The polling company reported Thursday that while 80% of heterosexual young adults experienced happiness the previous day, about 65% of their non-straight peers felt the same. The survey also found that 63% of straight young adults described their emotional and mental well-being as 'good' or 'excellent,' compared to 38% of queer young adults."[13]

Satan, operating through social engineers with agendas, understands that the most vulnerable time in a person's life is when they are a child. Scripture refers to them as "tender shoots."[14] Psalm 128:3(NIV) says, "*Your children will be like olive shoots around your table.*" I have a trellis with new shoots, and I train those new vines by connecting them to the trellis early. Then, they grow in the direction I point them. You can train a child to conform to any ideology because God created them to be moldable for loving parents to nurture, protect, and direct a child's heart and life. What happens when those who live deviant lifestyles (yes, I said it) and/or wish to groom, use, and make hefty profits off these children? If there are no mamas or papas standing in the way, these thieves of innocence will bring death to them.

The massive clothing corporation Target launched its new series of LGBTQ clothes that includes items for children, sparking controversy as the marketing push prepared for Pride Month. Target's move came as several companies were coming under fire for LGBTQ marketing, such as Anheuser-Busch, related to their Bud Light campaign. In that instance, the backlash was so severe that top executives at Anheuser-Busch began distancing themselves from the incident.[15]

"Target is offering a 'tuck-friendly' bathing suit in this year's LGBTQ Pride clothing collection, which is seemingly designed for children, according to the Daily Mail."[16] The swimsuits appear in the Pride section, which is often set up toward the front of the stores, and have tags on them advertising the 'tuck-friendly construction' and 'extra crotch coverage,' which helps biological men conceal their genitals.[17] The Daily Mail identified the adult one-piece colorblock swimsuit, which retails for $40, as one of the tuck-friendly swimwear options, though it is not listed as such on Target's website. Customer product reviews mention 'tuck-friendly' tags on the garment, however, and it is pictured with such tags in photos taken by the Daily Mail.[18]

Although there were "fact-checkers" who tried to refute that these swimsuits were not for children but instead for women, I looked at the models' age pictured, and they were definitely targeting teens.

While some Target stores appeared to remove items from a designer offering T-shirts that read "Satan observes pronouns" or moved some items, it is questionable whether Target has had a true change of course.

"In a May 24 memo to Target employees, which was obtained by Business Insider, Target CEO Brian Cornell said 'one of the hardest parts' of its move to pull the merchandise was figuring out how that would impact the 'wellbeing and psychological safety' of the LGBTQ community. 'We stand with you now and will continue to do so—not just during Pride Month, but each and every day,' he said."[19] These agendas have become a large part of corporate messaging mandates seeking to increase their equity rating scores, and they're not just limited to the retail industry.

"The Los Angeles Dodgers announced that the Sisters of Perpetual Indulgence, a well-known San Francisco order of queer and trans 'nuns' that has existed since the 1970s, are once again welcome at the team's annual Pride Night. Last week, the baseball team rescinded the group's invitation after a Republican senator from Florida wrote a letter accusing the sisters, a group which came to prominence during the Aids crisis, of being anti-Christian activists. The group, which does charitable and protest work in addition to its street drag show performances, was set to receive an award during a ceremony before a 16 June game against the San Francisco Giants."[20]

With schools introducing LGBTQ-friendly curricula at younger and younger ages across the country and retailers and celebrities championing the LGBTQ community, it's easy to draw the conclusion that children are being groomed to not only accept these lifestyles glorified everywhere they turn but also to personalize and question their own sexual identity, whether presented through a baseball game, shopping for clothes, or going to the movies. Children cannot go through a day without being bombarded with this in a brainwashing fashion. There are no safe spaces for parents to take their kids without being confronted with in-your-face displays. Add to this recipe of over-sexualization and gender identity confusion two hours of violent and sexually provocative gaming, and children can become dangerous to themselves and others. Their world is saturated with violence, sex, and sexual perverseness. This is an intentional attack on their childhood.

With over 90 percent of children playing video games and more than 90 percent of games rated E10 or above containing violence, what impact does this have on young children? A study by Susan Tortolero, director of the Center for Health Promotion and Prevention Research at the University of Texas, examined the link between violent video game play and depression. "We know that violence in general—whether it's being a victim of violence, or just witnessing violence—is associated with mental health problems," she told Healthline. "We also know, given brain research, that our brain sometimes doesn't distinguish between what's real and what we see on TV." She found that playing more than two hours a day of violent video games is linked much more strongly with depression than playing less than two hours a day of nonviolent video games." In addition to depression, these children are more likely to act aggressively toward others.[21]

Another study published tracked 5,000 teenagers for four years and found that playing Mature-rated video games predicted later risky behaviors. "...With subsequent increases in sensation seeking, rebelliousness, hanging out with kids who smoke cigarettes and drink alcohol, thinking kids who drink and smoke are cool, and thinking that one would like to try drinking and smoking," explained Jay Hull, department chair of psychological and brain sciences at Dartmouth College. "In turn, changes in these variables were associated with subsequent changes in drinking, smoking, fighting, risky sex, and delinquent behavior."[22]

During the Sandy Hook mass shootings, playing long hours of extreme video game violence was cited as a behavior of the shooter. Trump singled out video games as a major factor for both shooters' actions in El Paso, Texas and Dayton, Ohio. "We must stop the glorification of violence in our society. This includes the gruesome and grisly video games that are now commonplace. It is too easy today for troubled youth to surround themselves with a culture that celebrates violence," he said.[23] House Minority Leader Kevin McCarthy, a California Republican concurred with Trump, stating that "the idea of these video games that dehumanize individuals to have a game of shooting individuals and others—I've always felt that is a problem for future generations and others."[24]

Both Democratic and Republican politicians have a track record of targeting video games as one cause of American mass shooters' actions. After the shooting at Marjory Stoneman Douglas High School in Parkland, Florida, in 2018, Trump held a series of school safety meetings at the White House to try to address the crisis, citing violence portrayed in media, including video games, movies, and the Internet. During one of these meetings, Trump said, "I'm hearing more and more people saying the level of violence on video games is really shaping young people's thoughts."[25]

The American Psychological Association and the American Academy of Pediatrics are on record against children and teens playing violent video games. A 2015 policy statement from the American Psychological Association says that research demonstrated a link "between violent video game use and both increases in aggressive behavior ... and decreases in prosocial behavior, empathy and moral engagement."[26] In the American Academy of Pediatrics July 2016 guideline on media violence, the Academy warned "more than 400 studies revealed a 'significant' link between being exposed to violent media in general and aggressive behavior, aggressive thoughts and angry feelings."[27]

"Other more recent psychological research does not show a direct correlation between playing violent video games and exhibiting violent behavior outside those games."[28] CNN, among other Legacy media, minimized the impact of video gaming with new studies attempting to exonerate the gaming industry. Could gaming companies with revenues from the worldwide gaming market estimated at almost 347 billion U.S. dollars manage to generate studies to refute any claims that their intensely violent and sexualized games contribute to mass shootings or any other negative factors?[29] We must use common sense. If 9/11 terrorists trained on video game computer simulators and were able to hijack planes and cause mass deaths, could video games train someone to turn to violence and mentor them how to do so? Any other conclusion is not only naïve, it's dishonest. Kids are being targeted by the gaming industry![30] And not just gaming, social media is setting unrealistic expectations and new normals for acceptance in appearance, relationships, and sexual promiscuity.

As children and teens increasingly go online for entertainment and connection, parents, scholars and policymakers are concerned that young people's biology is making them particularly vulnerable to, and in some cases even being exploited, by social media. Younger social media users are more likely than older ones to have body image issues, while kids who use Instagram or Snapchat before age 11 face a higher risk of online harassment. "It's time we stopped trying to make profits on kids' developing brains."[31]

The worst target that could possibly be on a child, apart from being aborted, is that of child exploitation and child sex trafficking. "Sex trafficking is a growing yet inconspicuous issue in the United States, and youth are especially vulnerable to exploitation. Commercial sexual exploitation entails forcing or coercing a person into engaging in sexual acts for the profit of those who run the industry (i.e., the traffickers). This industry is driven by a demand for child sex and fueled by its lucrative nature. Along with the inherent vulnerability of being young and not yet fully developed, youth have a variety of risk factors which make them especially susceptible to victimization, including experience with child abuse, homelessness, and online exposure. Children and adolescents who are targeted and sexually exploited can suffer damaging short- and long-term physical and sexual trauma to their bodies, as well as adverse mental and emotional trauma that can make it difficult to cope with the maltreatment they have been subjected to."[32] The sex trafficking of children is a rising problem in the United States, estimated to be in the hundreds of thousands of victims. "The issue is fueled by nationwide demand, and, with the rise of technology, the Internet has become a marketplace for the growing industry."[33]

Instagram, the photocentric social media platform owned by Meta, helps link and promote a "vast" network of pedophile accounts that openly advertise illicit, "child-sex material for sale," *The Wall Street Journal* reported. Investigations by researchers at Stanford University, the University of Massachusetts Amherst, and the Journal found Instagram does not just host illicit content on its platform: Its algorithms actually promote it. The platform connects pedophiles to content sellers through a niche recommendation system that enables people to search explicit hashtags. It then connects them to accounts that use the terms to promote "child-sex material for sale."[34]

According to *The Wall Street Journal*, the buyers and sellers of sexual content involving children are just one component of the sexualized child content conglomerate. "Other Instagram accounts that seemingly belong to the platform's pedophile community gather pro-pedophilia memes or talk about their access to children, according to the Journal. The number of accounts that exist mainly to follow child-sex content is at least in the hundreds of thousands, if not millions, current and former Meta employees who have worked on child-safety initiatives at Instagram told the Journal."[35]

> **THERE IS AN OVERT ATTEMPT TO NORMALIZE SEX WITH CHILDREN AT AN ALARMING RATE AS MORE CHILDREN EXPERIENCE PORNOGRAPHY AND ARE ENCOUNTERING GRAPHIC CONTENT.**

There is an overt attempt to normalize sex with children at an alarming rate as more children experience pornography and are encountering graphic content.

Studies have shown that children are getting exposed to child porn at younger ages as more kids have access to devices at younger ages as well. "New research from the security technology company Bitdefender reports the 10-and-under age group now accounts for one in 10 visitors to porn video sites. And when it comes to consumption, the same study shows children under the age of 10 now account for 22% of online porn watching for juveniles under the age of 18. Gone are the days where kids used to hunt down dirty magazines in the house. Now, everything and anything imaginable is available with one click."[36]

Sadly, parents are not innocent in this corruption either. Children's exposure to pornography often starts at home.

"Investigators with the Franklin County Internet Crimes Against Children task force say they are seeing a concerning amount of cases involving children inadvertently learning about pornography through internet searches on home computers, tablets, and smartphones."[37]

They have seen where children have been exposed through a parent's or friend's device, and "the next thing you know they're down the rabbit hole of pornography," says Sergeant Jeff Zech, who has been part of the ICAC team for 6 years.[38] "Investigators say it's a growing issue that many parents may not realize, but they're part of the problem." [39]

Children's mental health is under immense attack, and there's no wonder why this is occurring with all the agendas being pushed on children. "Three large healthcare groups—the American Academy of Pediatrics, the American College of Emergency Physicians, and the Emergency Nurses Association—issued a joint letter Wednesday warning of an ongoing and worsening crisis: children presenting in emergency rooms with mental health issues that hospitals are not equipped to handle. According to the report, 'Emergency department (ED) visits by children and youth with mental and behavioral health (MBH) emergencies in the United States have been increasing over the last decade. At the same time, there has been an increased prevalence of depression and suicide in pediatrics.'"[40]

The report stated that the problem is particularly prevalent among black school-aged children, "who have a suicide rate that is two times higher than white children."[41] Most concerning, the report shows that emergency rooms "have a wide variation in their capability to care for pediatric patients with MBH conditions" and that "There is often inconsistent screening for self-harm risks and substance use in patients presenting for both mental health concerns and other complaints."[42]

Sadly, these same pediatric groups have affirmed gender transitions and the gender confusion being propagated on children in the last decade. Do they not see the connection between their actions and the mental health emergencies among youth?

In Matthew 18:6 (NIV), Jesus said, "*If anyone causes one of these little ones—those who believe in me—to stumble, it would be better for them to have a large millstone hung around their neck and to be drowned in the depths of the sea.*"

Your kids are being targeted. It's time for us as parents, and decent government officials that are not involved with these heinous sins, to go after the hunters. Guns have been blamed for violence. Gaming has been presented as harmless and even helpful. Celebrities are the salespersons for transgender ideologies, sexual promiscuity, and infatuation with drug and alcohol use. We must stop letting the world exploit kids, and parents must do their part to protect and lead the way in what is right.

IT'S TIME FOR US AS PARENTS, AND DECENT GOVERNMENT OFFICIALS THAT ARE NOT INVOLVED WITH THESE HEINOUS SINS, TO GO AFTER THE HUNTERS.

CHAPTER 3

THEY'RE COMING FOR YOUR CHILDREN

I woke up at the beginning of 2022 with a strong word in my spirit, "They're coming for your children." It was so strong that I told my son, "I feel God is calling me to wake up parents as every offensive evil hell can unleash is coming for the children of this generation." We must reach these youth and alert parents to the dangers and wickedness that their children are facing from every possible angle. It is rooted in the occult and Satan's desire to destroy this generation, because they are destined to bring in an awakening and usher in the return of Jesus. Just as Herod sought to kill all the babies because he knew a Redeemer was coming, the enemy knows his time is short and there are deliverers coming, those raised up by God to bring His presence and glory. Isaiah 11:6b (NIV) says, *A little child shall lead them.* An outpouring is coming and, therefore, Satan is attempting to come for the children—first with abortion and now the transgender assault on their identity, resulting in confusion and suicide. Parents have authority over their children and the enemy, but they must see the battle and understand how to use the weapons of God's warfare.

> AN OUTPOURING IS COMING AND, THEREFORE, SATAN IS ATTEMPTING TO COME FOR THE CHILDREN—FIRST WITH ABORTION AND NOW THE TRANSGENDER ASSAULT ON THEIR IDENTITY, RESULTING IN CONFUSION AND SUICIDE.

"'We're here, we're queer, we're coming for your children,' some of those in the crowd shouted in a NYC Drag March. The march came to an end at the Stonewall Inn, located in Greenwich Village, whose site says it is "Where Pride Began." [43]

This is not a game nor a vague taunt. As early as the 1980s, I read to my husband from a homosexual publication picked up at a restaurant. It openly stated, "We will seduce your sons."[44] At the time, it was easy to dismiss this as unlikely. My husband somewhat did. We can look back and see that they were not only serious but there was also a well-planned attack to do so. Will we be caught off guard this time with agendas that seek to mutilate childrens' bodies and change their identities?

"In July 2021, Breitbart News reported the San Francisco Gay Men's Chorus unpublished a music video where singers promised to 'convert' children to their LGBTQ ideology once the clip went viral online. Lyrics to the song include:

> *You think we're sinful. You fight against our rights. You say we all lead lives you can't respect. But you're just frightened. You think that we'll corrupt your kids if our agenda goes unchecked. It's funny. Just this once, you're correct.*

> *We'll convert your children. Happens bit by bit. Quietly and subtly, and you will barely notice it. You can keep him from disco, warn about San Francisco. Make him wear pleated pants. We don't care. We'll convert your children. We'll make them tolerant and fair."* [45]

When the rumblings of this messaging started in the 80's, no one believed it was palatable. No one believed it was possible. "Coming out of the closet" was made vogue, and most of the population politely kept silent, thinking there was no harm intended. We were spun a host of politically correct words that sounded good and felt like we should be kind and let this small group of people "live and let live" the way they wanted. But even in that early presentation, the polite "right side" deferred out of kindness, referring to freedom of speech and that everyone has a right to their opinion. In our value system, we knew babies were people, men were not women, children were to be protected, and that homosexuality could never replace the family. These were assumptions that seemed like common sense, for they had always been the norm. We thought, "If we be nice to them, they be nice to us" (Gollum in *The Lord of the Rings*). But just as the choir sang in San Francisco, it happens bit by bit, quietly, subtly. No one could have projected that we would come to a time that children in kindergarten would be having books read to them about sex, much less by a professing drag queen, sharing they may not be a boy or girl, that just because their sex organs looked one way, their gender may not match their organs! That's just what these social engineers were counting on.

Consider the horrific story of Bruce and Brian Reimer as chronicled by Michael Knowles in his book *Speechless: Controlling Words, Controlling Minds*:

> On August 22, 1965, Janet Reimer gave birth to twin boys, Bruce and Brian, in Winnetoba, Canada. From the moment Janet and her husband Ron brought the boys home, they noticed that they had trouble urinating... The doctors recommended circumcision as a simple fix for the problem, and Dr. Jean-Marie Huot performed the

procedure on Bruce the following month. But Huot did not perform a conventional circumcision but rather opted for electrocauterization, which went awry and burned Bruce's penis beyond recognition. After the debacle, the Reimers declined circumcision for Brian, whose problem soon disappeared on its own.

Early the following year, the distraught parents watched a news report about developments in the field of "gender identity" on a Canadian television station. The reporters interviewed Dr. John Money of John Hopkins University, and the Reimers made plans to visit in the hope of giving their mutilated son some semblance of a normal life. Money told the Reimers that he could not fix the poor boy's genitals, but he could make him look like a little girl. Since sex did not determine "gender," according to Money, Bruce could live a normal life as "Brenda," blissfully unaware of his masculine birth so long as his parents kept the secret.

The prospect of studying the development of identical twins, each raised with a different "gender identity," offered the perfect test of Money's theories. But Bruce, now Brenda, never felt like a girl. "Brenda's interests are strongly masculine," wrote clinician Joan Nebbs in a report on Brenda's psychological state during childhood. "She has marvelous plans for building tree houses, go-carts with CB radios, model gas airplanes." Moreover, the child has "strong fears that something has been done to her genital organs, and worse yet, "some suicidal thoughts."

Dr. Money's psychological interventions might better be called psychopathic. Money instructed the boys to simulate sex, with Brian performing the male role and Bruce the female... Even years later, Bruce could not recall the therapy sessions without crying.

After Brenda threatened suicide in his preteen years, the Reimers came clean about the discrepancy between his natural sex and his coerced "sexual identity," at which point he underwent surgery to reconstruct his male genitals, adopted the name David, and lived the rest of his life as a man. But neither Brian nor David ever recovered from the physical and psychological torture Money had inflicted on them in the name of "science" and "gender identity" theory. Brian developed schizophrenia and took an overdose of drugs to end his life at the age of thirty-six. After three suicide attempts, David followed suit two years later when he sawed off a shotgun, drove to a parking lot, and put a final end to his misery... The radicals who peddle gender ideology as compassionate never seem to mention the Reimers.[46]

This should be a glaring case study of attempts to change a child's sex and an indictment of psychiatric manipulation. Is there no accountability for any whim a psychiatrist has to experiment on a child's body and psyche? Parallel situations are happening in psychiatry today involving transitioning children, altering their sexual organs, and experimentation. Parents must wake up and recognize this is no longer subtle. Today, the stories of children all over the "civilized" world sound horrifically similar in many ways. When they openly say they are coming after your children, it is more than a real threat—it is a promise!

I was alone on a commercial flight from Columbus to Houston and was seated next to a man in his late 30s, the age of my sons. He pulled out a computer and began to watch a drag show. I was shocked that he had no concern that a woman was sitting next to him and children were across the aisle, and no regard that the content he was watching was vulgar. His conscience was clearly seared as he watched the disgusting content the entire flight, while also treating the flight attendant rudely. I had to twist my body in the seat and look out the window to block my line of sight from the content. In the past, any man would have been ashamed and embarrassed to view this in front of anyone, much less a woman old enough to be his mother. He was clearly miserable. I prayed for him as I tried to give him a shoulder. These drag female impersonators have become mainstream, as they read library books to children and perform for minor children. And why is this not inappropriate and evil? Yet they call out conservatives and parents as evil.

> WHEN THEY OPENLY SAY THEY ARE COMING AFTER YOUR CHILDREN, IT IS MORE THAN A REAL THREAT— IT IS A PROMISE!

RuPaul's Drag Race champion Jinkx Monsoon recently took aim at conservatives for using children as "political shields" in the child grooming debate. He claimed, "They're using children as a shield, like they've done many, many times. That has always been their tactic. What the GOP is doing is objectively evil."[47]

Not only do they rail that they are coming for your children, but they are also determined to pervert the Word of God. So-called churches across the world fly the Pride flag, paint their steps in rainbow colors, and ordain gays and lesbians to stand in pulpits. During "Pride" month this summer, The Edina Community Lutheran Church in Edina, Minnesota, recited "the sparkle creed" during its service, signaling its embrace of the LGBTQ+ agenda. Anna Helgen, co-pastor of the church, invited the congregation "to rise in body or spirit and let us confess our faith today in the words of the Sparkle Creed:"[48]

> NOT ONLY DO THEY RAIL THAT THEY ARE COMING FOR YOUR CHILDREN, BUT THEY ARE ALSO DETERMINED TO PERVERT THE WORD OF GOD.

"Let us confess our faith today in the words of the sparkle creed: I believe in the non-binary God whose pronouns are plural. I believe in Jesus Christ, their child, who wore a fabulous tunic and had two dads and saw everyone as a sibling-child of God. I believe in the rainbow Spirit, who shatters our image of one white light and refracts it into a rainbow of gorgeous diversity. I believe in the church of everyday saints as numerous, creative and resilient as patches on the AIDS quilt, whose feet are grounded in mud and whose eyes gaze at the stars in wonder. I believe in the calling to each of us that love is love is love. So beloved let us love."[49]

When the Scripture speaks of the great apostasy in the last of days, is this not it? [50]

What is the church going to do to answer this apostasy? We can care for the person enough to boldly denounce the sin. If we do not care to confront, then do we care at all? Apathy is not the answer, and neither is cowardice masked in a cloak of faux love. Real love cannot stand by and allow them to come for our children. Real men and women of God cannot pretend it's all right and remain silent—not violence but not silence either.

> *Behold, I have given unto you power ... over all the power of the enemy: and nothing shall by any means harm you.*
> —Luke 10:19 (AKJV)

> *Your children shall be taught of the Lord, and great is the peace of your children.*
> —Isaiah 54:13 (NKJV)

CHAPTER 4

THE NASTY NANNIES: CELEBRITIES, SCHOOLS & HOSPITALS

A nanny is a person employed to look after a child, a person or institution regarded as interfering. What happens when these institutions become nasty? My first experience with a nasty nanny was in the '60s when it first became vogue for mothers to work outside the home and leave their children at daycare centers. I was four years old, and the loud, heavyset woman in charge required us to put our heads on the table before lunch. She would walk up and down the aisle hitting anyone who was not silent or compliant on the back with a belt. I wore a Liddle Kiddles doll locket (think of an LOL doll), which she confiscated and couldn't find when it was time for my mother to pick me up. I wasn't there long, as my mother caught on to the negative atmosphere, but it definitely left a scar on my heart.

Parents are either unaware, too naïve, too busy, or have given in to allowing schools, celebrity culture, medicine, and radical leftist governments to brainwash their children. Many parents are content to allow screens to babysit their children, which allows

> **MANY PARENTS ARE CONTENT TO ALLOW SCREENS TO BABYSIT THEIR CHILDREN, WHICH ALLOWS THEM TO TEND TO OTHER PRIORITIES WHILE THEIR CHILDREN ARE PASSIVELY MESMERIZED AND SEDATED.**

them to tend to other priorities while their children are passively mesmerized and sedated. Perhaps they are unaware that their child, who "is continuously watching television, using a tablet, computer, or smartphone," is at a "significantly higher risk of developing developmental difficulties than a child who does not use the same type of technology."[51] Specifically, their "communication, fine motor skills, problem-solving, or personal and social abilities" may be delayed or impaired.[52] Something tells me that those behind the games, programming, and social media on the screens know this and capitalize on it.

From the time a child wakes until they go to bed, voices are jamming messages into their heads from media, gaming, school, peers, celebrities, music, and even doctors. These messages are laden with similarly connected agendas: sexual perversion, occult imagery, and addictions! It starts seemingly innocently, but line upon line, precept upon precept, the child is psychologically broken down. Cartoon characters wrapped in beautiful colors of the rainbow movement teaching "love" with catchy melodies the child sings. Then, they head to school where teachers cover their walls and clothes with the same messaging in classrooms, sentence structure, and other examples used in every discussion. Kids and friends that are early adopters quickly start "identifying" themselves with the names their "new mommy" has taught them. Like surrogate parents, institutions and teachers are training the children.

Add to that every ride in the car, a headset, a mobile device, their favorite celebrity voices on TV, and social media are all "bought and paid for" by pharmaceutical companies who stand to make great sums of money off these new victims of their experimentation. If the nasty nannies do it just right, they will earn millions from each child as they develop into adulthood—from vaccinations, medicines, condoms, painkillers, abortions, puberty blockers, transition surgeries, hormone therapy, overdoses, rehab, more drugs to replace old drugs, cancer, chemo, more surgeries, and, eventually, hospice and death when there's nothing left to earn from these "useless people" who are "basically meaningless, worthless" (to quote Yuval

Noah Harari).[53] Don't forget to donate your organs on your way out. They'll make that last dime on every soul!

In addition to the indoctrination youth are receiving from curricula, teachers, and peer pressure, educators themselves have become predators of students.

> The Broome County Sheriff's Office announced it's holding Johnson City Middle School Principal Daniel Erickson, 55, on the felony charge of luring a child and attempted rape in the third degree.
>
> Erickson, of Greene, NY, was arrested on July 7 following an investigation into suspicious behavior involving a minor at Johnson City High School.
>
> According to the sheriff's office, Erickson had been communicating via Snapchat with a 16-year-old girl. Over time, he made statements indicating that he was going to have sexual intercourse with the student.
>
> The sheriff's office said Erickson agreed to meet her in a remote location with the intention to have sex. He brought items such as a Grimace Shake from McDonald's, chicken nuggets and a box of condoms. However, detectives were at the location when he arrived and he was taken into custody without incident.
>
> Sheriff Fred Akshar said in a news release, "As a father, I know this is a nightmare scenario for any parent. We entrust

our schools with the care and safety of our children, and to have an individual violate that trust, abuse their power and prey on a very student charged in our schools' care is beyond disgusting."[54]

Sadly, these stories have become all too common. In addition to the psychological abuse many children experience as teachers and schools pressure and alienate students to agree with agendas that violate their brains, bodies, and values, how many children have been physically and sexually abused or lured into other traps because schools groomed students?

As a student in the late '70s, my history teacher, Mr. Boyer, would share with our history class vivid accounts of his homosexual activity over the weekend. Rarely will students share these situations with parents because they accept what the teacher shares as normal. "Mom put me in this class, so this must just be what the adult world does and believes." I questioned if this was right and thought it probably wasn't, but to complain or "tell" creates a level of vulnerability that most students have learned will result in a bad grade or ridicule. Even if a child questions what's being said, eventually, by enough exposure, the activity is normalized. The tender conscience of a child is violated and eventually seared as with a hot iron, becoming unfeeling and no longer resisting untruth.

One student exposed to LGBTQ and other agendas at school later tearfully told her mother she believed her mother knew what she was being taught, and by sending her there gave her approval. Kids are looking for someone to teach them about life, themselves, the world, family, and sexuality. When we delegate it to someone else, we sure better know who we are handing their lives over to. If not, it could end in death. Nasty nannies don't really care. It's what's in it for them.

Imagine taking your child to the hospital because they broke their arm roughhousing with their brother, and in the process, the hospital puts you through an interrogation as they contemplate child abuse on your part. Then, when it is clear that the child was not abused, they argue with you that your child should be vaccinated for COVID-19 and what a dangerous parent you are. Then, the staff member begins a discussion with your child about their preferred pronouns and sexual identity. After the interrogation, and the berating, and the violation of your faith and values, they finally examine the broken arm but end up casting the wrong arm! This actually happened to a family.

> KIDS ARE LOOKING FOR SOMEONE TO TEACH THEM ABOUT LIFE, THEMSELVES, THE WORLD, FAMILY, AND SEXUALITY. WHEN WE DELEGATE IT TO SOMEONE ELSE, WE SURE BETTER KNOW WHO WE ARE HANDING THEIR LIVES OVER TO.

Medical professionals, like educators, the financial system, and so many other institutions (think the military), are more focused on indoctrination into agendas than medical practice. It is frightening to think some of the most dangerous places for children to go are places that were intended to help bring healing to their bodies—but instead become a place where children are aborted or children's bodies are mutilated to remove breasts or sexual organs. A retired nurse said, "I couldn't do it anymore. We have to pay so much attention to a person's pronouns and 'identity' that we can't even properly pre-op them for surgery. If they say they are a woman but have male parts, there are important protocols to protect organs for surgery—but it's hard to know fantasy from reality, and that can be dangerous when performing even routine surgeries, and post-op too. It's all just confusion."

Satan understands that where there is confusion and striving, there's every evil work. If we look at every institution and environment, especially for children, there is confusion. And we wonder why children and youth are suicidal or struggle with identity issues. This is pure evil, and we know it is by design, at least Satan's design.

We were on a cruise ship for an anniversary and met a couple that seemed nice. He was a child psychologist. As they visited with us, we discovered they met in church as teens. We talked about how church used to be the center of social life. I asked him what he thought had changed to impact kids negatively. He held up his cell phone and said, "This." I agreed wholeheartedly. We were having a great conversation about them moving to take a new job in California and the challenges youth face until I mentioned I was so sad that children were being given puberty-blocking drugs and had transition surgeries performed. He and his wife bristled. His wife said, "They should be able to love who they want to love and identify the way they want to." I was surprised!

I had shared Scripture earlier and they seemed to agree with everything, but then this was a serious point of contention. He said, "People have been hurt and they have to make decisions based on that hurt, which includes changing their sexual identity." I said, "What does God's Word say about this, and what does He think? Surely, you don't think Jesus wants to leave people, especially children, in the broken state that the enemy put them in through abuse or for any other reason. He would not want them to change the way He created them. He is the Savior of the spirit, soul, and body, and who the Son sets free is free. There is healing and restoration in God. Would God sentence them to a life of sin and brokenness because someone hurt them? God wants them whole, not further violated." He could not answer but was clearly bothered.

I went back to my room and began to pray, asking God if I had been wrong to share this. I clearly heard the Lord say in my spirit, "I set you up to talk to him. This is his last warning. I have been trying to confront him, but he has chosen his profession and money over me." Wow. I fell on my bed and began to cry and pray. Instead of me feeling bad, concerned I offended him, I began to pray for him and his wife in strong intercessory prayer. "His last warning," kept resonating in my heart as I prayed over them. Later, I read an article that said California has hired over 10,000 psychologists and psychiatrists to handle transitioning youth.[55] I knew when I read it, he was one.

Women's influencers speak up for abortion rights and "it's my body, my choice," as long as we're talking about abortion and not vaccinations. Why so much obsession with dismembering children before they're born and then afterward? The loudest voices don't seem to raise children themselves

> **THE LOUDEST VOICES DON'T SEEM TO RAISE CHILDREN THEMSELVES BUT WANT TO CONTROL OTHERS' CHILDREN AND REPRODUCTION.**

but want to control others' children and reproduction. Think of any women's talk show host, and you will find a majority are not married or, if so, are married to the same sex and are childless. Many Hollywood celebrities have adopted children from poor nations and are experimenting and transitioning these children to another sexual identity.[56] These disinformation divas control the narratives that married women and young girls adopt as truth via social media and movies. They brainwash other women to embrace drag queens, same sex marriage, trans women's rights, abortion, and push a toxic male, anti-faith militancy.

> A New Jersey drag queen and former school board member said shielding children from seeing drag performances does "a disservice to their young minds."

> Eric L. Pinckney, whose drag name is Miss Savannah Georgia, shared his frustration with parents protesting "Drag Queen Story Hour" and other "drag performances" for children in an op-ed in USA Today.[57] He said his favorite performances are "those center stage, right in front of young children, reading books to them…."

What happened to mothers reading books to their children? We don't need disinformation divas spreading lies to children, canceling women and silencing fathers. We don't want female impersonators. We need mamas, real mamas with hearts to reunite with their children!

In response to the woke agenda behind the drag story time hour found in libraries across America, Hollywood actor

Kirk Cameron went on his own book tour across the country promoting Christian values, Breitbart reported.

"If we want to see the future look like the kind of place we grew up in, or our grandparents grew up in, we need to start investing and planting seeds today that will grow into these future trees of liberty and blessing for our kids," Cameron said.

"One of the ways we do that is by being the ones who tell them these stories, not allowing cross-dressing men to tell our children stories that lead our kids in a different direction," he added.

"Libraries used to be safe places for families, but many of them now seem to be agenda-driven places that welcome drag queens to hold story hours for children," Graham said in a statement. "This is just plain wrong, and I'm so glad Kirk Cameron has decided to tell a different story—a story with Biblical values."[58]

If as a four-year-old over 50 years later, I still have scars from the nasty nannies in my life, how much more are the wounds of this generation of children who are babysat by devices, pedophiles, and drag queens?

When we see through the eyes of eternity, Jesus said it would be better to cut your hand off if it offends you or pluck out your eye than miss heaven (Matthew 5:27-30, NLT).

How much more important is it to pluck our children out of the hands of nasty nannies?

Who are their teachers? What shows are they watching? What platforms are they on: TikTok, Lapse, Instagram, SnapChat? What books are they reading? Who are their "friends"?

They are likely Nasty Nannies in disguise.

CHAPTER 5

FOLLOW THE SPORTS

THEY ARE COMING FOR YOUR CHILDREN
THE FIGHT WE MUST WIN!

I predicted how women would be canceled in sports competitions and scholarships in my *Nasty Gets Us Nowhere: Women and Men Succeeding Together* book. We have since seen titles stolen from female athletes in wrestling, swimming, track, weight lifting, and tennis. When searching for women's scholarships that have been awarded to trans women, Google search engines will only offer all of the scholarships offered to trans women as if it were a recruiting piece to join the movement to get scholarships. With a further search outside the controlled narratives, I found heart-wrenching stories of girls who had trained throughout middle and high school only to lose their opportunities to trans athletes. The number of their stories is growing, and instead of their coaches or sport's organizations standing up for their rights, they are shaming them into silence.

> Chelsea realized her potential as a runner when she broke two school records in her first meet as a freshman at Canton High School in 2016.
>
> "Since then I just kept going with it and got better and better," she recalled. "Track is really just about hitting those long-term goals that you've set for yourself."
>
> But in her first statewide competition, she was forced to compete against a transgender athlete—something she said she "had never really heard of" until it happened to her. For her, those goals were winning a state championship and going to college for track. In that race, the trans competitor bumped her out of qualifying for the next round of competition.

"It was just obvious to everyone there that they had a huge advantage. Everyone could see it," Mitchell said.

By her sophomore year, she says there were two transgender athletes regularly blowing biologically female track stars out of the water. Mitchell raced against them in all four years of high school and in every major race she competed in.

"Just two athletes took so many opportunities away from biological females," Mitchell told *The Post*. "Even though there were only two of them, they took 15 state championships away from other girls—and there were 85 girls that were directly impacted from them being in the races."

She herself lost two all-New England awards and four girls' state championships as a consequence.

"Having to lose four of them, time after time, and trying to pick yourself up and go back to the starting line again and again was really hard because you knew each time that there was no hope to win," she said.

In her junior year, she filed a Title IX complaint against the state's policies but remained anonymous for fear that exposure might hurt her college recruitment prospects."[59]

For all the gains women have made to have their own sports and equality, this seems like a huge defeat and discouragement for young women—to have to pick themselves up again and again with no hope of winning. How can this be legal or equitable? That's track and field, but the same results are happening in tennis. Why? Because men are physically advantaged over women biologically. It's a fact that is being minimalized as trans athletes cancel girls' sports.

Male tennis player Karsten Braasch, past his prime at 31 years old and ranked 203rd worldwide among male tennis players, stepped up when Serena and Venus Williams claimed that they could beat any male player ranked in the top 200 players. "And he destroyed them one after the other. Braasch first beat Serena 6-1 in a single set, winner-takes-all game. And when it was time for Venus to face him, Braasch trounced her 6-2 ....As good as the girls were, they couldn't even beat a man who was never exactly a contender."[60]

Similar stories are emerging in swimming competitions, as athletes like Riley Gaines have experienced. Harvard sent a letter to its female swim team athletes encouraging, and eventually strong-arming them, to accept Lia Thomas (a so-called transgender woman who is biologically a male) as a competitor. Riley Gaines was one of those female swimmers who came in second place to Lia Thomas.

"Swimmer Riley Gaines, an outspoken advocate against transgender athletes in women's sports, bashed a letter allegedly sent to the Harvard swim team gaslighting them about competing with transgender swimmer Lia Thomas."[61]

In case you're wondering what gaslighting is, *Psychology Today* defines it as "an insidious form of manipulation and psychological control. Victims of gaslighting are deliberately and systematically fed false information that leads them to question what they know to be true, often about themselves. They may end up doubting their memory, their perception, and even their sanity. Over time, a gaslighter's manipulations can grow more complex and potent, making it increasingly difficult for the victim to see the truth."[62]

Lia Thomas, a man living as a woman, became a household name in 2022 after he won first place in the women's 500-yard freestyle event in the NCAA's swimming championship. In the wake of the controversy, female members of the Harvard swim team were given a letter designed to gaslight them about competing with a man, stating that teammates "should set aside their personal beliefs and let Thomas compete."[63]

Gaines translated on Twitter:

> "Let my [sic] divert your attention from inherently feeling like something is wrong, by "asking you to focus on how great Lia has been. Let me emotionally blackmail you into accepting mistreatment because otherwise you are complicit in a potential death. Exchanging your fair treatment for someone else's benefit (a male in this case) is a justifiable cause. And the fair treatment of women is 'just politics' anyway. While we won't tell you what to do, we're telling you it is a bad choice to fight this. Let the men in charge at the NCAA decide your fate. Immerse your thoughts and feelings into something else to ignore the obvious injustice you face. Let other people decide if you are worthy of fair competition without your input or voice. Oh, and finally, don't talk." Make no mistake, this is bigger than just fairness in women's sports. They want to control how you think, how you feel, and what you say."[64]

In addition to winning the NCAA championship, Lia Thomas received a nomination for the NCAA "Woman of the Year" award but lost the bid after significant backlash.[65]

To no surprise, Thomas also expressed his support for the Biden administration's proposed change to Title IX that will effectively ban K-8 schools from protecting women's sports from transgender male athletes.[66]

Lia Thomas said, "I started swimming when I was five years old, and it has given me so many opportunities to learn, grow, develop and connect with my peers—opportunities I wouldn't have gotten if I didn't have access to athletics. That's why it breaks my heart to see trans kids across the country lose out on these opportunities."[67]

No, Lia. If trans athletes compete, young girls will not be given access and opportunities to have the experience you received as a young boy to compete and succeed. Even more so, what is heartbreaking is to try to convince children they are not the sexual identity of their chromosomes and sell them a lie that there is something wrong with the way they were created by God, male or female, rather than some variation. To push agendas on unsuspecting innocent children and alter them according to the image a politician, medical

> TO PUSH AGENDAS ON UNSUSPECTING INNOCENT CHILDREN AND ALTER THEM ACCORDING TO THE IMAGE A POLITICIAN, MEDICAL PROFESSIONAL, TEACHER, OR COACH WANTS THEM TO ASSUME IS PURE CHILD ABUSE: EMOTIONALLY, SOCIALLY, AND PHYSICALLY.

professional, teacher, or coach wants them to assume is pure child abuse: emotionally, socially, and physically. Pretending to make Lia the winner by eliminating competitors is not doing him a favor either. Will we pretend that people are dogs and put them into dog racing events at the tracks? Insanity.

Of course, he won the competition. He is a biological male, and his chromosomes are male (XY),[68] giving him a physical advantage that no amount of training or effort by female competitors can compensate for. In other words, to make a trans athlete "feel" affirmed, women were manipulated, by "feelings," to throw their dreams away so a confused athlete who could not compete with his own equals could win. This is nonsensical, but we are told to believe. This erases male and female in competitive sports and puts us back into one category: males and males who think they are women. Male sports.

Perhaps we can save a future generation a lot of nonsense and require that regardless of how someone identifies—whatever name they want to assume or identity they want to maintain they possess—for competitive purposes, they fall into two categories: XY (male) or XX (female)! They compete in the category of their chromosomes, not according to their clothes, hairstyle, or bodily alterations. Then the Lias of the world can dress up all they want, but when they compete, they do so as an XY in sports.

Hollywood celebrities have stepped up to condemn any woman calling herself a feminist who has expressed outrage over women being canceled in sports competitions, scholarships, and even pageant winners because transgender women (males) are competing for their awards.

Over 450 celebrities and feminist leaders signed onto an open letter in support of trans women and girls on Wednesday, which marked both the Trans Day of Visibility (TDOV) and the last day of Women's History Month. Notable signatories include actress Laverne Cox, singer Janelle Monae, soccer star Megan Rapinoe, politician Sarah McBride, and feminist icon Gloria Steinem.

"We believe that honoring the diversity of women's experiences is a strength, not a detriment to the feminist cause," they said in the letter…

The one-page declaration addresses the current onslaught of legislative attacks experienced by trans youth, and trans girls in particular. In the midst of a pandemic, over 20 states are attempting to ban trans athletes from playing on the athletic team that matches their gender. Many of these states are also attempting to criminalize providing trans healthcare to minors and prevent transgender people of all ages from correcting the gender listed on their birth certificates.

GLAAD goes on to condemn the actions of anti-trans feminists often referred to as Trans Exclusionary Radical Feminists, also known as TERFs. The letter claims that this "contingent of self-identified feminists" has helped to promote "damaging and violent ideas about trans people for years in the United States and internationally." It states that their aid of anti-trans efforts is, "in fact, not feminist at all."
"True feminists do not wish to limit any woman's identity or freedom to fully be herself," the statement reads. "Allowing

transphobic rhetoric to go unchecked also strengthens the legislative efforts of anti-trans politicians—who now cloak their bigotry in language about protecting or supporting women."[69]

So, women are being attacked, even feminists, because they don't want biological women canceled and are now labeled transphobic? And anyone who feels this way is a bigot? How is it that only the feelings of trans women are considered and not the feelings of girls who have no hope of winning since they are competing with biology? What is the root of this confusion? They (GLAAD and trans advocates) continue to confuse the definition of a woman as anyone who "says" they are a woman or "feels" like a woman in their claims of discrimination. I cannot discriminate against a person

> **THE CURRENT ADMINISTRATION, INCLUDING THE NEWEST SUPREME COURT JUSTICE, CAN NO LONGER DEFINE WHAT A WOMAN IS, AND THAT IN ITSELF IS A TRAVESTY.**

who claims womanhood if they are not actually a woman. The real issue is "what is a woman?" The current administration, including the newest Supreme Court Justice, can no longer define what a woman is, and that in itself is a travesty.

In the 13th hour of Judge Ketanji Brown Jackson's confirmation hearing Tuesday, Sen. Marsha Blackburn, R-Tenn., asked the Supreme Court nominee: "Can you provide a definition for the word 'woman'?" Jackson, appearing confused, responded, "I'm not a biologist." Blackburn chided Jackson, claiming "the fact that you can't give me a straight answer about something as fundamental as what a woman is underscores the dangers of the kind of progressive education that we are hearing about."[70]

Historically, there has never existed any confusion over what a woman is. A woman has always been defined by her biological characteristics, including her sexual organs. The same is true in the animal kingdom concerning male or female. This was undisputed in science or society until the last decades. Because Christianity (and other major religions as well) view women in this traditional definition and scripturally, there is an effort to paint Christianity as a religion of hate, male-dominated, patriarchal rule where women are less than men, but this absolutely is not true.

> JESUS TREATED WOMEN WITH GREAT RESPECT AND HONOR AND ELEVATED WOMEN TO A PLACE OF EQUALITY.

Jesus treated women with great respect and honor and elevated women to a place of equality. Jesus spoke to a woman at a well in Samaria. She was a woman of disrespect due to her multiple relationships and her living with a man who was not her husband. It was at a time and in a culture where this was less honored by society. Jesus valued her and offered her eternal life, the water that would satisfy her longing. Upon her belief in Him, He gave her purpose.

Scripture also says, "*There is neither Jew nor Gentile, neither slave nor free, nor is there male and female, for you are all one in Christ Jesus,*" (Galatians 3:28, NIV).

This is a statement of equality that in Christ we are valued the same, but we are not the same creation. Women are given positions of honor in the Old Testament, like Deborah, a judge over Israel, and in the New Testament, like Lydia, a businesswoman, and Philip's daughters, who were prophetesses. Motherhood is also honored throughout the Bible, like the ultimate mother, Mary. Men, likewise, are honored, as well as those of different ethnicities, social standing, and profession.

Christianity elevates every person as an individual with value, made in the likeness and image of God. *"Male and female, He created them,"* (Genesis 1:27b, NKJV). We can celebrate who God created us to be by accepting that we are created on purpose with His design in mind. We don't need to reject our sexual identity or biology or change it. To do so is to reject God's plan and design for us. We are loved and accepted by God the way He created us. To attempt to change this or compete with the opposite sex, trying to be them when we were not created this way, is to dishonor ourselves and the other sex.

This is Satan's desire: to steal from both male and female the beautiful design God made. Scripture tells us that Satan is the author of confusion (1 Corinthians 14:33). We can accept our value and discover who we are in Christ. Rather than changing our bodies, we need a change in how we view our identity; and that is a spiritual transformation, not gender reassignment or rejection of our created purpose.[71]

Fast forward five years or less, and there may no longer be any titles or scholarships held by our girls. It's easy to be silent until it affects your daughter or granddaughter. Remember, they're coming for your daughters.

CHAPTER 6

I'M GLAD YOU WERE SO MEAN, MAMA!

I listened to the podcast story of Erin Friday, attorney and mother, who eventually started a parents' advocacy group in response to the horrific story she had to walk out with her daughter.[72] When her 11-year-old daughter's seventh grade class taught a comprehensive sex-ed class, they used the Genderbread curriculum and pictorials depicting that you could have a female body but a boy brain. They shared that the sexual identity spectrum could be anywhere from one end with Barbie to the other end with G.I. Joe, and then there's a full spectrum anywhere in between. Instructors distributed a worksheet with many kinds of gender identities associated with fun names students from which one could choose to identify. Erin discovered her daughter and a few friends that hung out at their house sitting in the front yard talking about which "fun" identity they were going to choose. It was clear that it was "not cool to be a boring white girl," as none of them chose it. Who would choose that with so many other exciting options?

When she discovered what was going on, she was horrified and thought, "I am a class parent and help the teachers; we have become friends. How could they do this to our kids without telling us?" She had volunteered and received the volunteer award. "Why are these teachers that are considered friends teaching all this nonsense?" Upon questioning, she found out that the school brings in a third party to teach sex-ed. Why she was the only parent questioning this ideology was more disturbing to her.

From the interjected gender discovery in class, her daughter first chose to be pansexual (sexually or romantically attracted to people regardless of their gender). A year later, her daughter went from pansexual to lesbian (attracted to the same sex), and then over the pandemic, landed on being trans (wanting to live as the opposite sex) for a year and a half. Erin thought they had been smart, engaged parents, checking their daughter's social accounts, but she found that her daughter had fake shadow accounts where she had a trans identity and was getting fed information from trans groups.

During COVID, she found that the public school had changed her daughter's name to a male name on class rolls and transcripts and now used male pronouns to address her daughter. "They had never met her daughter or her, because it was the pandemic, and yet, they were making this decision. What an overreach." The school told Erin they needed a safe space for her daughter, insinuating she was not safe as a parent. Then, the house of cards began to fall.

Her daughter's mental health had severely plummeted. Erin tried to share with them that after her daughter came out as a new name, she battled depression and acted mean, whereas beforehand, she had been a sweet kid.

She said, "Now, she had switched to dressing Goth, decorated her room in EMO, almost like demonic things. She was not like the person I knew anymore. Her whole personality had changed, and she was not the child she had been."

Erin pulled her daughter from the school. They quickly engaged a psychologist but didn't vet her properly, and she turned out to be a "gender-affirming" psychologist who told them they needed to acknowledge her daughter's new identity or she would commit suicide. Erin got a quick education and learned that Diane Ehrensaft from UCSF was the psychologist's mentor, who promotes the transgender child and decries the satanic panic people have over it. She promotes concepts such as when a child unbuttons their onesie, that is gender communicating. If a little girl rips barrettes out of her hair, she's gender communicating.

Erin explained that her daughter had always liked girly things like American Girl dolls and My Little Pony as a young child, but the psychologist insisted she had been hiding her gender identity. The psychologist tried to tell Erin that her memory of her child was false. Notably, there's no science behind this. The doctor's contentions were all smoke and mirrors, to put it kindly.

As a mom, she was terrified and not doing well, questioned herself as a parent, and wondered what she could have done differently. How was she not smart enough to see this? She had opened her home to damaged children and wanted to be a parent to all kids but realized that their influence was to change her daughter's gender identity. "I felt sorry for these kids, too, but in hindsight, I should have barred them."

It was a long going in and going out process to help her daughter out of this, and she threw everything at her she could to help her. The most important thing she felt was to have a relationship. Erin said, "I decided to set boundaries, and I was not going to let those boundaries be crossed. I took her phone. Your child will hate you, but your love for your child has to be strong enough to take their vitriol. There were nights I cried myself to sleep, and some days, I didn't get out of bed after my daughter told me I was mean or she hated me. But now, there is not a day that goes by that my daughter doesn't say she loves me and thanks me. You can take the hate when you know what the end will be."

So, Erin's advice is: Take the phone, drop the friends, change schools, and get them away from people who try to tell them they're transgender. Be the fall person. There is a level of embarrassment for them to have to say they were wrong, but you shoulder all that and let them blame you. Erin sent her daughter to "give-back camps" as a service project that kept her busy, learning, and giving back. "I made it very clear: 'Your mother, who you used to respect and love, does not believe in this.'" I started protesting with signs. I put Abigail Shrier's book in every room. They

> **TAKE THE PHONE, DROP THE FRIENDS, CHANGE SCHOOLS, AND GET THEM AWAY FROM PEOPLE WHO TRY TO TELL THEM THEY'RE TRANSGENDER.**

listened to de-transitioners' podcasts and cult grooming techniques together on long drives. She compared the trans movement to a cult. Today, Erin and her daughter have a great relationship, and she has accepted she is a girl and is happy to be so.

Erin shared that there are common threads among gender confused children as all their stories are similar. She said if she knows if a child's a boy or girl, she knows the markers: bullied, into anime, same-sex attracted, porn is a huge component, and sometimes autism.

California continually gets worse at taking parental rights and pushing child transitions. Insurers are getting closer to being required to cover surgeries, and parents' insurances paying for it—with parents not even being made aware of it.[73 74 75 76]

Parents are considered nefarious, evil, bad, terrorists, Erin shared. "Parents should know if their kids are going into a trans closet and changing clothes or being given trans tape at school to tape up their genitals or given binders to flatten their breasts. California just engaged 10,000 new school counselors who are actually new indoctrinators (secret keepers). Parents don't know that their kids are going to a counselor every day at school.

Erin identifies the following powerful, preventative measures: (1) Know the curriculum your child is assigned; (2) Know their teachers, and look for pride flags and gender fluidity books; (3) If anything alarms you, pull your kid out! Don't wait for an issue; (4) Be there for class read-alouds; (5) Go to school board meetings; (6) Reinforce two sexes at home, and give them responses to say when they are asked about pronouns; (7) Never allow your kids to take their school or medical surveys; (8) Read all their assignments; (9) Use the Switch phone with no Internet connection; and (10) Beware of social media; even Pinterest has messaging capabilities. "If I can't stand up for children, I have no morals. They can't cancel us all. All of us must do something."

> "IF I CAN'T STAND UP FOR CHILDREN, I HAVE NO MORALS. THEY CAN'T CANCEL US ALL. ALL OF US MUST DO SOMETHING."

It's extremely sad that children can be targeted by schools, medical representatives, celebrities, and drag queen story hour, but counselors, psychologists, and even in some places, ministers, are not allowed to question the child's "transitioning," pronouns, etc., or to counsel them in another direction. Everyone can push and almost force trans agendas on young, innocent, unsuspecting children looking to adults for life's truths, but no adult, including parents, is allowed to disagree or offer an alternative view of any sort? Christians with biblical answers aren't allowed to share their view of origin and gender? This is clearly a demonic plot to silence any view of the God that made them, and who made no accident in doing so. How can pharmaceutical companies and misdirected psychiatrists make billions if everyone accepts themselves as they are and are taught to embrace their gender as a gift and learn to love their body and identity as intentional and acceptable by a loving Creator?

I am familiar with another situation where a child's father had passed, and she was emotionally struggling. She had also been molested by two different persons earlier in childhood, and that trauma resulted in a belief that men were not safe. Instead of helping the child deal with the trauma of these situations, the psychiatric counselor had her write her mother a letter informing her mother she was transsexual! In the wrong body! The mother was obviously beyond upset. She confronted the counselor and said, "Before you draw these extreme conclusions, can you affirm that my daughter is healed from the trauma and pain of her father passing and the sexual abuse?" The counselor said, "No." "Then, how could you possibly determine that she could make such a life-altering decision as this in a state of depression and pain?" the mother demanded. The counselor had no words. Make no mistake, there is an agenda being pushed!

Once the mother removed her daughter from the environment, she rededicated her life to Christ. Eventually, her daughter told her, "Mom, the counselors thought you were mean, and I did, too, at the time, but I am so glad you were mean! Thank you for being mean, Mama. I'm not trans; I still like boys. I was just afraid and hurt."

Mental health issues are plaguing our nation's young people[77] as a result of family breakdown, over-sexualization, experimentation, addictions, and the resulting pain, but counselors will only accept the new "identity" and not address the root pain behind the confusion or these drastic life-altering decisions. Instead, children are given the option to choose "trans" as an escape from painful memories and hurts and to deflect the real issue, determining they are in the "wrong body." Everyone wants a fresh start, and the fantasy of starting all over as a new person, with a new name, and even new sex can be inviting if a child has been through trauma and struggles with self-rejection. How irresponsible is it to steer impressionable children toward decisions that have forever consequences, like puberty blockers, hormones, and mastectomies? We can understand why suicide rates skyrocket after trans surgeries.[78] The emotional pain coupled with the physical pain and mutilation of their bodies is too much to bear.

We are given real "change" and a fresh start through Christ. To become a "new creature in Christ" is to understand we have a new beginning and we are loved, regardless of any past pain or failings (2 Corinthians 5:17, KJV). Trans ideology is a deflection that pretends to fix a problem on the outside that comes from the inside. We can't change someone's inner hurts by a new outside identity or a new name. No hormone blockers, surgeries, or dress-up can change the hurt on the inside. Only by receiving healing from God—administered through those who love and are committed to real transformation, a spiritual new birth—can the core root issues be addressed. Transgender ideology is a lie. It will not bring the real change that it promises. To mislead children to believe that it will is criminal at best.

> **TRANSGENDER IDEOLOGY IS A LIE.**

Children Learn through Play and Imagination

First expressions of children and their personalities are seen in role playing.[79] It's perfectly normal for brothers and sisters to pretend, play dress-up and house, to role-play mommy and daddy; for sisters to dress up their little brothers; for girls to love to play sports or trucks with a brother, or for him to play dolls with his sister; or for boys to mimic their mothers or girls to do more masculine activities to hang out with their fathers. These are normal activities of childhood and the male/female exchange. "I'll play with dolls if we can play dinosaurs next," a brother said to his sister who was a year older. Adults do that as well. My husband loves to ride motorcycles. I enjoy riding, but I also like going to an antique store or tearoom. We share the experiences in a give and take; and if those were reversed, it would not make him a female or me a male. How offensive that those who call themselves "doctors" could confuse these into gender dysphoria. In the extremely rare cases of gender confusion, studies affirm that 84-88 percent return to their birth sex by adulthood.[80]

The best gift we can give our children is character, and we do that by requiring what is acceptable and doing the work that is necessary. As the Bible instructs in Proverbs 22:6a (KJV), "*Train up a child in the way he should go.*" Part of that training is affirming that God created them: "*Male and female he created them,*" (Genesis 5:2, ESV). There is no "spectrum" except that which so-called science and medicine have tried to create in an effort to deny God's creation and make themselves into "gods." They will answer to the one true God for their perversion of the souls and bodies of children, just as the pornographer, the trafficker, and the abuser will.

Distraught parents of adult children who have gone into harmful lifestyles ask me, "What can I do to fix this?" We cannot take false responsibility for the lives of other adults. We are not responsible for our children as adults, but we are responsible to them—to love them as a person but disagree with their choices. We can still love but disagree and not accept lies. As an adult, we are all responsible for our own lives, choices, and decisions.

When our children are underage and live in our homes, we are completely responsible for them. No government organization or psychologist or medical person has the authority to take a parent's rights to protect and train their child. This is a God-given call and responsibility. Parents must take this commission seriously, refuse to miss the opportunity to vehemently protect them, and stand up to any force that would dare violate their purity, identity, and belief system. It is a much harder conversation with parents of

> **IT IS MUCH EASIER TO MOLD A CHILD THAN REPAIR AN ADULT.**

broken adults than to prevent the indoctrination to begin with. It is much easier to mold a child than repair an adult. Why do you think the trans-revolutionaries are targeting children? They understand this better than many parents. Make no mistake. Their goal is to "mold a child in the way they want them to go, and when they are old, they will not depart from it." Millions of dollars will be made in the process.

Thirty seconds of human anger can cause brokenness in the belief system of a child.[81] Children draw conclusions about themselves when hurtful experiences or physical, emotional, or spiritual abuse happens. A little hidden voice talks from within and speaks defeat, failure, fear, and hopelessness. No matter what we change on the outside, the inside is where the problem exists. What is hidden in secret has a way of surfacing in situations and times when we least expect it. When that happens, it can feel overwhelming, but God, in His love and mercy, will let root issues surface that need to be dealt with. We try to mask our issues or hide them underneath achievement, personal possessions, addictions, and even relationships, but if that brokenness hasn't been healed, the pain will show up. Pain seeks pleasure and escape from the pressure. How can we help ourselves, our families, and children be freed and healed from the attacks that Satan has wielded against us?

We are told to forgive our abusers and ourselves, and we know we should, but sometimes we don't know how to forgive. This can trap us into feeling shame and confusion. Forgiveness is a choice we get to make, "to forgive as we have been forgiven." We choose forgiveness. Sometimes in our mind, we need to remove the command of "I have to forgive." If we "have to," it feels like slavery. If I "get to," it is a choice. God gave us the free will to make that choice. His Word tells us to guard our hearts, because everything in life flows out of our hearts. It is helpful for our hearts to experience the compassion for someone else that leads us to choose forgiveness. To choose forgiveness is to choose to follow in the footsteps of Jesus, freedom, and a fresh start. To forgive yourself and forgive others releases you from replaying the offense and being stuck in its trauma.

Those who hope in the Lord will not be dismayed. Situations can look hopeless, but there is always hope. In the heat of the moment, it's easy to react in our flesh out of our wounds and to make hasty decisions. High emotion equals low intelligence.[82] Refrain from making decisions when you are emotional. That's the play of the enemy to get us to draw extreme conclusions. Trans-revolutionaries are taking advantage of children and families in high emotion and pain to make low intelligent decisions. God forgive them, but save our children from their lies.

Forgiveness is a start, but there is work to be done. If we want to stay free, Jesus said we must not only clean the house and our lives of demonic lies, spirits, and their influence. We must also kill them with the fruit of God's Spirit, the truth of His Word, and the freedom to live for Him instead of being driven by past inner vows, hurts, and struggles.

Deliverance from demonic strongholds that came during painful trauma, abuse, hurt or from overbearing or demanding parents and situations is often needed. Alongside that, we must do the homework to renew our minds and free our souls from hurt.

The spirit is willing, but the flesh is weak. We can receive a breakthrough through deliverance by God's Spirit, freeing us from pain. The work in our spirits can be done immediately, but our souls, which encompasses our minds, wills, and emotions, must have renewal. A breakthrough is like when we receive salvation. The breakthrough is a start but not where we stop. Those areas need growth, healing, and character development. There is work to be done to redeem and restore the areas that hurt, break inner vows, and resolve issues from trauma and pain in our lives that have wreaked havoc. It has become unnatural for us to do certain things that are healthy when we are so unhealthy. We must relearn the right responses to show our love, to initiate love, and receive it. Children are no different. They need affirmation of who they are in Christ and what they have in Him. They also need healing from any deviations that have broken their hearts or harmed their identity as a child of God, created in His image, and the sex He gave them.

CHAPTER 7

CRITICAL RACE THEORY, CURRICULA & CONTROL

How do government officials, principals, educators, and school boards think they have the license to decide what children should be taught when it comes to morality, sexual behaviors, and views on their identity and race? Education Week, which touts itself as "America's most trusted resource for K-12 education news and information since 1981,"[83] presented an article in defense of their CRT and LGBTQ curricula many consider indoctrination and how the backlash started that began, in their words, to "censor" educators and books.[84] Comically, most conservatives and parents would find the actions they consider hinder education to be a positive move in the right direction to protect children from indoctrination through radical theories of sex-ed and racial fairness under the guise of Critical Race Theory. Critical Race Theory is denounced by many, including racial minorities, as actually condoning the same racial inequality that brought racial segregation in the first place.

> CRITICAL RACE THEORY IS DENOUNCED BY MANY, INCLUDING RACIAL MINORITIES, AS ACTUALLY CONDONING THE SAME RACIAL INEQUALITY THAT BROUGHT RACIAL SEGREGATION IN THE FIRST PLACE.

> Critical race theory has its roots in the Critical Theory of the neo-Marxist Frankfurt School, developed by thinkers such as Max Horkheimer, Theodore Adorno, and Herbert Marcuse, and continued in the work of Jürgen Habermas and others. Questioning both the value and the possibility of objective knowledge, and seeing claims to universal truth as the seeds of oppression…

And it's clear that many public schools are indeed incorporating plenty of CRT-inspired ideas in their curricula. Consider, for instance, the Albemarle County School District in Virginia, which adopted an anti racism policy in 2019. The details of the policy and related curriculum are documented in the official complaint filed in C.I. v. Albemarle County School Board, a lawsuit brought by five families who object to the ideology being taught in their schools.

According to the complaint, the county's schools teach children that all "whites" are inherently privileged due to their race, while all people of color are inherently disadvantaged and subordinated... and CRT's central claim about the systemic and pervasive nature of racism in our country. One article used in the curriculum states that in order to avoid being racist, "white people ... must acknowledge and understand their privilege," while people of color must "recogniz[e] how race and racism have been internalized." Students are told that being opposed to affirmative action, claiming reverse discrimination, saying "we all belong to the human race," or seeking objectivity by recognizing that there are "two sides to every story," are forms of racism.

This curricular content clearly draws on (and oversimplifies) CRT's view of legal neutrality and objectivity as tools of oppression that perpetuate systemic injustices. Similarly, in what could be a summary of key take-aways from CRT popularizers like DiAngelo and Kendi, a student handout presents a wide variety of actions and attitudes—including being "colorblind," the "celebration of Columbus Day," "denial of white privilege," support of "anti-immigrant policies," and "over-familiarization with POC [people of color]"—as "passive racism" that directly supports more "active" racist actions like "hate crimes" and "lynching."

The curriculum does not limit the teaching of such ideas to a single course, but requires that they be incorporated into multiple subject areas, including English, social studies, science, and even math. Crucially, these ideas are not presented as offering a controversial perspective that students can discuss and critique. On the contrary, this ideology is presented as uncontested truth to which students must assent and conform. The punishment for failure to do so is not only being labeled racist, but official disciplinary actions such as detention, suspension, or the requirement to attend a "restorative justice" session.[85]

Should children be shamed for acts they didn't commit and forced to say, "I have white privilege?" Should children be required to see themselves as victims and less than another because of their ancestry? CRT seeks to simply dehumanize and degrade people of all backgrounds based on race or gender. Do two wrongs make things right? Racism toward any group of people is completely unacceptable; it matters not what the skin color is. Is heterosexuality evil because it constitutes the majority of sexual identification? How is villainizing any group of people not risky, dangerous behavior, especially when

> CRT SEEKS TO SIMPLY DEHUMANIZE AND DEGRADE PEOPLE OF ALL BACKGROUNDS BASED ON RACE OR GENDER.

the audience is to shame children for something that they were not responsible for doing? How can we hold a child responsible if his/her father was a criminal? CRT punishes and guilts the innocent into shame, personal rejection, and hatred. In the guise of equality, it uses discrimination of minorities (whether of skin color or sexual orientation) to turn children against heterosexuality, equating the evils of slave trade with the discrimination of LGBTQ persons. CRT actually reignites racial hatred and tensions to victimize people, ultimately for state control. These are the roots of all Marxism.

Education Week has a problem with any resistance to CRT. In an article, "The Evolution of the Anti-CRT Movement: A Timeline," Education Week laments:

> Dozens of state laws restricting lessons on race and racism. School policies restricting transgender, nonbinary, and gender nonconforming students from participating in sports, using bathrooms aligned to their identities, and not being addressed by their preferred pronouns. And thousands of books removed from classroom and library shelves. The backlash to expanding diversity, equity, and inclusion efforts started in 2020, but has split and spiraled over the course of two years into several initiatives that impact students' schooling experiences. Both at the state and district levels, these efforts have been driven primarily by Republican lawmakers and right-wing groups who claim books and lessons about LGBTQ topics are inappropriate and that lessons on race and racism can teach white students to "hate themselves."

How did we get here?"[86]

Education Week blames Trump for removing the first brick in their utopian wall of diversity.

> Former President Donald Trump's executive order banning some types of diversity training for federal employees was the origin for the list of eight "divisive concepts," later seen in dozens of bills and laws restricting lessons on race and racism. Although the executive order was revoked by President Joe Biden, the language remains widely adopted by Republican lawmakers, and in state legislation, across the country.

What are Divisive Concepts?

> Many people are pushing a different vision of America that is grounded in hierarchies based on collective social and political identities rather than in the inherent and equal dignity of every person as an individual. This ideology is rooted in the pernicious and false belief that America is an irredeemably racist and sexist country; that some people, simply on account of their race or sex, are oppressors; and that racial and sexual identities are more important than our common status as human beings and Americans."[87]

To address CRT and gender ideology, Trump signed Executive Order 13950, which required federal agencies to assess compliance with the order's mandates in any diversity, equity, or inclusion training.

The order described "divisive concepts" in this manner:

"Divisive concepts" are:

> (1) one race or sex is inherently superior to another race or sex;
> (2) the United States is fundamentally racist or sexist;
> (3) an individual, by virtue of his or her race or sex, is inherently racist, sexist, or oppressive, whether consciously or unconsciously;
> (4) an individual should be discriminated against or receive adverse treatment solely or partly because of his or her race or sex;
> (5) members of one race or sex cannot and should not attempt to treat others without respect to race or sex;
> (6) an individual's moral character is necessarily determined by his or her race or sex;
> (7) an individual, by virtue of his or her race or sex, bears responsibility for actions committed in the past by other members of the same race or sex;
> (8) any individual should feel discomfort, guilt, anguish, or any other form of psychological distress on account of his or her race or sex; or
> (9) meritocracy or traits such as a hard work ethic are racist or sexist, or were created by a particular race to oppress another race.

The term "divisive concepts" also includes any other form of race or sex stereotyping or any other form of race or sex scapegoating."[88]

President Joe Biden repealed the order on the first day of his presidency in 2020.[89] [90]

EW complains the next brick removed was when:

> [T]he first three divisive concepts laws were passed in Oklahoma, Tennessee, and Texas in May 2021. The early versions of the laws all included similar language, banning teachers from teaching that students should feel guilt or anguish on account of their race or sex, or that anyone was inherently racist or sexist....[91]

Next, parents challenged a few educators for their radical views, and some educators lost jobs.

> "Matthew Hawn, a teacher in Tennessee, was fired from Sullivan County Schools for teaching white privilege as a fact, just a few days before the state passed its divisive concepts law. Hawn appealed the decision to his school board and lost."[92]

> "Just days before Arizona's divisive concepts law was about to go into effect, a county judge ruled that it violated the state's constitution, as it was vaguely written and tucked into a broader budget bill. Arizona's supreme court later upheld that decision, making the state's challenge the first and only successful one to block divisive concepts laws from impacting schools. A handful of other states have followed Arizona's lead and are either awaiting a decision or have had their cases dismissed."

"In March, Florida Gov. Ron DeSantis, a Republican, signed the Parental Rights in Education law, which is called the 'Don't Say Gay' law by its opponents because it restricts LGBTQ students and teachers from talking about their identities in classrooms. The law bans education about sexual orientation and gender identity for elementary students and requires that secondary school students are taught about these topics in a 'developmentally appropriate' way, as defined by the state. The law has spurred many copycat bills across the country."[93]

"Starting in the latter half of 2021, parents' complaints at school board meetings started shifting from lessons on race and racism to books about those topics, or books with LGBTQ characters. As of April, two million students in 86 school districts across the country have had their access to books restricted because of book bans put in place this school year." [94]

What Education Week fails to mention is the pornographic nature of these books and their degradation of marriage, family, and the religious beliefs of a majority of Americans. A Gallup poll conducted found that "a staggering 69 per cent of respondents believe people who identify as 'transgender' should remain in the sports that correspond to their actual biological gender. This marks a 7-point increase from a similar survey taken two years prior.... The results reflect an ongoing backlash against transgenderism at both a political and cultural level."[95]

Two districts in Oklahoma—Tulsa and Mustang—saw their accreditation downgraded by the state board of education after the state said they had violated the state's divisive concepts law through professional development lessons for educators on inherent bias… This was the first instance of a district's accreditation being impacted by an anti-CRT law, and the board's choice of punishment was harsher than the one recommended by state rules.[96]

In a great win for parental rights, Governor Glenn Youngkin introduced a policy that requires teachers to not hide information about a student's gender identity from their parents, use a student's sex assigned at birth and their legal name according to school records, and also requires transgender students to use bathrooms and play on sports teams that are aligned with their sex assigned at birth.[97]

Moms for Liberty impacted school board elections by requiring candidates to take a pledge and endorsed 500 school board candidates across the country this year, electing 49 percent. "In some of those districts, such as Charleston and Berkeley, in South Carolina, the election of far-right members to school boards in November led to the firing of superintendents and other drastic changes."[98]

ARE CHILDREN IN SERVITUDE TO THE STATE, OWNED AND INDOCTRINATED FOR THEIR PURPOSES, OR DID GOD INSTRUCT PARENTS TO "TRAIN UP A CHILD IN THE WAY HE SHOULD GO"?

Interestingly, what a majority of Americans would consider a win for the protection of children's minds and hearts by withholding sexually explicit material from them is considered an attack on free speech by the strong left-leaning teacher's unions and publications like Education Week. Do they view your children as theirs? Are children in servitude to the state, owned and indoctrinated for their purposes, or did God instruct parents to "*train up a child in the way he should go*" (Proverbs 22:6, KJV)? If parents will continue to stand up, keep up the pressure on political leaders to prohibit and remove the indoctrination of educators, it will be possible to spare a generation from repeating the egregious errors of segregation and the hedonistic anti-family and anti-marriage practices that destroyed many civilizations and are now destroying our education system.

You have to love the people of Arizona who have now created a hotline for parents to report schools and teachers, a customer service hotline if you will.

> "Arizona's Department of Education introduced a hotline last week for the public to report classroom lessons promoting critical race theory (CRT), gender ideology, and 'inappropriate sexual content,' topics that have long faced conservative criticism."

> The "Empower Hotline," which "empowers" concerned parents by encouraging them to report lessons that "detract from teaching academic standards," was a key promise of Republican Superintendent of Public Instruction Tom Horne's recent campaign, which aimed to prioritize math and reading instruction while declaring "war" on unnecessary and potentially harmful discussions about emotions and identity, according to the Arizona Republic.

THEY ARE COMING FOR YOUR CHILDREN
THE FIGHT WE MUST WIN!

The Department of Education's website allows for Arizona residents to report "inappropriate lessons that detract from teaching academic standards," which includes topics such as those linked to CRT and "social and emotional learning" programs accused of promoting "woke" concepts regarding race, gender, and sexuality.

"Some say critical race theory is a graduate study, not taught in K-12 schools. The evidence is to the contrary," Horne said, demanding that teachers "teach academics [and] not use their power over a captive audience, to promote their personal ideology."

"That is unprofessional conduct," he added.

He also assured educators that "as long as they are teaching academics, they have absolutely nothing to worry about."

"I want to be sure that we get rid of distractions, and the teachers are teaching the academics bell-to-bell the way they're supposed to be doing," he said."[99]

Imagine if schools and teachers had to account for their actions and the results of their job performance. For too long, tenure gave teachers the "right" to stay employed in school systems whether they were delivering real education for kids or not. Test scores have sunk to historical lows in the world, especially for developed countries like the U.S.

While speaking at a Moms for Liberty Joyful Warriors Summit

concerning his 2024 run for president, Trump pledged, "On day one, I will sign a new executive order to cut federal funding for any school pushing Critical Race Theory, transgender insanity, and other inappropriate racial, sexual, or political content on our children," before advocating for moving the "education system back to the states."[100]

He added:

> "Under my leadership, the 1619 project, you remember that beauty, climate change extremists that are destroying our country… the ridiculous 87 different genders the left says there are out there, think of it, and… we're going to cut it out. We're going to get it out. We are going to be pressing three basic things plus reading, writing, and arithmetic."

Trump stated that the "Marxism, fascism, communism, and the radical left socialism" he says is being thrust on students in classrooms across the country is not only hostile to religion, but "it now resembles established religion of its own," adding:

> "The Marxist left, and other lunatics preaching radical ideology, have become a cult with their own creeds, and their own mantras, and their own rituals. Instead of taking children to church, they believe in taking children to drag shows. You see what's happening?… Instead of teaching them to say their prayers, they teach them to recite their pronouns."

Trump said that he would direct his Department of Justice to legally pursue schools that engage in "these militant and country-destroying practices" under the "Establishment Clause and the Free Exercise Clause of our Constitution."

Moreover, he reiterated his plan to "implement massive funding preferences for all states and school districts" that commit to the following actions:

- "Abolishing teacher tenure for grades K-12 so we can remove bad teachers."
- "Adopting merit pay so we can reward the great teachers."
- "Implementing complete curriculum transparency so that parents have the right to see 100 percent of the material their children are being taught in school."
- "And very importantly, adopting a program of universal school choice."
- Furthermore, Trump advocated for local elections for school principal positions."[101]

This is the formula to take back education from leftists and stop the misinformation that is flooding our school systems and controlling impressionable minds. This is our opportunity; let's not lose it. We can expect a tremendous backlash from teachers' unions, lobbyists, woke corporations, big tech, and big, big money from the pharmaceutical industry to buy the election at all costs. Instead of just raising their hand, some parents stood up, and if they will refuse to sit down, this is a battle that we can win—the fight for our children's education. Either way, at whatever costs, get them out of this indoctrination!

And many parents are opting to do just that!

> Public school enrollment declined by 1.4 million students between fall 2019 and fall of 2020, dipping to 49.4 million, a loss of nearly 3 percent, and remains at the lowest point in a decade… Parental satisfaction with K-12 education plunged between 2019 and 2022, according to Gallup. Prior to the onset of COVID-19, 51 percent of parents said they were either completely or somewhat satisfied with their child's education. Three years later, that satisfaction level was 42 percent, the lowest in more than 20 years… distance learning during school lockdowns provided a glimpse into the classroom that made parents question their school's ability to educate their children."[102]

Some parents were surprised to see how little the school was actually doing for their children and did not miss the negative peer pressure on their child. Many parents who homeschooled during the pandemic, who may never have considered it otherwise, continued as they saw their children flourish academically and socially.[103]

MANY PARENTS WHO HOMESCHOOLED DURING THE PANDEMIC, WHO MAY NEVER HAVE CONSIDERED IT OTHERWISE, CONTINUED AS THEY SAW THEIR CHILDREN FLOURISH ACADEMICALLY AND SOCIALLY.

Studies have shown that homeschooled children tend to have higher standardized test scores, persevere through college longer, and have higher GPAs in college. For a long time, the most commonly expressed concern was worry that homeschooled children would be disadvantaged socially. Wow! Has this ever changed!

Once again, studies have reassured those considering homeschooling that homeschoolers are doing well on "all measures of social, emotional, and psychological development." In fact, many families now live in communities where the hardest part is deciding which activity to say "no" to!

With the rise in homeschooling popularity, there are literally countless ways creative homeschooling families can achieve socialization opportunities through volunteering, co-ops, sports, youth groups, and working in the community.[104]

Home School Legal Defense Association (HSLDA) is an organization that has helped families of all different backgrounds, single parents, and those with special needs children succeed at home education and has resources to help parents tailor their child's education to their unique gifts and personality. HSLDA says, "So, does homeschooling work? The short answer is, 'Yes, it can wildly succeed and be one of the best decisions your family will ever make.'"[105]

Our family chose home education, and it did wildly succeed. Other families are choosing religious schools and charter schools as some states are offering educational funds redirected back to parents to choose how and where their children are to be educated. The most important decision we will make about our children is who will train them. It is a God-given right and responsibility of every parent to train up their child in the way they should go and to protect their children from negative, radical outside influences. This standard needs to be applied in choosing a college or university as well. Jesus said, "When the student is fully trained, they will become like their teacher," (Luke 6:40, NIV).

CHAPTER 8

ART AND THE DISREGARD FOR LIFE

Proclaimed tech futurist Yuval Noah Harari, the philosophical voice of the World Economic Forum heralded by Bill Gates as "the prophet," doesn't see human life as being from God, so he says there are "useless people" among us.[106] Thus, it's perfectly acceptable to the humanist to eliminate them, to take their lives through abortion, and to fight to do so. The same people will fight to keep someone who has taken human life from facing justice in court. Their good is evil, and their evil is good. At the core of these arguments is a worldview that either rejects God and His principles for life or believes God created human beings in His likeness and image, male and female, and that all human life has beauty, dignity, and value, regardless of whether a person is unborn, disabled, young, old, male, female, or of any ethnicity and background. If you believe this, then it dictates how you see life, art, culture, and view others. If you reject this view, then engineering who should live and who should not (eugenics), as Hitler attempted, becomes the philosophy that guides all decisions, including justice and artistic expression

Therefore, those who believe in God and the sanctity of life become the number one enemy of the humanist, Marxist, and fascist.[107] In their minds, the Christian is the dangerous person that holds back technology, advancement, art, and an utopian world that exalts LGBTQ equity. It's, therefore, not a philosophy. It's a religion to them, and Christians and other undesirables are viewed as "useless eaters"[108] and haters who refuse to deny God and His commands for life.

This is also why they detest the Constitution of the United States of America,[109] because it protects the rights of the individual to have life, liberty, to pursue happiness, the right to religious freedom, free speech, to protest, to have a free press, to own property, and to defend one's life, family, and freedom from tyranny, albeit with a gun if necessary. These rights cause humanist demons to shriek in terror. They hate that ALL people have rights and freedom. On one hand, globalists scream equity and equal rights, but on the other hand, they want those rights to exist for them but not for those with whom they disagree.

The World Economic Forum has an agenda of depopulation,[110] abortion as a UN right, LGBTQ as the forefront of equity, and taking the rights of others in the name of LGBTQ. They wish to possess children's spirits, souls, and bodies by displacing parents and creating the UN Rights of the Child to conform children to the image of their god of equity and LGBTQ. The World Economic Forum is driving this agenda via ESG (environmental, social, governance) to control the money flow to those who support their ideology, starving out any opposition. The view that artificial intelligence (AI) is replacing human beings and that we have a population of useless people that need to be "dealt with" screams the opposite of human rights.[111] [112] They want some people to live and human rights just for "certain ones." The rest that don't align with

> THE VIEW THAT ARTIFICIAL INTELLIGENCE (AI) IS REPLACING HUMAN BEINGS AND THAT WE HAVE A POPULATION OF USELESS PEOPLE THAT NEED TO BE "DEALT WITH" SCREAMS THE OPPOSITE OF HUMAN RIGHTS.

their agendas and belief systems are not worthy of life and should be silenced, at best, and ultimately eliminated. This battle is being played out daily in business, arts, schools, and medicine.[113]

The social engineers at the World Economic Forum, and may I add many in its leadership, fall into the LGBTQ "friendly" category in their personal sexual expressions (identities) and have become involved in the education of American children over the last decades.[114] Now at early ages, they are confusing children about their identity and forcing them to question whether they are a boy or girl, the most basic trait in humanity.[115] Once the child is confused, they reprogram and indoctrinate them. Convincing the child that they are a victim of social inequity gives them power or control over the child. The victimized child is weaponized against anyone who does not accept the belief system that they have programmed them to believe. Do you see why we are beginning to see violence from LGBTQ youth against Christian schools?

> **WHERE ARE THE PARENTS, TEACHERS, DOCTORS, AND BANKERS WHO DISAGREE WITH THIS PROPAGANDA BEING FORCED ON TINY KIDS WHO ARE LOOKING FOR THEIR IDENTITY, ACCEPTANCE, AND THE UNDERSTANDING OF HOW TO LIVE LIFE?**

This is the formula for Nazism, Marxism, and any totalitarian takeover.[116] Capture the youth and use them against the Constitution. If only the children knew the truth! Who will tell them? Where are the parents, teachers, doctors, and bankers who disagree with this propaganda being forced on tiny kids who are looking for their identity, acceptance, and the understanding of how to live life?

These same social engineers are the ones who advocate to abort children. How do we help youth understand that the people training them and spending more time with them than their parents have an agenda against them? Social engineers have succeeded in killing 63 million of them via abortion,[117] and the ones that remain are now subjects of their indoctrination.

The correlation between abortion and violence against children is undeniable. In fact, after the acceptance of Roe v. Wade, abortion skyrocketed, and so did child abuse. This death of children has amounted to over 1,800 children in the U.S. being murdered in a year by their parents.

> According to data from the National Child Abuse and Neglect Data System (NCANDS), 51 States[118] reported a total of 1,809 fatalities.[119] Based on this data, a nationally estimated 1,840 children died from abuse or neglect in FFY 2019, a slight increase from the FFY 2018 number of 1,780. However, it is a 10.8 percent increase over the FFY 2015 number of 1,660.[120]

Thankfully with the Supreme Court conservative ruling (thanks to Donald Trump nominees), our justices have recently upheld the Constitution in some major decisions,[121] but our nation and Constitution is hanging by a thread, and those seeking to rule from global thrones know it.

> ... OUR NATION AND CONSTITUTION IS HANGING BY A THREAD, AND THOSE SEEKING TO RULE FROM GLOBAL THRONES KNOW IT.

Nonetheless, violence against children, and especially sexual violence against children, is at an all-time high. And now, youth are perpetuating violence, too, and learning new ways to fund it from adults in the art community.

We often observe the skirmishes but miss the battle plan. We must understand the big picture of anarchist's goals to stop them at their game. We get sidelined or distracted with small items, and they are going for a complete takeover of all beauty, life, and freedom.

How a culture values life, order, justice, and creation can be seen in its arts. Throughout history, art has been used to reflect people's beliefs and culture. It can steer culture in a direction that either aligns with God's Word and view of life and justice or induces lust and other vices that kill and destroy.

Ezekiel 28:12-15 is a description of Satan and the artistry with which he was created by God. The creativity that flowed from him led heaven's artistic worship of the Creator of all life, but then in vanity and pride, Satan exalted himself and led a rebellion against God. The Bible recounts:

> *You were the seal of perfection, full of wisdom and perfect in beauty. You were in Eden, the garden of God; every precious stone was your covering: The sardius, topaz, and diamond, beryl, onyx, and jasper, sapphire, turquoise, and emerald with gold.*
>
> *The workmanship of your timbrels and pipes was prepared for you on the day you were created.*
>
> *You were the anointed cherub who covers; I established you; you were on the holy mountain of God; you walked back and forth in the midst of fiery stones. You were perfect in your ways from the day you were created, till iniquity was found in you.*
>
> —Ezekiel 28:12b-15 (NKJV)

Satan used his beauty, power, and position to create rebellion. He corrupted himself through pride and vanity. Today, he still seeks to inhabit humanity's arts, music, and creativity, to lead a rebellion against God, destroy justice (what is just) and human life with sin and corruption.

When I was studying color, design, and imagery for logos to represent our movement to take back our children from those who are bent on their destruction, I was shocked to find that every color and positive image I found interesting had been co-opted by the LGBTQ movement.

> Pride Month was first recognized in 1994 when a coalition of education-based organizations in the United States designated October as LGBT History Month. The federal government first recognized the month in 1999 when President Bill Clinton declared June "Gay & Lesbian Pride Month." In 2009, President Barack Obama declared June LGBT Pride Month. On 1 June 2021, President Joe Biden declared June LGBTQ Pride Month."[122]

A month of Pride plus 11 more individual days of celebration on the calendar? I ask, is there any other group of people who garner this amount of celebration? This is not equity, folks. This is a takeover, a form of adoration, and worship wrapped in artistry masquerading as social justice.

I picked up a beautiful "art magazine" in Europe, and to my shock, a controversial performance artist connected to Podesta and Clinton emails, Marina Abramović, was featured in revolutionary themed pictures with self-described nonbinary artists of varying mediums. Heralded as a hero and role model for youth, she is pictured with masked young female revolutionaries with backdrops of burning cities. Who is Abramović?

> …Abramović worked with Jacob Samuel to produce a cookbook of "aphrodisiac recipes," called *Spirit Cooking,* in 1996.[123] These "recipes" were meant to be "evocative instructions for actions or for thoughts." For example, one of the recipes calls for "13,000 grams of jealousy," while another says to "mix fresh breast milk with fresh sperm milk."[124] The work was inspired by the popular belief that ghosts feed off intangible things like light, sound, and emotions.[125]

In my opinion, with these witches' brews, she is inviting spirit entities, performing satanic rituals, and selling this as art and performance to ignite passions in her participants. Quite literally, she is engaging people in demonic-inspired experiences that invoke infatuation with supernatural evil. She calls it "art."

> In 1997, Abramović created a multimedia *Spirit Cooking* installation. This was originally installed in the Zerynthia Associazione per l'Arte Contemporanea in Rome, Italy, and included white gallery walls with "enigmatically violent recipe instructions" painted in pig's blood.[126] According to Alexxa Gotthardt, the work is "a comment on humanity's reliance on ritual to organize and legitimize our lives and contain our bodies."[127]

Abramović also published a *Spirit Cooking* cookbook containing comico-mystical, self-help instructions… *Spirit Cooking* later evolved into a form of dinner party entertainment that Abramović occasionally lays on for collectors, donors, and friends…[128]

Among a tranche of emails leaked from John Podesta and published by WikiLeaks in the run-up to the 2016 U.S. presidential election was a message from Abramović to Podesta's brother discussing an invitation to a spirit cooking….[129]

Video featured in the documentary *Out of Shadows*, an exposé of Hollywood's infatuation with occult, pedophilia, and cannibalistic practices, shows celebrities at one of Abramović's parties eating cake that was made to so closely resemble life-size humans with internal organs that it was hard to distinguish the difference.

As she was accused of invoking witchcraft and satanism, Ben Davis, Art News, said this about Abramović's performance parties:

"I don't think Marina Abramović is a Satan-worshiper. On the other hand, I myself criticized the 2011 LA MOCA gala Abramović organized, pictured several times in *Out of Shadows*. Dubbed *An* Artist's Life Manifesto, it saw her serve up low-paid naked women as human centerpieces for wealthy guests. Accompanying promos saw Abramović loudly declare her love of U.S. banks and financiers as the new Medicis even as the fallout of the Great Recession was still mauling surrounding society."[130]

Occultist or not, her "performance art" is intended to shock and is beyond disturbingly grotesque and twisted. Yet Abramović is heralded as a young woman's hero in the art world, and celebrity and music culture and is featured with artists like Jay-Z on social media.

Gagosian Quarterly discussed the usage of crypto to fund female LGBTQ art and featured Nadya Tolokonnikova, artist and co-founder of the Russian protest and performance art group "Pussy Riot." Tolokonnikova said, "Myself and a lot of other artists started to get interested in the new technology, NFTs. I believe that the crypto art movement will be recognized later as an art movement in the same fashion as the Russian avant-garde movement of the Futurists. It is revolutionary to me in the way it states that digital art is art… ."[131] Artists featured with Abramović, Pussy Riot, and Tolokonnikova sold their first NFT series in early 2021.[132]

> Tolokonnikova founded UnicornDAO, its mission being to build infrastructure for a feminist and queer revolution on the blockchain, largely through collecting and showcasing art by women, non-binary, and LGBTQ+ creators. UnicornDAO has raised more than $5 million for a variety of female and LBGTQ+ empowerment initiatives, including LegalAbortion.eth, which secured half a million dollars for nonprofits championing reproductive rights in the aftermath of the reversal of Roe v. Wade.[133]

This goes back to her view that unborn children have no value, as echoed by her artistic mentors and their satanic rituals that mock life.

All of this is driven through NFT and seems like an innocent way to help ensure that artists receive royalties correctly by providing proof of ownership through blockchain.

Non-fungible tokens are unique digital assets that use blockchain technology to represent ownership and authenticity. Digital assets include art, music, video, virtual real estate, tickets/event access, virtual pet, fashion, and much more.[134]

Blockchain is a decentralized digital technology that provides a secure and transparent record of transactions that was developed primarily for Bitcoin and other cryptocurrencies but is now being used to provide trust and transparency in other industries.[135]

The struggle with this type of currency is that it has and is being used in money laundering schemes, payment for anarchists to start protests and escalate them to violent proportions, and even sex trafficking as a way to pay for sex slaves and other deviances.[136] Value for art and other digital assets can be inflated to avoid suspicion as there is little to no regulation in this new economic arena.

Nadya Tolokonnikova said it herself, "I started from selling one of my visual pieces," (an NFT), "called Panic Attack, for around 400,000 dollars, which was an insane sum for me, especially in the middle of the pandemic when I got money for hardly anything, just surviving on Patreon and selling merch…."[137]

Nadya has been in prison for "hooliganism" multiple times for riots, protests, and an obscene public performance,[138] like her hero Abramović. Is she being funded by elitists who have a nefarious plan to destroy free societies like America? Is art the cover-up for paying off Marxist revolutionaries for their rioting and destruction of property?

> "Fundraising in the crypto space often involves DAOs, decentralized autonomous organizations. A DAO is a governance structure that has no centralized authority; rather decision-making power is distributed across its members, all of whom hold governance tokens to vote on how the money is spent or how many members to include. DAOs raise funds in a variety of ways but commonly require members to exchange their own fiat currency for a proportional share of governance tokens."

> "For Tolokonnikova, a DAO can be pretty much everything you want it to be. 'It's a group of people who decide how you're going to govern this entity that they form. And you write your own constitution. The DAO is a working model for different types of governance, and it was appealing to me because of my interests in political theory; I'm an activist forever.'"[139]

The organization's philosophy is aimed at giving LGBTQ+ artists representation in the art world, but funding social agendas that support abortion and LGBTQ+ is the outcome of their activism. And who is willing to pay $400,000 for one of their works?

The high-end gallery of Paul Gagosian produced the large 214-page magazine—four color; luxury, heavy gauge gloss paper; photography and art; beautifully designed—funded by ads from all brands elite: Gucci, Chanel, Louis Vuitton, Prada, Loewe, David Yurman, Saint Laurent, Issey Miyake, The Peninsula Beverly Hills, Poliform, Kagn,

Ligne roset, Tiffany & Co., Dior, Givenchy, Bottega Veneta, and Brioni among others.

Additionally, the magazine featured art from Jim Shaw depicting the United States' Uncle Sam being ground through a meat grinder and negative imagery of Donald Trump, Steve Bannon, and other conservative leadership.[140]

One of the most notorious high-profile consumers of art was none other than Jeffrey Epstein.

> Convicted sex offender Jeffrey Epstein, who died by apparent suicide on August 10 while in jail facing additional charges related to alleged sex trafficking in New York and Florida, cultivated an expansive network of powerful and influential contacts in a wide array of fields—art very much among them. In addition to his dealings in the worlds of finance, science, and technology, the reputed billionaire engaged with art institutions, collectors, and cultural enterprises now reckoning with their affiliations with a figure whose history is being closely examined.[141]

Epstein sat on the board of the New York Academy of Arts, donated over $800,000 to the MIT Media Lab, and was heavily involved in the Wexner Center for the Arts.[142]

> With respect to 25-year-old aspiring artist Maria Farmer, the *New York Times* reported she met Epstein at a gallery show in connection with her graduation, after which Epstein "called her to offer her a job acquiring art on his behalf."[143]

Maria would later become one of Epstein's victims.

> Mark Epstein, Jeffrey's brother, served as chairman of the board of Cooper Union—the renowned college of art, architecture, and engineering in New York City.[144]

Hunter Biden's "artistry" also received enormous sums from undisclosed purchasers. Is it possible art is being used to launder money as part of the performance to lead a revolt against God and true freedom?

Isaiah 3:12 (AMP) describes the destruction of the last days: "*O My people! Children are their oppressors, and women rule over them. O My people! Your leaders lead you astray and confuse (destroy, swallow up) the direction of your paths.*"

There are those who are destroying life and using artistry in its various forms of expression to allure and create fantasy, to entertain and ignite imagination for evil. I enjoy art, fashion, and design immensely, for our Creator is the author of all beauty. Too often, in fear and religion, the church has pulled away from these areas, leaving the door wide open to the enemy and the Marina Abramović, Nayda Tolokonnikova, and Jeffery Epsteins of the world.

We must recognize youth and children are led by artists who seek to draw them in through creativity, music, modeling, fashion—and use them for sexual exploitation and activism. Rather than rejecting the arts as evil and taking it away, let's raise our vision and dare to dream that God could use us in these arenas to reflect His beauty and creation. Arts have always been reflective of the culture and a way Satan introduces sin into imaginations. Art tells a story. What we imagine, we will become. The arts have declared a revolution against a biblical worldview, using perversion and witchcraft, and have declared a war on the Creator who values all human life and freedom. Let's reclaim artistic creative expression, fund true beauty instead of perversion, and reflect God's

> RATHER THAN REJECTING THE ARTS AS EVIL AND TAKING IT AWAY, LET'S RAISE OUR VISION AND DARE TO DREAM THAT GOD COULD USE US IN THESE ARENAS TO REFLECT HIS BEAUTY AND CREATION.

goodness in the arts. Art is an expression of true freedom only found in God. We can use it to tell His story of the value He places on human life.

CHAPTER 9

GOD'S CHILDREN ARE NOT FOR SALE

The plight of child trafficking has been given more mainstream attention than ever with the release of the movie *The Sound of Freedom*, in spite of Hollywood and mainstream media criticism. I had the honor of meeting real-life hero Tim Ballard, who left his career to rescue children; actor Jim Caveizel; and the Angel studios team at a recent Flashpoint "Truth and Freedom Tour" hosted at our Faith Life Now headquarters in New Albany, Ohio, by Gene Bailey. The movie was screened at the event, within a few miles of the location of the previous home of Jeffrey Epstein,[145] a prophetic event to be certain.

After the movie's screening, during the evening session of the tour, under the 2,500-seat tent in the coolness of the evening, the overflowing crowd prayed against the darkness and satanic attack aimed at children and carried out by evildoers across our world in high places, and some who had just been down the street.

I was asked to take the stage, alongside two other female ministers, to pray over our nation's children. Over 40 youth charged to the front of the auditorium and prayed fervently. Mothers, grandmothers, and ministers came forward and joined in praying as they held onto the tent poles that had been driven into the soil of New Albany. It was an electrifying moment—some described it as a "charis"[146] moment—where God brought two different generations

> OVER 40 YOUTH CHARGED TO THE FRONT OF THE AUDITORIUM AND PRAYED FERVENTLY. MOTHERS, GRANDMOTHERS, AND MINISTERS CAME FORWARD AND JOINED IN PRAYING AS THEY HELD ONTO THE TENT POLES THAT HAD BEEN DRIVEN INTO THE SOIL OF NEW ALBANY.

together, an older generation fighting on behalf of a younger generation seeking God, filled with His spiritual fire.

I believe this occurrence was God-ordained and chosen to happen in New Albany, Ohio. New Albany is the location where Jeffrey Epstein found the money, power, Manhattan apartment, and even the jet to run his sex-trafficking ring. That ring ensnared high level politicians, financiers, bankers, presidents, celebrities, and governments into luring and entrapping innocent girls as young as 14 years old into sex trafficking and defiling them.

He carried this out at Little St. James Island, a seven-story Manhattan apartment (a converted school), West Palm Beach, and across the nations in various countries, carrying passengers such as Bill Clinton to Africa.[147]

> One of the more perverse aspects of the Jeffrey Epstein story is how the predator's power flowed from a man who made his fortune selling lingerie to generations of women and teens in malls across America. Epstein's emetic symbiosis with his chief benefactor, Leslie Wexner—known as the "Merlin of the Mall" because at one point his company owned Victoria's Secret, Abercrombie & Fitch, Express, and Bath & Body Works—is explored in *Victoria's Secret: Angels and Demons*, a three-part docuseries... (This after other Epstein confidante, Ghislaine Maxwell, was sentenced on Tuesday to 20 years in prison.)
>
> *"Turning a blind eye* is a very key phrase with this series," says director Matt Tyrnauer. Epstein had been introduced to Wexner in the mid-1980s by an insurance executive and

soon became money manager to the mall magnate at a time when his company (then called the Limited, later renamed L Brands) was riding high. The documentary shows how Epstein was given full power of attorney, replaced Wexner's mother on the board of the Wexner foundation, and even shacked up in a house on the property of Wexner's Xanadu in Ohio. Epstein's money, Upper East Side mansion, and even the *Lolita Express*—originally a Boeing 727 owned by L Brands—would all come from Wexner.[148]

Epstein reportedly committed one of his first sexual assaults against Maria Farmer, an artist who worked for him, in his $8 million New Albany home. Farmer testified via affidavit and reported to the *New York Times* that "he and his friend Ghislaine Maxwell, the daughter of the late British press baron Robert Maxwell, assaulted her in a bedroom in the home."[149]

In addition to Wexner, Epstein's island, Little St. James in the U.S. Virgin Islands (which was nicknamed "Pedophile Island") served as "a private getaway for the rich and famous," including Bill Gates, Bill Clinton, Prince Andrew, Alan Dershowitz, Chris Tucker, Kevin Spacey, and Naomi Campbell.[150]

The then first lady of the U.S. Virgin Islands, Cecile de Jongh ("Cecile"), was Epstein's "'ready partner' in helping Epstein 'freely transport and exploit young women' with 'impunity' to his private islands."[151] Her husband, John de Jongh, was the territory's governor when his wife "ran Epstein's business operations for several years."[152] In fact, the year John took office in 2007, Epstein paid Cecile "$200,000 in salary and bonuses" as well as the tuition for de

Jonghs' children's private education.[153] Among many other acts in furtherance of Epstein's scheme, Cecile facilitated the procurement of visas for Epstein's young victims, and even arranged English classes through the University of the Virgin Islands as a cover for their visits. "Ultimately, [the University of the Virgin Islands] structured a bespoke class to enroll victims and provide cover for their presence in the territory—the same year Epstein donated $20,000 to the university through one of his companies."[154]

As for Bill Gates, *The New York Times* reported that "beginning in 2011, Mr. Gates met with Mr. Epstein on numerous occasions—including at least three times at Mr. Epstein's palatial Manhattan townhouse, and at least once staying late into the night, according to interviews with more than a dozen people familiar with the relationship, as well as documents reviewed by *The New York Times*."[155] To no surprise, when you "Google" Gates' visits, you are bombarded with "false claim" pages from various "fact-checkers."

Clinton's close connection to Epstein is well documented.

> Billionaire and accused sex trafficker Jeffrey Epstein visited the White House 17 times during former President Clinton's first few years in office, newly unearthed visitor logs reveal. The logs, obtained by the *Daily Mail* through a FOIA request, reveal several visits by Epstein beginning with an invitation just one month after Clinton's inauguration in January 1993 by Robert Rubin, who was assistant to the president for economic policy at that time. A spokeswoman for Rubin told the outlet that "to the best of Mr. Rubin's recollection he never met or spoke with Mr. Epstein."

The logs show Epstein, who died in 2019 of an apparent suicide in jail, visited the White House on 14 separate days and made two visits in a single day on three occasions between 1993 and 1995. Most of the visits were to the West Wing, making it likely that he met with the president.[156]

Epstein was among a group who actually launched the Clinton Global Initiative.[157]

Launched in 2005, the Clinton Global Initiative was an arm of the Clinton Foundation dedicated to connecting world leaders who are uniquely suited to "implement solutions to the world's most pressing challenges." Epstein's name never appeared on any Clinton Global Initiative founding documents, but Lefcourt reiterated his client's involvement in the organization's formation in a 2016 ABC News interview. In addition to his work launching the Clinton Global Initiative, Epstein also donated $25,000 to the Clinton Foundation in 2006 through his own personal charity, according to the *Daily Beast*. That donation came after Epstein developed a close personal relationship with Bill Clinton during a month-long trip to Africa in 2002.

"Jeffrey is both a highly successful financier and a committed philanthropist with a keen sense of global markets and an in-depth knowledge of twenty-first-century science," Clinton told *New York* magazine through a spokesman following the trip. "I especially appreciated his insights and generosity during the recent trip to Africa to work on democratization, empowering the poor, citizen service, and combating HIV/AIDS."

Clinton flew on Epstein's private plane on at least 26 occasions between 2002 and 2003, including as many as ten flights without his secret service detail, according to flight logs published by Fox News in 2016. Clinton distanced himself from the accused pedophile and characterized the 26 flights as representing just "four trips," all of which he took in the company of his secret service detail, in a statement issued Monday evening.[158]

Unlike other politicians and celebrities connected to Epstein, Trump ousted Epstein when reports circulated about him assaulting a woman at Trump's Mar-a-Lago Club.

Jeffrey Epstein turned Donald Trump's Mar-a-Lago into another of his hunting grounds for young girls, leading Trump to bar him from the Florida resort, court papers claim. "Trump allegedly banned Epstein from his Mar-a-Lago Club in West Palm Beach because Epstein sexually assaulted a girl at the club," according to the papers filed in the Sunshine State as part of an ongoing legal battle between Epstein and Bradley Edwards, who represented many of Epstein's underage accusers in civil suits against him. The filing is dated April 2011, well before Trump ascended to the presidency. "I knew him like everybody in Palm Beach knew him," Trump told reporters at the White House of Epstein during an appearance with Qatari Emir Tamim bin Hamad Al Thani. "I had a falling out a long time ago, I'd say maybe 15 years. I was not a fan of his, that I can tell you."[159]

Of the hundreds of names on Epstein's island, we have yet to see any convictions except Ghislaine Maxwell, who was sentenced to a mere 20 years, yet Epstein possessed blackmail materials on many visitors.[160] Where are the convictions? We continue to hear rumblings with lawsuits aimed at many of the Who's who of America.

OF THE HUNDREDS OF NAMES ON EPSTEIN'S ISLAND, WE HAVE YET TO SEE ANY CONVICTIONS EXCEPT GHISLAINE MAXWELL, WHO WAS SENTENCED TO A MERE 20 YEARS, YET EPSTEIN POSSESSED BLACKMAIL MATERIALS ON MANY VISITORS. WHERE ARE THE CONVICTIONS?

All three of the Epstein lawsuits against America and Germany's largest banks expose how global child sex trafficking provides the blackmail control leverage on thousands of targeted VIP puppets in politics, the judiciary, top corporations, law enforcement and media outlets, all the while pumping out 24/7 propaganda to shape, misdirect and control public perception of reality. Child sex trafficking serves a crucial control mechanism within the highly profitable organized crime industry that keeps puppet national leaders on a leash, and how it works hand-in-hand with the world's largest banks owned and operated by the Rothschild banking cartel for money laundering black ops purposes.

Though child sex trafficker Jeffrey Epstein has allegedly been dead for four years now, his name is still in the daily headlines even in the mainstream legacy media. Why? Because the globalist slave empire is likely coming down.[161]

Let's pray so!

Epstein's crimes required a network of people who were willing to abuse and traffic children for their own personal lascivious lifestyles, addictions, and perversions. It also required those who consumed these children like they were a meal at a restaurant and those who turned their heads for profit. All are guilty of such gross crime. A nation or justice system that cares so little for children is morally depraved, and hell will swallow them unless sincere repentance and restitution is made.

> **A NATION OR JUSTICE SYSTEM THAT CARES SO LITTLE FOR CHILDREN IS MORALLY DEPRAVED, AND HELL WILL SWALLOW THEM UNLESS SINCERE REPENTANCE AND RESTITUTION IS MADE.**

> Profiting from the wickedness of human enslavement has literally been ongoing for well over four centuries… The slave trade involves more children and adults trafficked as modern slaves for labor and commercial sex exploitation than any previous time in history, along with diabolical trafficking of human organs and illegal arms, virtually all of it covertly money laundered by the world's largest central banks….[162]

It's certainly no wonder why the leftist media are criticizing *Sound of Freedom* as I will discuss in the next chapter. The movie that unveils a part of their deception. Nonetheless, the movie's power has been recognized by many, including viewers who broke into spontaneous applause and cheers at key moments, including Caviezel's retort that has become the movie's tagline —"God's children are not for sale."[163]

Sound of Freedom is a remarkable example of how to expose the *"fruitless deeds of darkness."*[164] There is nothing that is more dark or has been more concealed than the sex trafficking of innocent children. There is something extremely satisfying about beating the media at its own game—a mainstream movie turned blockbuster. When politicians, large banks, Fortune 500 companies, law enforcement, and the judiciary conspire to cover for sex traffickers and pedophiles, this is how citizens of the Kingdom occupy.

> THERE IS SOMETHING EXTREMELY SATISFYING ABOUT BEATING THE MEDIA AT ITS OWN GAME—A MAINSTREAM MOVIE TURNED BLOCKBUSTER.

CHAPTER 10

MISSING CHILDREN

The children crossing our southern border, often fleeing dire circumstances in their home countries, enter the U.S. with the hope of finding safety and security. Instead, as many as 85,000 of them are missing.[165] While the term "missing" should be alarming to all of us, it is misleading as it suggests that these children are simply lost or unaccounted for and only need to be "found." It is also a misnomer because it suggests we don't know why they are missing or what is happening to them. But, thanks to courageous individuals like Tim Ballard, we now know the devastating truth.

> THE CHILDREN CROSSING OUR SOUTHERN BORDER, OFTEN FLEEING DIRE CIRCUMSTANCES IN THEIR HOME COUNTRIES, ENTER THE U.S. WITH THE HOPE OF FINDING SAFETY AND SECURITY. INSTEAD, AS MANY AS 85,000 OF THEM ARE MISSING.

And apparently, it is easy. According to Tim Ballard, "'It's literally more difficult to adopt a cat out of the shelter than it is for a sponsor to show up and check one of these kids out and take them into the belly of the United States,' he said, describing that belly—the U.S. government—as the 'number one consumer of child sex material in the world.'"[166]

While I initially questioned how 85,000 children go "missing" and do not make headline news, the reasons became very apparent after *Sound of Freedom*, which grossed more than $174 in six weeks and hit number one at the box office, surpassing *Indiana Jones* and *Mission Impossible*.[167]

Left-wing news and media viciously banned the movie—not for its acting or script—but because of their insistence that child sex trafficking isn't happening! Consider the vitriolic comments made by Miles Klee of *Rolling Stone* in his article titled, "'Sound of Freedom' Is a Superhero Movie for Dads With Brainworms: The QAnon-tinged thriller about child-trafficking is designed to appeal to the conscience of a conspiracy-addled boomer:"

> "[Jim] Caviezel, best known for being tortured to death in Mel Gibson's *The Passion of the Christ*, has become a prominent figure on the conspiracist right, giving speeches and interviews in which he hints at an underground holy war between patriots and a sinister legion of evildoers who are harvesting the blood of children. It's straight-up QAnon stuff, right down to his use of catchphrases like "The storm is upon us."
>
> Ballard, Caviezel, and others of their ilk had primed the public to accept *Sound of Freedom* as a documentary rather than delusion by fomenting moral panic for years over this grossly exaggerated "epidemic" of child sex trafficking, much of it funneling people into conspiracist rabbit holes and QAnon communities. In short, I was at the movies with people who were there to see their worst fears confirmed."[168]

Sam Adams of *Slate* similarly mocked the movie, starting with the article subtitle, "People acted like they were at *Top Gun*." According to Adams:

"*Sound of Freedom* … arrived in theaters surrounded by a cloud of innuendo put forth by its star and its noisiest right-wing supporters—conspiratorial insinuations about who doesn't want this story to be told and what real-world traffickers are really up to."[169]

He continues:

"Although the movie makes no reference to QAnon or its associated conspiracy theories, which only began to leak into the mainstream the year before it was completed, Caviezel has been enthusiastically using his press tour to profess his belief in an international black market where a barrel of children's body parts goes for a thousand times the price of oil. Ballard himself has circulated wild and unsupported figures about the extent of the sex-trafficking industry, including the claim that 10,000 children are smuggled into the U.S. for sex every year, which was picked up and used as a campaign talking point by Donald Trump."[170]

So-called news sources like *Rolling Stone* and *Slate* are either completely on board with sex

> SO-CALLED NEWS SOURCES LIKE ROLLING STONE AND SLATE ARE EITHER COMPLETELY ON BOARD WITH SEX TRAFFICKING AND ARE PART OF A DELIBERATE EFFORT TO SUPPRESS THE TRUTH OR THEY ARE SO BLINDED BY THEIR FAR-LEFT POLITICAL AGENDA THAT THEY CAN'T EVEN SEE THE EVIL THAT IS BEFORE THEM.

trafficking and are part of a deliberate effort to suppress the truth or they are so blinded by their far-left political agenda that they can't even see the evil that is before them. As Ballard said, "If you're making pedophiles happy and making them salivate over your policies, I think it's time to push pause and reconsider your policies."[171] Likewise, if you're a news outlet and you're trashing films because child sex trafficking isn't that bad, it is time for some serious soul-searching.

Notably, this negative coverage of Ballard is an abrupt about-face to what media previously reported. Ballard noted that in the past, "*Rolling Stone*, MSNBC, CBS, CNN, and more—posted 'glowing' stories about the operation that occurred on October 11, 2014."

> "'They applauded it. They said that we were good guys. They said, 'Congratulations, you rescued children.' Eight years later, those same outlets are pretending that didn't happen. … They're lying about it. They're changing their story. They want to pretend it's not happening," he said, explaining that he believes the motive is that they do not want to have a wider conversation about what is happening to children and the 'consequences to children that their agendas and their policies are having.'"[172]

There's no doubt that this news is intentionally suppressed due to its entrenchment with radical political agendas, primarily the LGBTQ propaganda aimed toward children on every mountain of influence. Ballard suggests that this agenda includes the normalization of pedophilia.

"They know that this is going to shine a light on all of their agenda that they've been working on. ...So they'd rather just pretend none of it's happening. And it's easier just to say, 'Well, maybe sex with kids isn't even that big a deal after all.' I mean, that's where they're going now,' he said, pointing to a United Nations-backed report issued months ago and saying, 'it's time to consider decriminalizing sex with children.'"[173]

> I CAN ONLY PRAY THE DAY NEVER COMES WHEN THE SLOGAN USED TO MAINSTREAM GAY MARRIAGE, "LOVE IS LOVE," IS APPLIED TO ADULT-CHILD SEXUAL RELATIONSHIPS.

There is no question that the LGBTQ's agenda, brainwashing children that they can decide their own gender, plays right into the pedophile ring's hands. I can only pray the day never comes when the slogan used to mainstream gay marriage, "love is love," is applied to adult-child sexual relationships.

The left-controlled media is clearly aware that the disappearance of unaccompanied children would also shed light on the proliferation of illegal immigration and the current administration's failure to protect our southern border. Ballard advocates for this measure, believing it to be the most compassionate policy in preventing traffickers from exploiting vulnerable children.

The issue of sponsors lacking proper background checks when taking custody of unaccompanied minors raises alarming concerns about the children's safety and well-being.

"Tens of thousands of children—unaccompanied, young children—are disappearing into the belly of the beast, and they have to know that's happening, but they care about their agenda more than that," he said, explaining during the interview that "no background checks were done by the sponsors who came to get them."[174]

This is unacceptable. God instructs us to "*rescue those being led away to death; hold back those staggering toward slaughter. If you say 'But we knew nothing about this,' does not he who weighs the heart perceive it?*"[175] We can't say we don't know what's going on. As believers, we have a part to play in the rescue of these children. One of my favorite quotes from the *Sound of Freedom* movie was, "When God tells you what to do, you cannot hesitate." The charge is clear.

CHAPTER 11

FOLLOW THE SCIENCE

Throughout the COVID pandemic, we heard the echoing voices of mainstream media, "Follow the Science!" We were constantly brainwashed that science wouldn't lie to us, that medical professionals were following the science and knew more than us. Never mind that the scientists, doctors, and media voices were given bonuses to echo these mantras and force 65 million vaccines into arms without typical protocols to test for efficacy or safety.[176]

Now, the scientists and medical professionals are at it again. They attempt to sell us that biological sex and gender identity are not the same. This is the narrative articulated by thetech.org:

> Biological sex refers to the physical features of a human body (or anatomy). But just as important if not more, gender identity is one's internal sense of being. That may align more toward being a male, female, or anywhere in between. Some people who identify as non-binary may not have an internal sense of being a male or female at all. Sex reassignment surgery involves changing a person's anatomy. Whether a person identifies as a male or female shouldn't change after surgery. And it doesn't change their genetics either!"[177]

A quick biology lesson for those of us who haven't had a course in over 25 years: Whatever set of chromosomes a person is born with cannot be changed, regardless of surgeries or outward appearances or feelings that a person is not the sex of their organs at birth. Our bodies are made up of trillions of cells which are either XX chromosomes (female) or XY (male). This cannot be changed. So how is "science" in the classrooms across the nation pushing this agenda on innocent children? Wait for it...

Their explanation is, "Chromosomes do not define gender." Sometimes people do not "identify" with the biological sex assigned at birth. This means they are transgender."[178]

We are witnessing the redefinition of everything that we have known as science, medicine, education; every societal norm is breaking the rules and rebuilding our culture, a Fourth Industrial Revolution. Make no mistake, this is their revolution.

> WE ARE WITNESSING THE REDEFINITION OF EVERYTHING THAT WE HAVE KNOWN AS SCIENCE, MEDICINE, EDUCATION, AND EVERY SOCIETAL NORM IS BREAKING THE RULES AND REBUILDING OUR CULTURE, A FOURTH INDUSTRIAL REVOLUTION.

This tech article goes on to mention that there are medical conditions that impact some people's chromosomes, naming these as Androgen Insensitivity Syndrome and Congenital Adrenal Hyperplasia. They do mention, "Having these issues does not make a person transgender."[179] In the rarest of cases, less than .003 percent of persons are born with a condition and are classified as intersexual.[180]

I learned about these conditions years ago as a youth leader when one of the youth in my church group came to me with a question. Her psychology professor at a Christian university was claiming that transgenderism was normal behavior and should be embraced based on the fact that some were born as "intersexual," being both sexes.

I contacted a doctor friend, and he quickly shot down this psychology professor's misinformation to students. He said the chromosomes are still detectable, whether male or female, but in super rare circumstances, exposure to the other chromosomes (likely chemicals/birth control) can produce more pronounced breasts in male babies or a more pronounced vulva in females, replicating the look of a male body part. These are not genetically altering to the child but rather present as more of a deformity. But this professor was using a rare anomaly to alter student's views of transgenderism.

Scientific American magazine spins an interesting twist on transgender clinics and ideology in an emotionally riveting piece intended to tie Nazism to those who reject the trans movement.[181] This article reminds me of the propaganda that was put out during the women's lib/abortion movement. The two—abortion and women's liberation—are tied together because they were intentionally connected. Sell an emotional story of a woman having a backroom abortion and dying a gruesome death. Then, use

> ABORTION IS BIG MONEY, AND WHO BETTER TO USE TO CHAMPION THE CAUSE THAN WOMEN?

that emotion to sell all future women on "their rights" to abortions until 64 million babies have been brutally murdered before seeing the face or feeling the touch of their mother. Abortion is big money, and who better to use to champion the cause than women?

The *Scientific American* piece smells like the same game but pushing the trans movement for children. Their article begins with a homosexual man in 1930s Germany taking his life by firearm on his wedding night because he had to marry a woman. (Aghast!) His supposed last words to a Dr. Hirschfeld, also a practicing homosexual Jewish man, were, "The thought that you could contribute to a future when the German fatherland will think of us in more just terms sweetens the hour of death." (Drama!) Hirschfield was so moved, thus he was inspired to leave his practice and fight for queer rights and sexual health and started an institute for sexuality, or sexual deviation, depending on your view. At the time, homosexuality was believed to be a mental illness. Hirschfield sought to prove that there was a third sex, proposing the term sexual intermediaries for nonconforming individuals. He included in this group the homosexual, transvestite, a spectrum of bisexual practice, and those who had no fixed gender.

Scientific American normalizes this behavior, using "history to bear witness" to its normalcy and goes on to criticize UK laws to prevent child transitions.[182] "In the wake of a U.K. Court decision in 2020 limiting trans rights, an editorial in *The Economist* argued that other countries should follow suit. An editorial in *The Observer* praised the court for resisting a "disturbing trend" of children receiving gender-affirming care as part of a transition."[183]

And then follows *Scientific American's* unscientific agreement, "Hirschfield's study of sexual intermediaries was no trend or fad; instead, it was a recognition that people may be born with a nature contrary to their assigned gender. And in cases where the desire to live as the opposite sex was strong, he thought science ought to provide a means of transition."

Hirschfield went on to perform a transition surgery in 1930. In that era, it surely would have been called barbaric, but with today's spin on words, *Scientific American* describes it as "gender-affirmation."[184]

How affirming! And then in typical fashion, the clinic is described as "full of life everywhere, furnished, plush, a place of education, to free the individual,"[185] He partnered with a surgeon there to perform the transformation of genitals and employed the five trans women who received surgery. (Scarily, this sounds akin to today's transition centers in Children's hospitals staffed by trans people.)

According to *Scientific American*, "This should have been the bedrock on which to build a bolder future."[186] Yet, Hitler's troops would invade the clinic and destroy and burn the exhaustive library and research Hirschfeld collected, setting the trans movement back for decades. To make matters worse, one of his partners, Gohrbrandt, would leave to join Hitler as a chief medical adviser and further their grim experiments in concentration camps. Instead of seeing these surgeries as "Frankenstein-ian," *Scientific American* would have us believe that Hirschfeld was a great hero who freed people to believe their feelings. But Gohrbrandt was a butcher. Both of their ideologies are flawed and lead to the same conclusion—destruction, mutilation of a body, sterilization, and intense pain.

Hirschfeld would flee to Paris to regain his institute with his live-in partners, Giese and Tong, a medical student. Hirschfeld would die of a sudden stroke in 1935 while on the run, Giese died by suicide, and Tong disappeared.

Scientific American's conclusion? "The Nazi ideal had been based on white, cishet (cisgender, heterosexual) masculinity masquerading as genetic superiority."[187] (Translation: Anyone who resists the trans movement is likened to these Nazis, bigots.) "What began as a project of 'protecting' German youth and raising healthy families had become under Hitler a mechanism for genocide."[188] (Translation: If you try to protect your kids from LGBTQ+ propaganda, you, too, are a Hitler, or at best a racist, Nazi.)

And of course, their conclusion is, "Studies have shown that supportive hormone therapy, accessed at an early age, lowers rates of suicide among trans youth."[189] But there are those who reject the evidence that trans identity is something you can be "born with." Richard Dawkins was recently stripped of his "humanist of the year" award for comments comparing trans people to Rachel Dolezal, a civil rights activist who posed as a black woman, as though gender transition were a kind of duplicity."[190]

Scientific American, with great swells of pride and sob stories, reminds you to: believe the science or you can no longer be a scientist or a doctor. Believe transitioning children is acceptable, normal, and affirming or you can't be a real parent or politician—and you might even be of the likes of Hitler, especially if you're a white heterosexual. What they don't get is that pushing these agendas via schools spending more time on pride than preparation in reading, writing, and math mimics the playbook for fascism, Marxism, and all other communist ills. Taking parent's rights from them and demanding they comply or have their children taken from them is too. Canada has already taken steps to do this.[191]

What was science yesterday is obviously no longer science today. We used to think the world was flat, but we discovered it's not. We used to believe there were two genders because of the science of chromosomes and biology, but trans doctors were trying to tell us differently all along, and we just wouldn't listen. Stupid us. We used to believe there was a God who created people in His likeness and image, but science has helped us to understand there is no God, just a great explosion that instead of being destructive proves that chaos and confusion can create a perfect world. I'm not buying it, and neither should you.

What happens when science or those who purport to be scientists have other agendas and refuse to collect data that goes against their bias? We don't have real science. Sadly, we see more medical tyranny than ever masquerading as science. As I documented in my book *Fight Like Heaven: A Cultural Guide to Living on Guard*, the medical system is designed without checks and balances, ensuring that big pharma and medical institutions will drive science in the direction of their profits.

> The American Medical Association (AMA) recently suggested that taxpayers fund uterus transplants for transgender women as an attempt to force pregnancy and as a way to help them feel like real, biological women who can give birth.

> In its *Journal of Ethics* issue, titled "Patient-Centered Transgender Surgical Care," suggestions were offered in order to reduce the cost of the surgery:[192]

> > "Even though there has been no uterus transplant to date in transwomen that we know of, some clinicians have maintained that there are no absolute barriers in anatomy, hormones, and obstetric considerations that would rule out the possibility of successful UTx in transwomen," the association claimed in June of this year.[193]

However, the AMA has been consistently chastised for proposing the idea and has also been accused of taking an "activist stance." They argued that transgender women's inability to bear children may cause "psychological dissonance," undermining their health and well-being. The report comes as some pioneering uterus transplant doctors sincerely believe they are on the verge of helping transgender women give birth to their own children, despite the fact that the majority of those familiar with biology and other online users have scoffed at the idea."[194]

Dr. Avery Jackson III, a board certified neurosurgeon, Founder and Chief Executive Officer of the Michigan Neurosurgical Institute, reached out to me after hearing me speak about the seven mountains of influence. He said, "The Holy Spirit gave me revelation on how the enemy used science and medicine to ambush all seven mountains of our society." Dr. Jackson took this revelation and created The Body Healthcare, a faith-based healthcare organization.[195]

> IN THE PAST, IT WOULD HAVE BEEN CONSIDERED LUDICROUS AND DANGEROUS TO SUGGEST THAT DOCTORS REMOVE HEALTHY ORGANS FROM A HUMAN BEING, LET ALONE TRY TO TRANSPLANT A UTERUS INTO A MALE'S BODY.

And it's true! Slowly but surely, the science and medical fields are being hijacked and compromised to stand for agendas that evidence and years of study prove aren't true. In the past, it would have been considered ludicrous and dangerous to suggest that doctors remove healthy organs from a human being, let alone try to transplant a uterus into a male's body.

Science and medicine have not only twisted age-old facts, but they have also used their agenda-driven theories to control the media, Wall Street, and Hollywood—and are using their voices and money to spread propaganda and cancel those that hold a different opinion.

HOW MANY PEOPLE REGRET TRANSITIONING AND WHY?

No one knows how many experience transition regret because no one is tracking patients, but there are indications of growing numbers... and the reasons for regret are telling.

- A detransitioner is someone who identified as trans, nonbinary, or another gender identity but then regrets the medical interventions and re-identifies with their natal sex.
- A desister is someone who identified as transgender but stopped identifying before medicalizing.
- There are also people who regret transitioning without detransitioning, sometimes because they feel it would be too hard to detransition.

WHAT WE KNOW ABOUT REGRET

- Studies show that 80% to 88% of prepubescent children who believe that they should be the opposite sex, but do not socially transition (change name, pronouns and outward appearance) would grow up to be comfortable with their unaltered, natal bodies. A large portion are same sex attracted.

- Recent studies show that most people detransition within 4-6 years of transitioning.
- Reddit/Detrans, a platform for those questioning transition was created in November 2017. In the last 6-months, an average of 60 new subscribers join every day. While not every member is a detransitioner and not all detransitioners join, the significant growth indicates rapid increase and interest in detransitioners.[196]

It is far past time for all of us, especially parents, to stop believing "the science." We must question and question everything we are told and do our own research. Research is being tainted by profits, and only those with discernment will know how to navigate their future with wisdom and prevention. We must not put our trust solely in the words of a psychologist, doctor, or medical professional. As the joke says, "Doctors don't know everything. They're just practicing." And they're certainly not God! And what do we make of science? For decades, science has been used to undermine the Bible and create an ever-growing population of atheists, especially among the young. But does science really support the overarching belief attributed to science that there is no God or Creator?

Headlines lately have not been encouraging for the faithful. A Gallup poll shows that the percentage of Americans who believe in God has fallen to 81 percent—a drop of 10 percent over the last decade and an all-time low. This accelerating trend is especially pronounced among young adults. According to a Pew Research Center poll, 18-29-year-olds are disproportionately represented among so-called "nones"— atheists, agnostics, and the religiously unaffiliated.

Pastors and other religious leaders have attributed this trend to many factors: young people being raised outside the church, an unfamiliarity with liturgy and church culture, even COVID-19.

...Perhaps surprisingly, our survey discovered that the perceived message of science has played a leading role in the loss of faith. We found that scientific theories about the unguided evolution of life have, in particular, led more people to reject belief in God than worries about suffering, disease, or death. It also showed that 65 percent of self-described atheists and 43 percent of agnostics believe "the findings of science [generally] make the existence of God less probable."[197]

"In recent years, many scientists have emerged as "celebrity spokesmen for atheism."[198] People like Richard Dawkins, Lawrence Krauss, Bill Nye, Michael Shermer, and Stephen Hawking have published popular books arguing that science proves God to be unnecessary or implausible. "The universe we observe has precisely the properties we should expect if, at bottom, there is no purpose, no design... nothing but blind, pitiless indifference," Dawkins famously wrote.[199]

However, science actually reveals the truth and existence of God.

First, scientists have discovered that the physical universe had a beginning. This finding, supported by observational astronomy and theoretical physics, contradicts the expectations of scientific atheists, who long portrayed the universe as eternal and self-existent—and, therefore, in no need of an external creator.

Evidence for what scientists call the Big Bang has instead confirmed the expectations of traditional theists. Nobel laureate Arno Penzias, who helped make a key discovery supporting the Big Bang theory, has noted the obvious connection between its affirmation of a cosmic beginning and the concept of divine creation. "The best data we have are exactly what I would have predicted, had I nothing to go on but the five books of Moses...[and] the Bible as a whole," writes Penzias.

Second, discoveries from physics about the structure of the universe reinforce this theistic conclusion. Since the 1960s, physicists have determined that the fundamental physical laws and parameters of our universe are finely tuned, against all odds, to make our universe capable of hosting life. Even slight alterations of many independent factors—such as the strength of gravitational or electromagnetic attraction, or the initial arrangement of matter and energy in the universe— would have rendered life impossible. Scientists have discovered that we live in a kind of "Goldilocks Universe," or what Australian physicist Luke Barnes calls an extremely "Fortunate Universe."

Not surprisingly, many physicists have concluded that this improbable fine-tuning points to a cosmic "fine-tuner." As former Cambridge astrophysicist Sir Fred Hoyle argued, "A common-sense interpretation of the data suggests that a super-intellect has monkeyed with physics" to make life possible.

All this underscores a growing disparity between public perceptions of the message of science and what scientific evidence actually shows. Far from pointing to "blind, pitiless indifference," the great discoveries of the last century point to the exquisite design of life and the universe and, arguably, to an intelligent creator behind it all.[200]

Dr. Jackson has not been silent and has a great answer to go with the revelation he received while he was listening to me speak. He told me in his email, "We have a strategy, The Body Healthcare, partnering with the church to take back dominion over all seven mountains! God had me create a national church/private trust entity to begin building a parallel healthcare system in it. We are giving everything that we have personally and professionally to this assignment so that we can protect people from the next wave of attempted control and fear-mongering."

There are medical professionals, such as Dr. Jackson, and scientists who have been ostracized, terminated, and silenced for questioning the status quo and popular narratives of culture (isn't that science?), but truth can only be kept silent for so long.[201 202 203]

Somehow, by the grace of God and the courage of those who refuse to remain silent can good science surface to expose the misinformation. Only until medical research is separated from pharmaceutical companies and their money machine can real science and medicine exist. And real science will not refute the Bible; it only continues to validate its accuracy when science is honest.

> **AND REAL SCIENCE WILL NOT REFUTE THE BIBLE; IT ONLY CONTINUES TO VALIDATE ITS ACCURACY WHEN SCIENCE IS HONEST.**

CHAPTER 12

MEDICAL GAMES AGAINST CHILDREN

THEY ARE COMING FOR YOUR CHILDREN
THE FIGHT WE MUST WIN!

Just when you think the medical games can't get any stranger, we have Professor and Doctor Diane Ehrensaft, Director of Mental Health and Chief Psychologist at the UCSF Benioff Children's Hospital Gender Development Center. Ehrensaft, who specializes in pediatric "gender-affirmative care for transgender and gender-expansive patients," claims that children can identify as a mythology-inspired creature who loves mermaids.[204]

According to Ehrensaft's biography, she focuses her research on "how genders before puberty develop as well as the mental health effects of puberty blockers and cross-sex hormones, which are part of chemical sex changes, on children."[205] She says that she "totally agree[s] we are in the midst of a gender revolution and the children are leading it. And it's a wonderful thing to see. And it's also humbling to know [children] know more than we do about this topic of being gender expansive."[206]

The transgender "revolution," according to Ehrensaft, "is the next phase of the '60s feminist movement, which featured challenging stereotypes about gender."[207]

Those like Dr. Ehrensaft are coaching children to confuse fantasy with reality, to deny biological reality (creating confusion), and to accept this twisted alternate reality that is required training for medical/hospital staff by their superiors. Question it and you could lose your livelihood.

Do you remember the story about the king who wasn't wearing any clothes, but his lords and ladies—not gender affirming in today's upside-down world, I guess—were required to pretend he was

162

wearing clothes? A fantasy created by some shifty tailors who made money selling a lie? Then, everyone had to go along with the lie and compliment his attire or be denounced by the king and his royals. Doesn't this look similar? It took a small boy who blurted out the truth— "Why isn't the king wearing any clothes?"—for everyone to acknowledge he was unclothed!

I reviewed a children's hospital reference manual addressing how to care for LGBTQ patients and families in pediatric settings. This manual explained terminologies, definitions, 11 flags symbolizing all of these, how to discuss gender pronouns—and, in my opinion, dodge parents who were not "gender affirming."[208]

I found much of this manual to be shocking and dishonest in its claims that if everyone does gender affirmation just right and creates "safe spaces"—where youths can be free with their gender expression, gender identity, pronouns, name changes, gender markers, sexual orientation, sexual behaviors, and dress—and even affirms those who identify as having no gender, then we will decrease suicides. That's a very tall order, it certainly would keep everyone jumping through hoops, and it would allow them to blame suicides on failures to perform these demands to perfection.

The manual instructs medical staff that: "it may be beneficial to reflect on the assumptions and stereotypes you may have learned through your life related to how a person dresses, wears their hair, makeup, etc., or acts, talks…" and that conversations around gender identity and/ or sexual orientation at appropriate times and for appropriate reasons should not be avoided. "Normalize and validate… Report any gender or sexuality related harassment, discrimination, victimization…

Importantly, there is no right or wrong way to be transgender or gender diverse. There may be several reasons why a transgender or gender diverse person does not transition either socially, physically, or both. Transition is not required to identify as a transgender or gender diverse person. It may not be obvious that a person identifies as transgender or gender diverse, which is why it is important to ask about name and pronouns to avoid making false assumptions about their identity. Gender-affirming care is a need of every patient because we all have a gender identity worthy of being affirmed."[209]

Then, staff are coached to introduce themselves with their name and pronouns and not to say words like ma'am or sir or to use the word "preferred" regarding pronouns, because this implies gender identity is a choice. They are further coached to train their staff on the manual's material and to display gender safe signage to communicate their commitment to creating inclusive environments.

Their stated goals are to reduce bullying, suicidal thoughts and tendencies, and illicit drug usage. Reduce drug usage? What about their usage of hormone altering drugs for a lifetime?

Their conclusion is that when we respect pronouns (and all the other terminology and identifications), these youths will have lower rates of suicide.[210] The numbers do not tell that story or outcome, and it's easy to just keep blaming suicides on those of us who disagree with their diagnosis and prognosis of how to solve the confusion and pain youths are facing rather than take responsibility that their "cure" isn't working.

How are hospitals, schools, and media culture contributing to the confusion to begin with? To me, that is the question and a large part of the answer. As we have learned with other medical scenarios, there must be a disease or manufactured problem before medical institutions can run to the rescue to "cure" the issue, and charge hefty sums to do so.

> **AS WE HAVE LEARNED WITH OTHER MEDICAL SCENARIOS, THERE MUST BE A DISEASE OR MANUFACTURED PROBLEM BEFORE MEDICAL INSTITUTIONS CAN RUN TO THE RESCUE TO "CURE" THE ISSUE, AND CHARGE HEFTY SUMS TO DO SO.**

Remember how we were repeatedly told that COVID-19 was not a lab leak and was not manufactured? We heard stories of wet markets and bats, special delicacies in China. The lid is only beginning to come off the distortions, outright lies, and agendas that raise more questions about the medical industry, with its culture of pharmaceuticals and surgeries and disregard for preventative or natural treatments.

> Scientists who wrote a paper dismissing the so-called "lab leak theory" of the origin of COVID-19 admitted they feared blaming China for accidentally releasing the virus, according to internal communications obtained by a House subcommittee.[211]

The United States House Select Subcommittee on the Coronavirus Pandemic majority revealed that one of authors and other collaborators of the March 2020 *Nature Medicine* article, "The Proximal Origin of SARS-CoV-2" secretly "worried about the 's—tshow that would happen' if 'China in particular' were deemed responsible for COVID escaping one of their research labs… in an interim report Tuesday."[212]

Their correspondence on the subject is astounding:

> "Given the s—tshow that would happen if anyone serious accused the Chinese of even accidental release, my feeling is we should say that given there is no evidence of a specifically engineered virus, we cannot possibly distinguish between natural evolution and escape, so we are content with ascribing it to natural process," Dr. Andrew Rambaut, a professor of evolutionary biology at the University of Edinburgh, wrote in a Feb. 2, 2020, Slack message to co-authors Dr. Kristian Andersen, Dr. Edward Holmes and Dr. Robert Garry.

> "Yup, I totally agree that that's a very reasonable conclusion," Andersen responded. "Although I hate when politics is [sic] injected into science—but its [sic] impossible not to, especially given the circumstances."

> Another scientist—who had joined the co-authors, then-National Institutes of Health Director Dr. Francis Collins and National Institute of Allergy and Infectious Diseases Director Dr. Anthony Fauci a day earlier on a conference call—also urged his colleagues to tamp down lab leak discussions that might imperil "science in China."

> "An accusation that nCoV-2019 might have been engineered and released into the environment by humans (accidental or intentional) would need to be supported by strong data, beyond reasonable doubt," Dutch virologist Dr. Ron Fouchier wrote in a Feb. 2, 2020, email. "It is good that this possibility was discussed in detail with a team of experts.

However, further debate about such accusations would unnecessarily distract top researchers from their active duties and do unnecessary harm to science in general and science in China in particular."

The FBI and Energy Department have since determined the lab leak theory to be the most likely explanation for the origins of the coronavirus pandemic.

The House report also shows the article faced initial rejection from *Nature Medicine* for not sufficiently disproving non-natural origins of COVID-19.

In an email to one of the publication's editors on Feb. 20, 2020, Andersen lamented not being able to "refute a lab origin" in an earlier draft.

"[T]he possibility must be considered as a serious scientific theory (which is what we do) and not dismissed out of hand as another 'conspiracy' theory,'" he said. "We all really, really wish that we could do that (that's how this got started), but unfortunately it's just not possible given the data."[213]

Andersen testified before the House committee:

"My initial hypothesis was a lab theory. When I stated that we were trying to disprove any type of lab theory, I was specifically referring to us testing our early hypothesis. This is textbook science in action," he said.[214]

This testimony was consistent with evidence in the House report, which contained correspondence which articulated his initial concerns about COVID-19 being engineered or genetically modified.

> "Eddie, can we talk? I need to be pulled off a ledge here," Andersen texted Holmes.

> In sworn congressional testimony from June 16, Andersen also said he thought at the time that the virus "could be engineered."

> Rep. Nicole Malliotakis (R-NY), a member of the House COVID subcommittee, asked why researchers like Rambaut were concerned about inflaming tensions with China—and why Andersen reversed course from his initial hypothesis within days of Fauci contacting him.

> "Something happened here," she said… "Politicians may flip-flop. Scientists do not flip-flop in a matter of 72 hours…"

> "Andersen has denied that a $8.9 million federal grant he received after authoring the paper was a quid pro quo for having completed the scientific study."

> Both Anderen and Garry have received millions in grants from NIAID since 2020.[215]

Were these scientists less concerned with the truth and the public's health than covering up their responsibility for what was carried out in Chinese labs and protecting their grants? How did their cover-up affect lifesaving interventions that were delayed and cost lives? And how do we trust the "science" of COVID-19 origins as well as the vaccines that "science" insisted were safe and effective, especially when they were recommended for pregnant women and children? How will these scientists and the NIAID be held accountable? The public now questions the science and medical community more than ever. Will we get the answers we deserve? Next time we're told to "believe the science," why should we? And even worse, can we ever trust the medical community again?

> NEXT TIME WE'RE TOLD TO "BELIEVE THE SCIENCE," WHY SHOULD WE? AND EVEN WORSE, CAN WE EVER TRUST THE MEDICAL COMMUNITY AGAIN?

How is this possible combination of politics affecting science and medicine playing out in gender confusion and huge hospital and pharmaceutical industry profits? How are medical personnel who disagree for religious reasons treated? In many settings, medical staff are told to wear badges that have their pronouns, to add pronouns to their email accounts, and even to acknowledge neopronouns: Ze, Zir, Zirs, Xe, Xem, Xyr. What? These are pronouns for those who do not want to associate themselves with any gender! And we thought Freud's ideas of sexuality in the '60s were bizarre. This is a whole new level.

In the manual I discussed earlier, clinical staff are further instructed, "The decision to disclose information about the child's gender identity or sexual orientation to others is the choice of the child. Hospital staff should be cautious to not 'out' (verbally or in written documentation) any individual without their consent—as this may present a serious safety risk to the child." The manual also includes how to sidestep parents who may not affirm the child's gender identity and how to find out if parents are affirming.[216]

Children's hospitals across the country are adding new buildings and clinics specifically designed to address gender confusion as not being confusion but rather as the way children identify. They are affirming them with puberty blockers, hormone therapy, transition surgeries, cosmetic surgeries, camps, support groups, political activism, and psychological coaching. And as long as they can get away with playing this game with our children's health and future, they will—all for a hefty paycheck.

> AND AS LONG AS THEY CAN GET AWAY WITH PLAYING THIS GAME WITH OUR CHILDREN'S HEALTH AND FUTURE, THEY WILL—ALL FOR A HEFTY PAYCHECK.

At the same time, at least a dozen states, including New York, California, and Massachusetts, have aligned with transgender advocates and many medical providers by ensuring that children are guaranteed access to care. And in July, the Biden administration proposed an expansion of the Obama-era protections.

"Gender-affirming care for transgender youth is essential and can be lifesaving," Dr. Rachel Levine, an assistant secretary at the U.S. Department of Health and Human Services, said in an interview with Reuters.

Levine, a pediatrician and a transgender woman, drew an outcry from conservative opponents of children's gender care and some medical professionals earlier this year when she told NPR radio: "There is no argument among medical professionals—pediatricians, pediatric endocrinologists, adolescent medicine physicians, adolescent psychiatrists, psychologists, et cetera—about the value and importance of gender-affirming care."[217]

And as "gender-affirming" care is being heralded as the cure to so many difficulties that ail young persons in their development, there are more voices of dissatisfaction. Those who have "transitioned" in adolescence are speaking up and even suing the medical practices of professionals they say took advantage of them.

> THOSE WHO HAVE "TRANSITIONED" IN ADOLESCENCE ARE SPEAKING UP AND EVEN SUING THE MEDICAL PRACTICES OF PROFESSIONALS THEY SAY TOOK ADVANTAGE OF THEM.

A lawsuit was filed on behalf of Layla Jane (Kayla Lovdahl in the lawsuit), a young woman who was medically transitioned as a 12-year-old girl. Layla Jane has sued the Permanente Medical Group, Kaiser Foundation Hospitals, and the clinicians who facilitated her transition from age 12 to 17 by administering puberty blockers and cross-sex hormones and performing a double mastectomy. The lawsuit, brought by the Center for American Liberty, alleges that defendants' medical negligence led to "substantial injury" through chemical and surgical sex-change interventions used while Layla Jane was a minor.[218]

"The law says children aren't mature enough to make serious decisions that could have long lasting consequences, like getting a tattoo, driving with friends, drinking alcohol, smoking cigarettes, or even voting," said Lovdhal. "So why is it acceptable for 13-year-olds to decide to mutilate their body?"[219]

The Center for American Liberty, also represents Chloe Cole, another young woman seeking legal action against the same institutions and doctors for facilitating her transition as a minor. Cole commented, "I was fifteen when you cut into my body, ripped out my breasts and stitched me back up like I was your rag doll," Cole charged, "You are on the wrong side of history and will always be remembered as child butchers."[220]

Counsel for Layla Jane and Cole are committed to holding the defendants accountable and intend to "strongly deter Kaiser's factory-line approach that permanently mutilates an unknown number of American children, subjecting them to a lifetime of harm, regret, and medical consequences."[221]

Parents must take a stand for their children and yes, question, and even fight any institution willing to confuse and take advantage of children.

CHAPTER 13

OBAMACARE FUNDS THE MOVEMENT

For years, we have been traveling through Canada to speak or vacation in a small beach home my parents purchased in the '80s. It has been eye-opening to see the progressive agendas unfurl in Canada and recognize where our U.S. government officials planned to take Americans. On one of these trips, I sat next to a Canadian who began to share with me how gender reassignment surgeries were being performed in Canada at the expense of the taxpayer, and how he, as a devout Catholic, resented that his tax dollars funded something that was opposed to his religious faith. He complained that it wasn't enough that the surgery, hormones, and follow up hormone therapy were 100 percent covered. There was a fight to cover painkillers for as long as they were needed.[222]

In the U.S., Hillary Clinton, as Secretary of State, pushed for a socialized healthcare system, then Barack Obama was driving a similar plan, later dubbed Obamacare. It became very clear to me that this socialized government plan, which would be funded by tax increases, was absolutely necessary to their plans to indoctrinate people, including youth eventually, by covering transgender surgeries. It began to make sense. If people had to pay for these very expensive surgeries on their own, very few would take place. But the government's "Affordable Care Act" could use taxpayers to fund these surgeries. There must be socialized medicine to "fund"— or could we say "launder"—the money from taxpayers to the

> THERE MUST BE SOCIALIZED MEDICINE TO "FUND"—OR COULD WE SAY "LAUNDER"— THE MONEY FROM TAXPAYERS TO THE PHARMACEUTICAL COMPANIES AND HOSPITALS WHO WOULD PERFORM THESE GENDER TRANSITIONS.

pharmaceutical companies and hospitals who would perform these gender transitions.[223] [224]

The story of Devin Payne illustrates how the Affordable Care Act was devised to achieve this scheme in the U.S. and usher in Canada's system of socialized "medicine."

> Devin Payne had gone years without health insurance—having little need and not much money to pay for it. Then Payne, who had a wife and four children, realized she could no longer live as a man. In her early 40s, she changed her name, began wearing long skirts and grew out her sandy blond hair. And she started taking female hormones, which caused her breasts to develop and the muscle mass on her 6-foot one-inch frame to shrink.

> The next step was gender reassignment surgery. For that, Payne, who is now 44, said she needed health coverage. "It is not a simple, easy, magical surgery," said Payne, a photographer who lives in Palm Springs. "Trying to do this without insurance is a big risk. Things can go wrong ... not having the money to pay for it would be awful."

> Payne learned in the fall that she might qualify for subsidies through the state's new insurance marketplace, Covered California, because her income fell under the limit of $46,000 a year. She eagerly signed up in March for a Blue Shield plan for about $230 a month, and began making preparations for the surgery that would change her life.

Among the less-talked-about implications of the Affordable Care Act is the relief it is providing to many transgender people, many of whom are low-income and who have struggled to obtain health coverage. Without insurance, many people were unable to afford the hormones, surgeries, and counseling needed to complete their transition. Nor would they have been covered in the event of surgical complications, which can include infections.

"We are still dependent on insurance and the medical community for us to be able to live authentically," said Aydin Kennedy, coordinator of the transgender health program at St. John's Well Child and Family Center in Los Angeles."[225]

No wonder there is such a push to normalize transgenderism and sex change surgeries—money. When the government can't get it from the individual because it's grossly infeasible, it legislates it, reassigns the expense to the taxpayer, then creates demand for it through policies, news, schools, media, and whomever else it can control.

A few years later in Manitoba, Canada, we were speaking at a conference. I was shocked to see a trans-clinic on almost every major corner of the city. Additionally, I opened the newspaper to see a two-page spread of emotionally moving stories of people who had gender reassignment surgery. There were at least seven stories, and not one of them shared any regrets. It seemed as if it was an ad for the transgender clinics rather than a news story. There was no objectivity. And the final paragraph of the article encouraged those who had any questions or thoughts of exploring their gender identity to stop by, as if it was as simple as a routine checkup. Because I was a youth leader, I had done enough research to recognize that there were many horrific stories of regret and a high incidence of suicide after gender-reassignment surgery.

Although I have essentially lost my faith in all that is left of the FDA since COVID-19, the fact remains that:

> Puberty blockers and sex hormones do not have U.S. Food and Drug Administration (FDA) approval for children's gender care. No clinical trials have established their safety for such off-label use. The drugs' long-term effects on fertility and sexual function remain unclear. And in 2016, the FDA ordered makers of puberty blockers to add a warning about psychiatric problems to the drugs' label after the agency received several reports of suicidal thoughts in children who were taking them.

> More broadly, no large-scale studies have tracked people who received gender-related medical care as children to determine how many remained satisfied with their treatment as they aged and how many eventually regretted transitioning. The same lack of clarity holds true for the contentious issue of detransitioning, when a patient stops or reverses the transition process.

> The National Institutes of Health, the U.S. government agency responsible for medical and public health research, told Reuters that "the evidence is limited on whether these treatments pose short- or long-term health risks for transgender and other gender-diverse adolescents." The NIH

has funded a comprehensive study to examine mental health and other outcomes for about 400 transgender youths treated at four U.S. children's hospitals. However, long-term results are years away and may not address concerns such as fertility or cognitive development.[226]

Despite the complete absence of long-term risks in children (as well as the obvious atrocity of the procedures used themselves), "more than half of states pay for gender-transition treatment through Medicaid" and only "nine states exclude youth gender care from Medicaid coverage."[227] As Ron DeSantis remarked days before Florida banned such coverage for children, "You don't disfigure 10, 12, 13-year-old kids based on gender dysphoria."[228]

Views about the speed of "treatment" varies among gender-care health practitioners.

A growing number of gender-care professionals say that in the rush to meet surging demand, too many of their peers are pushing too many families to pursue treatment for their children before they undergo the comprehensive assessments recommended in professional guidelines. Such assessments are crucial, these medical professionals say, because as the number of pediatric patients has surged, so has the number of those whose main source of distress may not be persistent gender dysphoria. Some could be gender fluid, with a gender identity that changes over time. Some may have mental health problems that complicate their cases. For these children, some practitioners say, medical treatment may pose unnecessary risks when counseling or other nonmedical interventions would be the better choice. "I'm afraid what we're getting are false positives and we've subjected them to irreversible physical changes," said Dr. Erica Anderson, a clinical psychologist who previously worked at the University of California San Francisco's gender clinic."[229]

Finland, Sweden, and the United Kingdom, once at the forefront of advocating children's gender care, have now limited the availability of treatment and even closed prominent facilities. The United Kingdom is shutting down its main clinic for children's gender care and overhauling the system after an independent review found that some staff felt "pressure to adopt an unquestioning affirmative approach."[230]

Meanwhile, the United States is moving forward at full speed with gender transitions. As mentioned above, the Affordable Care Act has forced insurance companies to cover medical and surgical sex changes. The Biden administration has promulgated a rule (albeit unconstitutionally) that "categorical coverage exclusions or limitations for all health services related to gender transition are discriminatory" and that a covered entity can't deny or limit coverage or claims, or charge more in cost-sharing related to gender transition."[231]

And how much do these procedures cost, and what about recovery time?

The procedures are long, complicated, and often painful. Vaginoplasty, for example, is a six-hour surgery with a recovery time of up to a year and a half, while phalloplasty has a similar recovery time and can take as long as 12 hours in the operating room.

While cost estimates vary widely, the Philadelphia Center for Transgender Surgery estimates that "bottom surgery" costs about $25,600 for male-to-female patients and about $24,900 for female-to-male. The center provides estimates for other common trans-related surgeries, such as breast augmentation ($9,000), bilateral mastectomy (up to $10,900), facial feminization (up to $70,100), and facial masculinization (up to $53,700).

These are out-of-pocket expenses for an estimated 14% of transgender people who are uninsured or whose insurance won't cover the procedures. And they don't include the price of ongoing therapy and other medical care, such as visits to a specialist for hormone therapy.

Under the 2014 Affordable Care Act and a handful of other laws with antidiscrimination provisions, insurers are required to cover medically necessary care for trans people. And an increasing number of them do. About 83% of companies surveyed by the Human Rights Campaign, for example, offer healthcare benefits that cover transgender care, up from 9% in 2010.[232]

Hormone replacement therapy has traditionally been utilized for an aging population to supplement hormone loss for health concerns related to aging. In recent years, hormones have increasingly become referenced more as a sexual enhancement drug. It's difficult to watch any news or media without ads for pharmaceuticals, and in particular those for ED, erectile dysfunction. The usage of little blue pills and testosterone replacement for men has skyrocketed. The negative impacts of breast cancer incidences with synthetic hormone therapy use for women has produced lawsuits that have resulted in many women saying no to synthetic hormones.[233]

Suzanne Somers helped champion bio-identical hormone replacement therapy instead of traditional synthetic hormone therapy, which also challenged pharmaceutical industry profits from menopausal women.

The abortion industry, with its disgusting by-product business of selling baby parts, was exposed and Roe v. Wade overturned, challenging the future of abortion profits.[234]

As pharma began losing control over women's health, was the trans or transition movement a replacement business? To what degree has abuse and over-usage of testosterone supplementation combined with pornography driven the sex-trafficking industry? The drug company supplies the drug addiction, but someone must supply the "victims"—the women and children who become the "fulfillment" centers for their drug induced addiction. Are these drug and trafficking syndicates related? We know illegal drugs are connected to trafficking, but what roles do pharmaceutical and medical corporations have to play as well?

> THE DRUG COMPANY SUPPLIES THE DRUG ADDICTION, BUT SOMEONE MUST SUPPLY THE "VICTIMS"—THE WOMEN AND CHILDREN WHO BECOME THE "FULFILLMENT" CENTERS FOR THEIR DRUG INDUCED ADDICTION.

As taxpayers, are we going to allow our hard-earned money to fund the mutilation of children? Does this make us complicit in this evil scheme? These are obviously "ugly" conversations that no one, including me, really wants to have, but we must if we want to save the innocent, the children. The propaganda and even censorship have raged to hide these conversations. We must have them.

> AS TAXPAYERS, ARE WE GOING TO ALLOW OUR HARD-EARNED MONEY TO FUND THE MUTILATION OF CHILDREN?

CHAPTER 14

GLOBAL CRIME
SYNDICATE

How does organized crime play into the war for our tomorrow? With the freeflow of fentanyl across our southern border[235], the atrocities of child-trafficking, human trafficking and child pornography, and the abundance of other illegal substances, we ask ourselves how can a government that sends satellites into orbit and develops AI technology not be able to stop these horrific acts, bring law and order, and eradicate these hideous, unspeakable crimes against children and women? Their seeming complicity begs us to question: do they really want to stop these crimes, or are power and money driving these decisions? Also, when it seems we are close to indictments and justice being served, why are the perpetrators of sinister demonic crimes only getting a slap on the hand and seeming to disappear from accountability? Is there a crime syndicate and how deep does it intertwine with global agendas, names, fortunes, and even U.S. Presidents and government officials?

IS THERE A CRIME SYNDICATE AND HOW DEEP DOES IT INTERTWINE WITH GLOBAL AGENDAS, NAMES, FORTUNES, AND EVEN U.S. PRESIDENTS AND GOVERNMENT OFFICIALS?

Organized crime is defined as "illegal activities, conducted by groups or networks acting in concert, by engaging in violence, corruption or related activities in order to obtain, directly or indirectly, a financial or material benefit."[236]

According to the United Nations, "organized crime thrives worldwide, affecting governance and political processes, and weakening the advancement of the rule of law. It encompasses, inter alia, illicit trafficking of firearms, drugs, protected species, cultural property, or falsified medical products and, among its most severe manifestations, human trafficking and the smuggling of migrants. It also includes the laundering of proceeds of crime and obstruction of justice. Moreover, with all forms of organized crime shifting ever more to being dependent on or incorporating online aspects, including the use of virtual assets, its reach and capability of harm is increasing. Organized criminal groups are flexible in changing or expanding their illicit businesses for profit. They misuse vulnerabilities and crisis situations such as the COVID-19 pandemic, economic downturns, natural disasters, and armed conflicts exploiting them for their own purposes."[237]

The term "oligarchy" refers to "government by the few, especially despotic power exercised by a small and privileged group for corrupt or selfish purposes. Oligarchies in which members of the ruling group are wealthy or exercise their power through their wealth are known as plutocracies[…] Most classic oligarchies have resulted when governing elites were recruited exclusively from a ruling caste—a hereditary social grouping that is set apart from the rest of society by religion, kinship, economic status, prestige, or even language. Such elites tend to exercise power in the interests of their own class."[238]

While street gangs and neighborhood mob organizations are certainly contributing factors in the chaos and confusion we witness in our cities across America (and the world), I want to focus on the global players who are profiting from the worst ills of society, for they are the force that drives criminal activity and "pays off" the nefarious actors or funds activism through NGOs ("Non-Governmental Organizations" that operate independently of any government, typically for social or political issues, i.e.,

BLM, Greenpeace, Open Societies, MoveOn, Media Matters, Energy Foundation). They drive political agendas and invoke fear in order to control officials and prevent them from interfering with or stopping illegal activities. Campaign contributions funneled through NGOs can later serve as a means to elect officials and call in favors or buy a crooked district attorney.

We recall scandals like the Anthony Weiner computer laptop, which contained many missing emails of then Secretary of State Hillary Clinton and her assistant Huma Abedin, not to mention evidence that Anthony Weiner (Huma's then-husband) had engaged in the solicitation of a minor (15 yr. old girl) for sex. The material was supposed to implicate others, including Clinton, in crimes. But according to New York Times investigative reporter James B. Stewart, "The discovery fell through the cracks because top FBI officials were "overwhelmed" by the Russia probe."[239]

"A determined New York FBI agent was 'scared' by what he had found and pressed his superiors to finish the job. 'I'm telling you that we have potentially ten times the volume that Director Comey said we had on the record,' the agent recounted to Stewart. 'Why isn't anybody here?'"[240]

"Reportedly, only 3,077 of the more than 300,000 emails found on the Weiner laptop "were directly reviewed for classified or incriminating information. Three FBI officials completed that work in a single 12-hour spurt the day before Comey again cleared Clinton of criminal charges."[241] Did the 90% of unreviewed emails implicate many powerful people, as the NYPD personnel reportedly claimed? If so, why are the FBI and DOJ shielding them?"

And who could forget the email server scandal? "Hillary Clinton's private email server contained information that was classified at a higher level than "top secret," the inspector general of the intelligence community told members of Congress in a letter obtained by CBS News. The server Clinton used as Secretary of State contained "several dozen emails containing classified information determined by the [intelligence community] element to be at the CONFIDENTIAL, SECRET, and TOP SECRET/SAP levels," the inspector general, Charles McCullough, wrote in the letter, which was first reported by Fox News. "SAP" stands for special access programs, which carry a classification level higher than top secret. Former CIA Director David Petraeus was sentenced to two years' probation and fined $100,000 for sharing similarly classified information with Paula Broadwell, his biographer and mistress."[242]

What about the Biden family?

Two congressional inquiries have revealed a number of instances where FBI personnel actively thwarted investigations by alerting Hunter Biden's attorneys in advance of a planned search of one of Hunter's storage facilities. And then there's the 51 current and retired intelligence officers together signing a letter saying that the Hunter Biden laptop was "a sophisticated Russia disinformation campaign," and did this to insure voters would not discover the laptop's authenticity prior to the 2020 elections.[243]

"Now there are further revelations that the FBI colluded with a foreign government — Ukraine — to silence Americans on social media. The House Judiciary Committee's subcommittee on the "weaponization" of the federal government reported last week that the FBI facilitated censorship requests coming from Ukraine's own intelligence service (SBU), passing them along to Facebook, Instagram, and YouTube. 'In so doing, the FBI violated the First Amendment rights of Americans and potentially undermined our national security,' the committee's report said. Bruner, author of *Compromised: How Money and Politics Drive FBI Corruption*, has been reviewing the committee reports, and concludes, 'getting to the bottom of all this, we see that it goes all the way to the top.'[244]

To bring this home, when parents tried to get involved with their local school boards to counter CRT and LGBTQ agendas in their children's schools, they were deemed terrorists by our FBI. "Rep. Jim Jordan (R-OH) challenged current FBI Director Christopher Wray about approving surveillance of parents who spoke up against policy decisions at local school board meetings and about a local field office's surveillance conducted against Latin-Mass Catholics as possible 'domestic terrorists.'"[245]

Sadly, it appears that our FBI and CIA are scandal ridden, but how long has this been going on?

"Conservatives tend to have two bad habits. First, they're prone to viewing the past through a nostalgic lens. Second, they tend to instinctively give law enforcement the benefit of the doubt. These tendencies help explain why conservatives for decades have been able to overlook the many abuses—constitutional, legal, and moral—of US intelligence agencies."[246]

In his article, "8 Historic Cases That Show the FBI and CIA Were Out of Control Long Before Russiagate," John Miltimore chronicles the history of UA intelligence agencies, which "reveals that government bureaucrats were out of control long before the 2016 presidential election."[247]

These include the following:

1. **That Time the CIA Considered Bombing Miami and Blaming It on Castro**

    It's no secret that the US government sought to assassinate Fidel Castro for years. Less well known, however, was that part of their regime-change plot included a plan to blow up Miami and sinking a boat-full of innocent Cubans.

    The plan, which was revealed in 2017 when the National Archives declassified 2,800 documents from the JFK era, was a collaborative effort that included the CIA, the State Department, the Department of Defense, and other federal agencies that sought to brainstorm strategies to topple Castro and sow unrest within Cuba. One of those plans included Operation Northwoods, submitted to the CIA by General Lyman Lemnitzer on behalf of the Joint Chiefs of Staff. It summarized nine "pretexts" the CIA and US government could employ to justify military intervention in Cuba. One of the official CIA documents shows officials musing about staging a terror campaign ("real or simulated") and blaming it on Cuban refugees. [..].

2. In 2014, the CIA Was Caught Red-handed Spying on the Senate Intelligence Committee.

In the summer of 2014, the CIA's inspector general concluded that the CIA had "improperly" spied on US Senate staffers who were researching the agency's black history of torture. As the New York Times reported:

> An internal investigation by the CIA. has found that its officers penetrated a computer network used by the Senate Intelligence Committee in preparing its damning report on the CIA.'s detention and interrogation program.

And that's not the worst part. The Times goes on to note that CIA officers didn't just read the emails of the Senate investigators. They also sent "a criminal referral to the Justice Department based on false information."

John Brennan, CIA director from 2013-2017, insisted during Senate hearings these were "very limited inappropriate actions" and that "the actions of the CIA were reasonable."

Sen. Ron Wyden (D-Oregon) disagreed.

> "That's not what the Inspector General [concluded]," Wyden said. "When you're

talking about spying on a committee responsible for overseeing your agency, in my view that undermines the very checks and balances that protect our democracy, and it's unacceptable in a free society. And your compatriots in all your sister agencies agree with that."

Brennan, who publicly lied about the episode, was not punished and even retained his security clearance until Aug. 15, 2018.

3. The FBI's "Suicide Letter" to MLK and His Wife

Before he had a day named in his honor and a monument on the National Mall, the government viewed Martin Luther King Jr. very much as a threat. In fact, his message of peace, love, equality, and civil disobedience had the FBI so scared that agents actually sent King and his wife a package containing a strange letter and tape recording. It contained details of the civil rights activist's sexual indiscretions and encouraged him to kill himself. ...

4. The CIA Forced Prisons to Participate in Mind Control Experiments in the 1950s.

If you've never heard of Project MKUltra, you might find it hard to believe. Also known as "the CIA Mind Control Program," the effort was launched by the agency in 1953. The program used drug experiments on humans, oftentimes on prisoners who were tested against their will or in exchange for early release. The experiments were undertaken so CIA agents could better understand how to extract information from enemies during interrogations. Here is a description from the History Channel:

> MK-Ultra's "mind control" experiments generally centered around behavior modification via electro-shock therapy, hypnosis, polygraphs, radiation, and a variety of drugs, toxins, and chemicals. These experiments relied on a range of test subjects: some who freely volunteered, some who volunteered under coercion, and some who had absolutely no idea they were involved in a sweeping defense research program. From mentally-impaired boys at a state school, to American soldiers, to "sexual psychopaths" at a state hospital, MK-Ultra's programs often preyed on the most vulnerable members of society. The CIA considered prisoners especially good subjects, as they were willing to give consent in exchange for extra recreation time or commuted sentences... [...]

5. The FBI's Systemic Forensic Fraud in Crime Labs

In the early 1990s, Dr. Frederic Whitehurst, an attorney and chemist who worked at the FBI as a Supervisory Special Agent, noticed troubling practices in the bureau's Investigation Laboratory.

There were "alterations of reports, alterations of evidence, folks testifying outside their areas of expertise in courts of law," said Whitehurst.[...]

At least 35 of these cases involved convicted criminals who received the death penalty, according to the National Whistleblower Legal Defense and Education Fund.

6. Operation Midnight Climax: Drugging Unsuspecting Johns and Filming Their Interactions with Prostitutes

In the 1950s and early 1960s, the CIA admitted to operating a "bawdy house" in a San Francisco apartment where "unsuspecting citizens were lured… for the CIA's drug experiments," according to a local news story report documented by the agency.

Private citizens were taken to the bordello by $100 prostitutes and drugged without their knowledge, usually with LSD," the *San Francisco Examiner* reported in 1977 after the CIA admitted to the operation. Agents sat behind a two-way mirror and filmed the interactions between the drugged men and prostitutes. [...]

7. The FBI Has Routinely Staged Acts of Terrorism.

In the wake of 9/11, the FBI has, on numerous occasions, targeted unstable and mentally ill individuals, sending informants to bait them into committing terror attacks. Before these individuals can actually carry out the attack, however, the Bureau intervenes, presenting the foiled plot to the public as a successfully thwarted attack.

In 2011, journalist Glenn Greenwald summarized several examples of this deceitful tactic:

> [T]he FBI subjected 19-year-old Somali-American Mohamed Osman Mohamud to months of encouragement, support and money and convinced him to detonate a bomb at a crowded Christmas event in Portland, Oregon, only to arrest him at the last moment and then issue a Press Release boasting of its success. In late 2009, the FBI persuaded and enabled Hosam Maher Husein Smadi, a 19-year old Jordanian citizen, to place a fake bomb at a Dallas skyscraper and separately convinced Farooque Ahmed, a 34-year-old naturalized American citizen born in Pakistan, to bomb the Washington Metro.

8. The CIA's Media Manipulation Campaigns

From the agency's earliest days, it has attempted to control the flow of information to the public. In his book Legacy of Ashes: A History of the CIA, former New York Times journalist Tim Weiner documented how much influence the agency's first civilian director, Allen Dulles, had among major media companies:

> Dulles kept in close touch with the men who ran The New York Times, The Washington Post, and the nation's leading weekly magazines. He could pick up the phone and edit a breaking story, make sure an irritating foreign correspondent was yanked from the field, or hire the services of men such as Time's Berlin bureau chief and Newsweek's man in Tokyo.

Weiner noted, "It was second nature for Dulles to plant stories in the press.[...]"

Considering the CIA's long history of intervening in other countries' elections and governments, it is particularly ironic that their claims of Russia's meddling in the US' democracy are taken at face value.

Nor is the corruption and deceit limited to the FBI and CIA. Former Director of National Intelligence James Clapper lied to lawmakers and the public in

2013 when he claimed [the] NSA did not collect any type of data on "millions or hundreds of millions of Americans." He was caught red-handed months later when whistleblower Edward Snowden revealed the extent of the agency's mass surveillance operations."[248]

Surely the FBI and/or CIA was complicit in Epstein's sex-trafficking, rape and pedophilia crimes. There's just no credible explanation given the notoriety of those involved, the sheer depravity of the crimes, the intricacies of the plot, the territory it spanned and the utter lack of justice surrounding this massive scheme. That Epstein was clearly murdered while on suicide watch cannot seriously be refuted by anyone with a pulse. In fact, it is safe to say we were all disappointed as death was too kind and his list of accomplices may go forever unidentified.

Revelations of the Jeffrey Epstein case reveal a justice system that let accused pedophile Jeffrey Epstein continue to abuse underage women. Epstein was given a plea deal by then Florida U.S. Attorney Alex Acosta, who later was investigated, and the DOJ said the decision was an act of poor judgment. "Letting a well-connected billionaire get away with child rape and international sex trafficking isn't 'poor judgment'—it is

SURELY THE FBI AND/OR CIA WAS COMPLICIT IN EPSTEIN'S SEX-TRAFFICKING, RAPE AND PEDOPHILIA CRIMES. THERE'S JUST NO CREDIBLE EXPLANATION GIVEN THE NOTORIETY OF THOSE INVOLVED, THE SHEER DEPRAVITY OF THE CRIMES, THE INTRICACIES OF THE PLOT, THE TERRITORY IT SPANNED AND THE UTTER LACK OF JUSTICE SURROUNDING THIS MASSIVE SCHEME.

a disgusting failure. Americans ought to be enraged," Senator Ben Sasse said in a statement.

Victims' rights attorney Brad Edwards, who sued the Justice Department in 2008 on behalf of two victims who alleged the Epstein deal was reached in violation of their rights, criticized the reports while praising Villafaña, the prosecutor who prepared a 53-page indictment against Epstein that was never filed because Acosta decided in 2007 to negotiate a deal with Epstein."[249]

What did that deal involve, and more importantly, *who* did it involve?

How could that information be used by intelligence agencies and others to control or, better, blackmail Epstein's clientele? The connection between world leaders, celebrities, politicians, and elite global leaders may be clearer if we knew. As discussed in a previous chapter, flight logs have turned over a Who's-Who's list of world leaders, politicians, celebrities, and at least 300 British nationals, Prince Andrew, Bill Clinton included.[250] [251]

It turns out, Clinton was a "much more frequent flyer on a registered sex offender's infamous jet than previously reported, with flight logs showing the former president taking at least 26 trips aboard the "Lolita Express" -- even apparently ditching his Secret Service detail for at least five of the flights, according to records obtained by FoxNews.com.[252] According to Conchita Sarnoff, of the Washington, D.C. based non-profit Alliance to Rescue Victims of Trafficking, and author of *TrafficKing*, Clinton was among Epstein's "inner circle" all of whom "knew [Epstein] was a pedophile."[253] "Why would a former president associate with a man like that?" Sarnoff asked. The answer is pretty obvious.

The book, *Filthy Rich*, details the relationship between Clinton and Epstein.

> Epstein had already donated $2,000 to Clinton back in 1992 when he ran for the Presidency. In time, he would donate $147,000 to Democrats and $18,000 to Republicans, and the cash got him access. 'Filthy Rich' says that in 1993, Epstein donated $10,000 to the White House Historical Association, contributing to the Clintons' efforts to redecorate the residence with gold drapes and other lavish decor. The book says: 'In return, Epstein received a perfunctory thank-you letter from the association and an invitation to a donor reception with the Clintons. 'He brought Ghislaine Maxwell as his date.' There they were, a serial pedophile and his alleged madam, meeting the Clintons for the first time—and it took place in the White House.

> A proper introduction between the two was arranged by Lynn Forester, a blond telecom executive who later married into the wealthy Rothschild family.

> She was supposedly 'smitten' with Epstein and became an 'evangelist for his financial services', the book says.

> During the dinner at Ted Kennedy's house in 1995 she spoke to Clinton about Epstein, rather than social policy she intended to talk about.

> In a revealing letter to Clinton in 1995 she wrote: 'It was a pleasure to see you. 'Using my fifteen seconds of access to

discuss Jeffrey Epstein and currency stabilization, I neglected to talk to you about a topic near and dear to my heart. Namely, affirmative action and the future'.[254]

Bill Clinton became so close to the Rothschilds that he spoke at the funeral of Evelyn de Rothschild at the request of his wife, Lynn Forrester de Rothschild, herself on the visitor log to Little St James Island, and the person who introduced the Clintons to Epstein. The Rothschild Foundation manages the Spencer House in London on Little St. James Street.[255] Maybe Epstein named his island, Little Saint James, as a nod to Rothschild? Coincidence or not, how is the world of elites connected, and how have they operated financially to affect nations, currencies, trafficking, drugs, military installations, wars, bribery, and control of smaller nations?

There are other nefarious plans linked to global family names and agendas, these involving world population agendas, climate change, recently called Climate Emergency by media fearmongers. "Climate anxiety"[256] is a new mental health "fear" children are facing as they are inundated with distressful stories of what will happen if we do not save the planet, kill the babies, erect solar farms instead of real farms, give up our cars, and eliminate livestock in favor of fake meats.

According to *Killing The Planet: How The Financial Cartel Doomed Mankind*, in 1977, the Rockefeller Brothers Fund sponsored a task force report entitled "The Unfinished Agenda: The Citizens Policy Guide to Environmental Issues."[257] The report is a self-described "consensus document" illustrating the "collective thinking of the participating environmental leaders ... about a world transition from abundance to scarcity, a transition that is already underway."[258] It called for the following increasing "family planning programs," "progressively increasing gasoline tax," and "escalating tax on natural gas consumption" as well as "all fossil fuels."[259] Accordingly, Rockefellers, via the charitable organizations they control, channel "massive funding" into the climate agenda.[260]

According to *Killing the Planet*, "Within the decade, the Rockefellers, with the help of their new friend, Bill Gates, will soon have total dominion over the earth's food supply. Genetically modified seeds are now being planted on every continent throughout the world... Never in the history of mankind has such power been wielded over the food chain. The Rockefellers who masterminded the production of genetically modified organisms and the birth of agribusiness had become the masters of the new feudal system and of the human race...."[261]

The Rockefellers control not only the food, but also the laws and policies controlling the food.

> The Rockefellers established an intermediary non-profit 501c3 organization—the Energy Foundation—to conceal their donor intent and to push their climate agenda at both the state and federal levels of government. In accordance with IRS regulations, wealthy individuals can fund a 5013c organization (such as the Energy Foundation), and direct it to transfer large sums of money to 501c4 organizations which can legally fund political campaigns and lobby for public policy. With this loophole, the Rockefellers shelled out tens of millions of dollars to the Energy Foundation, wrote off their expenditures as charitable contributions, and

channeled the money into campaign coffers of politicians who were willing to do their bidding."[262]

Rothschilds' protégé, George Soros, is also part of the green energy shakedown. Through his Open Societies Foundations, Soros has "funneled billions of dollars to major green activist foundations."[263]

Although these issues may seem far from our day-to-day lives, this type of corruption and control filters into and operates throughout local, state, and federal governments and destroys families. Their "family planning" funding green energy plans drives the abortion industry, degrades motherhood, sterilizes youth in transgender surgeries, and spins that the earth is overpopulated in spite of the fact that most of the earth is still unpopulated green space. It may be hard to convince those dwelling in cities, but there are plenty of resources and unpopulated land, and we are *not* in a climate crisis. However, we may find ourselves in a self-manufactured food crisis in the future if globalists have their way, turning millions of acres into solar farms throughout the food belt of America. If they take control of food and energy supplies, they can control the future. Gates and others have already "predicted" a coming food shortage.

> THEIR "FAMILY PLANNING" FUNDING GREEN ENERGY PLANS DRIVES THE ABORTION INDUSTRY, DEGRADES MOTHERHOOD, STERILIZES YOUTH IN TRANSGENDER SURGERIES, AND SPINS THAT THE EARTH IS OVERPOPULATED IN SPITE OF THE FACT THAT MOST OF THE EARTH IS STILL UNPOPULATED GREEN SPACE.

THEY ARE COMING FOR YOUR CHILDREN
THE FIGHT WE MUST WIN!

If we want to save the future for our children, we must expose darkness and the global crime syndicate, and we must start with what our hand finds to do at the local level. While we were busy and asleep, the enemy infiltrated our garden(nation) and sowed tares among the wheat (youth). We are now reaping the consequences of turning our governance over to evildoers who have corrupted themselves and everything holy.

CHAPTER 15

THE FUTURE
OF MONEY

Gary and I travel consistently and have contacts all over the world. For years, I have been tipped off about the future agendas coming to America by observing Canada, Europe, New Zealand, Cambodia, Vietnam, and Africa. While recently traveling in Europe, I was surprised when face recognition was required to be my "boarding pass." There was no paper boarding pass or scanning a QR code from my phone—my face was the entry. It was eerie as one by one we stepped in front of a screen, saw our faces appear on their security screen, and then heard the ding of acceptance, or as happened to a few outside of our party, a buzzer rejecting the person's admittance and then seeing them promptly removed to face scrutiny (pun intended).

While in France, I entered a ZARA store and had my clothes in hand to try on in the dressing room. Before admittance, I was asked to stand in front of a mirror that scanned my face and the items I had in my hands. While I was changing clothes, I heard a fight break out between the clerk who was "guarding" the dressing room and a mother who was not allowed to accompany her daughter to give her opinion as her daughter tried on clothing items. The mother was furious, and they left the store. There is no room for mothers or their opinions in a digital world.

When I approached the check-out, there was no individual attendant. My purchases were already added and waiting for my payment option as I lay them on the counter. My husband and I were expected to remove all the electronic tags from the clothes with the store's device, a new training experience for us. As we did that, I discovered the machine had charged me for items I had handed back to an attendant on the way to the checkout. When I reported this to the attendant (guard) on duty, it turned into a crisis. She didn't know what to do! The machine had failed to recognize I no longer had the items. No one seemed to know how to remove the item from my cart. In a moment of unsettling pressure, I agreed just to go ahead and purchase the $100 items rather than continue to wait and face their scrutiny. There seems to be no room for human decision or judgment in a peopleless, cashless world, I learned! After leaving with our purchase, we entered a McDonald's, and it was the same scenario—all electronic, personless. It occurred to me that I would not be able to travel, or buy food or clothes in this cashless, personless system if someone didn't want me to have the "privilege."

I couldn't help but see the parallel between this and voting electronically without paper ballots. Do you remember how we were told our election using electronic systems was the safest, most secure election? Here we go again, except this time it's your money! Let's look at the same computer tech used to affect elections and see how this is increasingly being used to impact your money and drive agendas that align with the New World Order a.k.a. The Great Reset/ Fourth Industrial Revolution.

> LET'S LOOK AT THE SAME COMPUTER TECH USED TO AFFECT ELECTIONS AND SEE HOW THIS IS INCREASINGLY BEING USED TO IMPACT YOUR MONEY AND DRIVE AGENDAS THAT ALIGN WITH THE NEW WORLD ORDER A.K.A. THE GREAT RESET/ FOURTH INDUSTRIAL REVOLUTION.

Professor J. Alex Halderman has made a career studying electronic voting security. His research has changed the concept of stolen elections from theory to reality.

"I know America's voting machines are vulnerable," J. Alex Halderman firmly stated, pausing to lift his head from the page he read to look up at a phalanx of U.S. senators, "because my colleagues and I have hacked them—repeatedly—as part of a decade of research studying the technology that operates elections and learning how to make it stronger."

It's not hyperbole to say a shudder swept through that August meeting room in the Hart Senate Office Building in Washington, D.C., as Halderman delivered a much-rehearsed line at the onset of a six-minute statement. Until the U-M computer science professor began his testimony before the Senate Select Committee on Intelligence in June 2017, the idea of a hacked American election felt to many lawmakers like a still-theoretical notion. Other technologists and elections integrity experts had warned members of Congress in such formal settings about abstract vulnerabilities, but state officials and election machine vendors had repeatedly insisted they had it all under control.

Halderman has little patience for such coddling. That his voting machine intrusions took place in laboratories rather than live elections made his message no less alarming to the committee.

"We've created attacks that can spread from machine to machine like a computer virus and silently change election outcomes," Halderman continued. "We studied touch screens and optical scan systems." Then, emphasizing each next word with a staccato delivery and direct eye contact, he stated: "And in every single case, we found ways for attackers to sabotage machines and to steal votes. These capabilities are certainly within reach for America's enemies."

After the aforementioned decade of warning lawmakers about the dangers posed by the machinery of U.S. elections, Halderman, 37, had delivered his message directly to the country's most powerful people. Since then, he has returned to the Capitol routinely to chat with legislators and their staff as Congress passed $380 million in funding for states to modernize their equipment and security practices. In addition, Sen. Richard Burr, the chair of the committee Halderman testified before, sought his input into an election reform package that, as of press time, has yet to be introduced.[264]

It's interesting that even with Congressional demonstrations and warnings, electronic voting machines have become accepted for voting, alongside a pandemic with out-of-control mail-in ballots, ballot harvesting, and video footage of people stuffing ballot drop off boxes at 3:00 a.m. Instead of addressing the dangers presented with electronic voting, did they choose to use the information to carry out the unimaginable? Fraud. Imagine if these electronic scenarios involved a Central Bank Digital Currency (CBDC) and your money. We are already hearing the legacy media tout the safety of a central digital currency. Tell that to Chinese citizens given poor social credit scores that are used to prohibit their travel and purchases, or to the Canadian truckers who had their bank accounts frozen when they didn't agree with their government.

Our ministry recently received this letter from a minister in Uganda we have financially supported for over twenty years:

> Dear Pastor, the American Government slapped a number of sanctions on Uganda some time ago because our President signed the anti-Homosexuality bill into law… Then yesterday the World Bank in New York sanctioned Uganda too for the same reason of anti-Homosexuality.
>
> Now our economy is under painful and unbearable sanctions.
>
> Inflation is going up so rapidly while our economic lives are getting so painful everyday.
>
> Please, remember to put us in your prayers as we go through these very painful economic times.

We cannot disregard or ignore those at the World Economic Forum and other globalists like Blackrock's Larry Fink, who wish to bring all businesses and the financial system into ESG (Equity, Social, Governance) as a determination of winners and losers (i.e., who gets a loan or is denied) by using DEI (Diversity, Equity and Inclusion).[265] The folks involved in this scheme will say it's not political, but any fool can see that it is purely political. If you disagree with their equity or diversity definition, (code for LGBTQ agendas), then you get a low score. If you don't embrace and support their social agendas, including gender transitions for youth, their governance rules and regulations, and the green agendas spelled out in Agenda 2030, they can decide you or your business don't qualify and you don't get the loan, the contract, the promotion, etc.

Major retailers' recent business decisions (which to most of us seem foolish) illustrate how much influence and overt control financial companies like Blackrock truly have.

Executives at companies like Nike, Anheuser-Busch and Kate Spade, whose brand endorsements have turned controversial trans influencer Dylan Mulvaney into today's woke "It girl," aren't just virtue signaling.

They're handing out lucrative deals to what were once considered fringe celebrities because they have to—or risk failing an all-important social credit score that could make or break their businesses.

At stake is their Corporate Equality Index—or CEI—score, which is overseen by the Human Rights Campaign, the largest LGBTQ+ political lobbying group in the world.

HRC, which has received millions from George Soros' Open Society Foundation among others, issues report cards for America's biggest corporations via the CEI: awarding or subtracting points for how well companies adhere to what HRC calls its "rating criteria."

Businesses that attain the maximum 100 total points earn the coveted title "Best Place To Work For LGBTQ Equality." Fifteen of the top 20 Fortune-ranked companies received 100% ratings last year, according to HRC data."

More than 840 US companies racked up high CEI scores, according to the latest report.

The HRC, which was formed in 1980 and started the CEI in 2002, is led by Kelley Robinson who was named as president in 2022 and worked as a political organizer for Barack Obama's 2008 presidential campaign.

The HRC lists five major rating criteria, each with its own lengthy subsets, for companies to gain—or lose—CEI points. [...]

The main categories are: "Workforce Protections," "Inclusive Benefits," "Supporting an Inclusive Culture," "Corporate Social Responsibility" and "Responsible Citizenship."

A company can lose CEI points if it doesn't fulfill HRC's demand for "integration of intersectionality in professional development, skills-based or other training" or if it doesn't use a "supplier diversity program with demonstrated effort to include certified LGBTQ+ suppliers." [266]

This is purely political! It's merely wrapped in a cloak of deception. Companies must use their "certified LGBTQ suppliers."[267] The result is if you are a progressive leftist who believes in the social agendas being forced on businesses and CEOs, then you win, and if you disagree, the socialist Marxists will pull your credentials and shut your life and your company down. Think COVID-19 lockdowns, except this time it's not just

> **THINK COVID-19 LOCKDOWNS, EXCEPT THIS TIME IT'S NOT JUST A LOCKDOWN, IT'S A LOCKOUT OF YOUR ABILITY TO PURCHASE, BUY, AND PROVIDE.**

a *lockdown*, it's a *lockout* of your ability to purchase, buy, and provide. And now the same system of sex ed "suppliers" are contracted to come to your school and teach children gender ideology.

Children's lives and future fertility threatened with transition surgeries, along with "green" depopulation agendas are just a few of their agendas used to penalize countries, businesses, and individuals who don't comply with ESG. New Zealand is the latest model for their green agenda and, why not? New Zealand's leadership also embraced leftist children's curricula that consider masturbation normal sexual behavior and support this behavior in children as young as five years old![268] New Zealand was placed under Emergency Orders for "Climate Emergency" long before COVID-19 ever hit their shore. Their prime minister at the time, Jacinda Arden, declared Emergency Executive Orders under a Climate Change Emergency, using the "emergency" to institute the most liberal abortion policy in the world.[269]

Can you see the dangers when companies or individuals are placed in a position where they either have to accept the HRC and Larry Fink's version of business or pay the consequences with their ability to provide? This is what the World Economic Forum's Klaus Schwab called "stakeholder capitalism,"[270] which maintains that all business in the world is connected and therefore must adhere to the world's mutual goals of green mandates, the WHO abortion for all mantras, equity to all in the LGBTQ+ groups, and population control to weed out undesirables. If you're Kamala Harris, you can even spin population control as a means of providing for our children!

Harris said:

> So I stand here before you, as Vice President of the United States, proud to make the announcements we are making today, which are historic. And I am very clear: I stand here on the shoulders of people like Vernice — (applause) — and her decades of work and leadership in the fight for environmental justice. [...]

> So, every day, all across our nation, we feel and see the impact of the climate crisis. I mean, if you watch the morning news, it will be the lead story. It's been every day for the last couple of weeks. It is the lead story. I think we finally, at least in our progress, come to the point that most people can no longer deny it because it is so obvious.

> And we have seen, around our country, where communities have been choked by drought, have been washed out by floods, and decimated by hurricanes. Here in Baltimore, you have seen your skies darkened by wildfire smoke. And you have seen the waters of the Chesapeake Bay rise, threatening homes and businesses that have stood for generations.

> It is clear that the clock is not only ticking, it is banging. And we must act.

> As Vice President, as I said, I've traveled across our nation to speak with thousands of Americans about this crisis. I have met with students and entrepreneurs, small-business owners, community leaders, nonprofit leaders, labor leaders — folks

with new approaches to reduce our emissions and accelerate our clean energy transition, but folks who often do not have access to the funds they need to make their ideas a reality. And that is a problem.

For years, one of the missing pieces in our strategy to fight the climate crisis is that we have not invested at scale in community climate action. For years, the people of the community — folks who know what their neighborhood needs and how to provide it — have not been given adequate resources to implement climate solutions that match the magnitude of the crisis we face.

And that's why we're here today.

Today, I am proud to announce the largest investment in financing for community-based climate projects in our nation's history. (Applause.) It's a good day.

And one of the reasons that it is so significant is because we also — frankly, we've got to make up for lost time. So, by dramatically accelerating our work, we know we can lower emissions.

And we will do that by providing $20 billion to a national network of nonprofits, community lenders, and other financial institutions to fund tens of thousands of climate and clean energy projects across America. (Applause.)

So, here is what that will mean: Okay, so imagine, for

example, the construction companies that build affordable housing here in Baltimore that, because of this investment, will now have the capital they need to install energy-efficient appliances in new units, to lower energy use, and to help tenants save on their electric bills.

Imagine, for example, the small-business owner who will now be able to receive zero-interest loans to electrify their fleet of delivery vehicles so we can reduce pollution and save on gas.

Imagine, for example — (applause) — right? Imagine, for example, the house of worship that will now be able to have access to loan guarantees so they can install solar panels on the roof of their building — (applause) — to generate affordable clean electricity for the entire neighborhood. Imagine.

You know, when President Biden and I took office, we set an ambitious goal. Yes, people said, "That can't be done." We said, "Well, you know what? We believe in dreaming with ambition and then seeing it through."

And so, we set an ambitious goal to cut our greenhouse gas emissions in half by 2030 and to reach net-zero emissions by 2050. The investment we are announcing today will help us to achieve these goals, and it will do so much more, because think also about the impact on not only the local economy, not only on an investment in the entrepreneurs and innovators from and in the community. Think about the impact on something like public health.

> When we invest in clean energy and electric vehicles and reduce population [pollution], more of our children can breathe clean air and drink clean water.[271] (Applause)

Later when her "population" remarks were criticized, the word "population" was crossed out and the word "pollution" was added to "clarify" what she really intended, however she made no correction when delivering her speech. And the climate goals do include reduced populations. How else do you handle an empty social security fund and a national debt of $31+ trillion? If you can't pay out because of mismanagement and out of control government spending, then you must reduce the population starting with the elderly. Many would argue that COVID-19 protocols helped accomplish this goal. Lack of election integrity may be the method to ensure unpopular candidates stay in control to accomplish the rest of their agenda. Financial controls drive the ultimate endgame to control purchasing power and reinvent a new "stakeholder capitalism" that is not capitalism, but more closely aligns with communism and state control of companies.

Referring to the time of the Great Tribulation (possibly the Great Reset?), Revelation 13 says:

> *The second beast was given power to give breath to the image of the first beast, so that the image could speak and cause all who refused to worship the image to be killed. It also forced all people, great and small, rich and poor, free and slave, to receive a mark on their right hands or on their foreheads, so that they could not buy or sell unless they had the mark, which is the name of the beast or the number of its name.*

THEY ARE COMING FOR YOUR CHILDREN
THE FIGHT WE MUST WIN!

This calls for wisdom. Let the person who has insight calculate the number of the beast, for it is the number of a man. That number is 666.

—Revelation 13:15-18 (NIV)

Lest you think that this is a bizarre thought from the Bible, even leftist fact-checkers, in an attempt to minimize concern, admit this very troubling information:

> We've seen a post online claiming that Bill Gates and Microsoft have a patent, numbered 060606, for a microchip that would be inserted into people's bodies, and would monitor their activity in return for cryptocurrency. There is a genuine patent Microsoft applied for in 2019, numbered W0/2020/060606. The application does mention technology allowing for people's activity to be monitored in exchange for cryptocurrency, but there is no mention of implanted chips. The patent application has not yet been granted.

> Specifically, the application is for a system whereby tasks are given to users, which, on participation or completion, can be rewarded with cryptocurrencies. Information is collected from a sensor, coupled with or potentially within the user's device, to determine whether those tasks have been completed.

> The patent application describes that user device as potentially being "personal computers, servers, cell phones, tablets, laptops, smart devices (e.g. smart watches or smart

televisions.)" It may also be a piece of wearable tech. The sensor is described as either a device in itself or built into the user device.[272]

How plausible is it that we are fast approaching the future of a digital currency that will be controlled using metrics of the government computations that align with the globalists' agendas?

God has always given His people answers and a way of escape from evildoers. We must remember:

> HOW PLAUSIBLE IS IT THAT WE ARE FAST APPROACHING THE FUTURE OF A DIGITAL CURRENCY THAT WILL BE CONTROLLED USING METRICS OF THE GOVERNMENT COMPUTATIONS THAT ALIGN WITH THE GLOBALISTS' AGENDAS?

No temptation has overtaken you except such as is common to man; but God IS faithful, who will not allow you to be tempted beyond what you are able, but with the temptation will also make the way of escape, that you may be able to bear it.

—1 Corinthians 10:13 (NKJV)

There is a new day coming, but it is not the day the evildoers are planning; it is a day where those who are faithful will *not* be marked with 666, but with His Name. The name of God will be on their foreheads because of their belief and commitment to Him, as recorded in Revelation 22.

*Then the angel showed me the river of the water of life, bright as crystal, flowing from the throne of God and of the Lamb through the middle of the street of the city; also, on either side of the river, the tree of life with its twelve kinds of fruit, yielding its fruit each month. The leaves of the tree were for the healing of the nations. No longer will there be anything accursed, but the throne of God and of the Lamb will be in it, and his servants will worship him. **They will see his face, and his name will be on their foreheads.** And night will be no more. They will need no light of lamp or sun, for the Lord God will be their light, and they will reign forever and ever.*

> THERE IS A NEW DAY COMING, BUT IT IS NOT THE DAY THE EVILDOERS ARE PLANNING; IT IS A DAY WHERE THOSE WHO ARE FAITHFUL WILL NOT BE MARKED WITH 666, BUT WITH HIS NAME.

—Revelation 22:1-5 (ESV) (emphasis added)

There are two kingdoms. One rewards the faithful with God's plans and eternal dynasty. The other will bring destruction to those who have served Satan and His tyranny to control and dominate mankind.

For the wrath of God is revealed from heaven against all ungodliness and unrighteousness of men, who by their unrighteousness suppress the truth. For what can be known about God is plain to them, because God has shown it to them. For his invisible attributes, namely, his eternal power and divine nature, have been clearly perceived, ever since the creation of the world, in the things that have been made. So they are without excuse. For although they knew God, they did not honor him as God or give thanks to him, but they became futile in their thinking, and their foolish hearts were darkened. Claiming to be wise, they became fools.

—Romans 1:18-22 (ESV)

We cannot serve two masters. Choose God or choose mammon (money and its control). In this day and hour, we must make a resolute decision to serve God, and Him alone, based upon His Word, and not serve money.

CHAPTER 16

PROPHETIC WARNINGS FOR OUR TIMES

THEY ARE COMING FOR YOUR CHILDREN
THE FIGHT WE MUST WIN!

The seeds of Satanic rebellion were sown into humans from Adam, who turned his allegiance to Satan, causing his lineage of the human race to be born with a sin nature. We were born into darkness. The anti-Christ spirit has been at work ever since with greater increase like birth pangs giving way to the culmination of events foretold in the book of Revelation.

Jesus said, "The enemy comes to steal, kill and destroy, but I have come that you may have life and life more abundantly" (John 10:10). If you read *Fight Like Heaven,* you understand the seeds of the enemy have been sown into the agendas of the United Nations, the World Economic Forum, and Agenda 2030, birthing a New World Order to be brought about through a climate agenda, which is unfolding before our eyes. The pandemic prepared the way with fear, isolation, and the breakdown of law as emergency orders took precedence over laws and constitutional freedoms. In churches, there was a great falling away. The next trick up their sleeve is to use "climate emergency"

> **THE NEXT TRICK UP THEIR SLEEVE IS TO USE "CLIMATE EMERGENCY" TO UNITE THE WORLD UNDER GLOBAL ELITIST CONTROL.**

to unite the world under global elitist control. To accomplish their mission, nations of the world will convene at the end of 2023 and agree to the terms of a seven-year covenant to realize their Agenda 2030 goals. This meeting is called COP28.

On March 8, 2023, on International Women's Day (started by socialist countries), the UN announced there was just 40 weeks to go to reach COP28, which is being held December 12, 2023. "The 'Conference of the Parties,' known as COP, is the decision-making body responsible for monitoring and reviewing the implementation of the United Nations Framework Convention on Climate Change. It brings together the 197 nations and territories called Parties— that signed on to the Framework Convention. The COP has met annually since 1995." The 21st session was held in Paris, and from it the Paris Climate Accord emerged, the first international climate agreement."[273] Dr. Sultan Al Jaber from Saudi Arabia is the President-Designate for the COP28.[274]

If you recall, one of the first actions President Donald Trump enacted was to remove the US from the Paris Climate Accord, which was a huge reason the WEF leaders said Trump must be removed. At the 2018 World Economic Forum (WEF) in Davos, President Donald Trump was a strong voice for a united America, letting the world know that our nation was stronger and more prosperous than ever. I was moved when I re-listened to his speech to see just what has been undone in the last four years in an effort to deteriorate America. Here are parts of his speech:

> I am here today to represent the interests of the United States of America ... America hopes for a future that every person can prosper... a safe home, a great job... the stock market is smashing one record after another. We have created 2.4 million jobs...small business optimism is at an all- time high...African American employment is at an all-time ever recorded historical high in the United States, and we have lowered taxes...cut 22 burdensome regulations to free our businesses and workers as never before.. I believe in America. As President of the United States, I will always put America first. America first, does not mean America, alone. When

America grows, so does the world ... .We support free trade but it needs to be fair trade…When people are forgotten it ceases to be free ... a nations' greatness is the sum of its citizens, pride, devotion, love of the people who call that nation home…. Let us resolve to use our power, not for ourselves but for the good of the people…. We have a whole new United States. There is a tremendous spirit. God bless you all.[275]

Joe Biden, however, immediately placed the US back in the Paris Climate Accords on his first day in office.[276] Under the Paris Agreement, all countries agreed to take collective measures "to limit global temperature rise to well below 2 degrees Celsius, and ... to strive for 1.5 degrees Celsius."[277]

Their goals require all nations and corporations to take a "stake" in accomplishing these goals. They also require extensive changes in business and lifestyles (a.k.a. giving up freedoms), especially in developed, prosperous countries like the US.[278] In doing so, free enterprise and freedom are being strong-armed to obey the dictates of the UN and World Economic Forum's agendas over their country's best interest. This prompted the backlash atmosphere, birthing the "America First Agenda," and winning Donald Trump his election. His agenda was completely against the world elites' plans to bring the US into the New World Order.

So what are the goals of the COP in the 40 weeks leading up to the COP28 on December 12, 2023 in Abu Dhabi (UAE), a prophetic event? Interestingly, before the COP28 meeting, Prince (King) Charles spelled out a program to accelerate sustainability measures to coincide with COP28, positioning himself to lead the world in this plan.

As part of the Sustainable Markets Initiative, The former Prince of Wales, launched the Terra Carta in 2021 — a mandate that puts sustainability at the heart of the private sector. Marking a year since the former Prince of Wales announced his Sustainable Markets Initiative at Davos in 2020, the Terra Carta is the guiding mandate for the Sustainable Markets Initiative, providing a proposed set of principles to 2030 that puts Nature, People and Planet at the heart of global value creation.

Deriving its name from the historic Magna Carta, which inspired a belief in the fundamental rights and liberties of people over 800 years ago, the Terra Carta aims to reunite people and planet, by giving fundamental rights and value to Nature, ensuring a lasting impact and tangible legacy for this generation.

In the 2022 Commonwealth Heads of Government Leaders statement, the leaders of all 56 Commonwealth Countries commended His Majesty King Charles III, when he was Prince of Wales, on the creation of the Terra Carta for Nature, People, and Planet, and recognised its value as a blueprint for public-private collaboration in making markets sustainable for the future.

The C40, a global network of mayors, from 96 of the world's leading cities have also affirmed their support for the Sustainable Market's Initiative, including the blueprint set out in the Terra Carta for the transition to a sustainable future.[279]

Their stated goals of the Terra Carta are a "Green & Just Transition: A green and just transition champions inclusivity and equity, resilient communities, sustainable development and the urgent need for quality green jobs for all."[280] Their "evidence" for a green and just transition emanated from the COVID-19 pandemic. They state:

> In response to the COVID-19 pandemic, which has highlighted the inextricable link between health, the environment and the economy, the C40 Global Mayors COVID-19 Recovery Task Force carried out analysis and modeling in late 2020 to determine what could happen if the world's major cities collectively prioritized a green and just recovery.

> The report assessed the potential impact of green and just recovery packages on GHG emissions, health, employment and economic investment. Six representative cities were included in the analysis to provide illustrative results from the regions where most C40 member cities are located, including Africa, Europe, Latin America, North America, Southeast Asia and Southwest Asia."[281]

Climate meetings are being held in these cities with strategies set to reach their climate goals and bring their "projects to the Dec. 12th meeting at which time the nations of the world will enter into a Global 'Covenant.'"[282]

The Terra Carta Accelerator Initiative, released on May 5, 2023 is being developed in response to King Charles III challenge to the Sustainable Markets Initiative to develop five land-based and five water-based initiatives *per year* through 2030.[283] Their stated goal is to reduce emissions by 40 percent (almost half of the world's emissions) in the next seven years, which will impact gas, travel, food...*everything*.

Control the energy and food and you control nations. They are selling the plan as "prosperity," but implementing it by enforcing strict limitations and removing freedoms. If they succeed, gone are the days of taking a vacation outside of your immediate area, and perhaps even a drive in the country. Gone are the days of starting your own business and having funding, when necessary, to grow it. Gone are the days where parents have rights over their children instead of the UN, just as we learned that *our body, our choice* only applies to abortion, but not to our choice over vaccines during the COVID-19 pandemic.

> CONTROL THE ENERGY AND FOOD AND YOU CONTROL NATIONS.

Their goal is to create a 15-minute city where people live en masse (think China), and have all they need within a 15-mile zone or perhaps even in their apartment building.[284] In doing so, cars are replaced with mass transit, cycling, or walking, or electric cars are required for any longer-distance travel. Companies cannot do business unless they agree to the requirements forced on them, not from their state or even federal government, but rather from the global "community." The biggest feature of this structure is governance: who will govern who. So who is involved?

Interestingly, COP28 set a 40-week agenda and events leading up to their December 12, 2023 meeting and used pictures of a pregnant woman travailing over the earth in its PR announcement.[285] Just like it takes 40 weeks for a child to be born, they announced their 40 weeks leading up to COP28 using a woman to represent mother earth.

I can't help but think of those Paul wrote about in Romans 1:25 (NIV) as having "exchanged the truth about God for a lie, and worshiped and served created things rather than the Creator—who is forever praised."[286] This agenda is also driven by world religious leaders who will also have ceremonies at COP28.

The Pope's seven-year plan that preceded these meetings, called "Laudato Si" calls to "implement environmental sustainability in different sectors of the church…"[287] "We need a new ecological approach that can transform our way of dwelling in the world, our styles of life, our relationships with resources of the Earth and in general our way of looking at humanity and of living life."[288] He further instructed that the years would be followed by a seven-year plan connecting climate control of seven sectors in a seven-year agreement. In this declaration, he called for repentance from the church for the way we have treated the earth, "Let us take care of Mother Earth…let us overcome the temptation of selfishness that makes us predators of resources…"[289] The Pope called for repentance to Mother Earth and the sins harming earth rather than repentance from the sin of killing children through abortion or sex-trafficking, or LGBTQ agendas against them.

The icon of the Congress of the Peoples (COP) and the Paris Climate

Agreements is the Eiffel Tower, the La Dame de Fer — French for "The Iron Lady." It is interesting indeed to have iron and clay mixing toward a one-world agenda that possibly involves the Pope, the King of England, Saudi Arabia, and world nations, including Israel joining in a seven-year agreement! The UN contends that SDGs (Sustainable Development Goals) are the best means to insure human rights and spread *peace and security* throughout the world.[290]

Each week since the 40-week announcement, voices from all over the world in leadership, and elites, have called for peace and safety (or security) through climate agreement. Al Jaber said, "We have 7 years to go to unite the world in an agreement. The clock is ticking."[291] The country of Oman wants 79 percent electric vehicles on the road by 2035.[292] California has outlawed gas weed eaters and mowers. Battery-powered mowers will be the only option.[293]

UN Secretary-General Antonio Guterres called for all people of faith to join together in praying for peace as the festivals of Ramadan, Easter, and Passover coincide together, "At a time of terrible divisions in the world, leaders from multiple faiths joined together at UN Headquarters in New York on Friday to observe a moment of prayer for peace."[294] The UN states its mission:

> Due to the powers vested in its Charter and its unique international character, the United Nations can take action on the issues confronting humanity in the 21st century, such as peace and security, climate change, sustainable development, human rights, disarmament, terrorism, humanitarian and health emergencies, gender equality, governance, food production, and more."[295]

King Charles said in Germany, "Together we must strive for the security, prosperity and well-being that our people deserve."[296] Peace and security is consistently in their weekly rhetoric. "There is no true security without climate security," stated Ambassador Lana Nusselbeh, Permanent Representative of the UAE to the UN.[297] Al Jaber described King Charles as an "inspirational advocate for environmental action" for COP28.[298] He further expressed he looks forward to collaborating with King Charles to work toward solutions.[299] The Bible warns us in 1 Thessalonians 5:3: "For when they shall say, Peace and safety; then sudden destruction cometh upon them, as travail upon a woman with child; and they shall not escape."[300]

King Charles' book, *Harmony: A New Way of Looking at Our World*, contends that the earth cannot support the population, among other ideas. However, as Terry Eagleton of The Guardian says, "There are, to be sure, limits to Charles's revolutionism. He wants the kind of change radical enough to do away with polluters and modernist architects, but not radical enough to do away with himself."[301]

Is King Charles' Terra Carta, an apostate replacement of the Magna Carta? The Magna Carta was drawn up as an agreement in 1215 between King John of England and the nobility.[302] It mandated freedom from tyranny, inspired our Constitution, and was the Great Charter of freedoms, basic human rights, a free church, and reforming law and justice, including freedom from excessive government control and property. Above all it guaranteed that the government would be limited by the written law of the land. Conversely, King Charles' Terra Carta—terra meaning earth—is a document to the earth which takes freedoms from the people and places control back in the hands of an aristocracy — himself, and the elites of the UN and WEF.

Interestingly, on November 29, 2021, Israel and the United Kingdom entered into a "Memorandum of Understanding" on "UK-Israel Strategic Partnership."[303] The Memorandum of Understanding provides that, "With a view to enhancing the friendly cooperation and exchanges between the Participants and further promoting the bilateral relations between the two countries; [Israel and the UK] reached the following understanding," concerning, among other things, cooperation on many fronts: defense and security; economic enhancement; climate innovation, development of low and middle income countries; and advancement of gender equality.[304] This agreement illustrates just how aligned Israel and the UK (and the UN) are on every issue advanced in Agenda 2030.

Recently, the UN released "the much anticipated" Climate Change 2023: Synthesis Report.[305] The report contains demands to step up lower carbon emissions, and "Equity and Inclusion." You may ask, "How does *this* agenda fit into *climate control*?" Here is their answer:

> "Ambitious mitigation pathways imply large and sometimes disruptive changes in economic structure, with significant distributional consequences within and between countries… shifting of income and employment…Adaptation and mitigation actions that prioritize equity, social justice, climate justice, rights-based approaches, and inclusivity, lead to more sustainable outcomes…The design of regulatory instruments and economic instruments and consumption-based approaches can advance equity. Individuals with high

socio-economic status contribute disproportionately to emissions…Climate resilient development is advanced when actors work in equitable, just and inclusive ways to reconcile divergent interests, values, worldviews, toward equitable and just outcomes."[306]

This is a lot of useless word-speak used to create confusion to accomplish their Marxist communist goals that include destruction of the US and depopulation.

The pathway to COP28 requires 35 trillion dollars to accomplish its goals.[307] King Charles, in his address to G7 leaders, said they are prepared to direct tens of trillions of dollars toward sustainable investment by 2023.[308] COP28 is the most significant climate meeting since the Paris Accords. In order to cut global emissions by half, the next seven years are sure to change everything!

Israel created a 429-page document on how we will adopt and implement these changes. Al Jaber said, "The world has a small window of opportunity to deliver major changes" and must work with other fully developed nations to reach the goal by 2027.[309] A seven-year agreement will come from the COP28 meeting; the World Bank is involved in issuing seven year benchmark bonds.[310]

There is something significant about the number seven in Bible prophecy. Recall the prophecy in Daniel 9:25-27 where an overview of Israel, the building of the temple, the coming of Jesus as the Anointed One, His death, and the covenant Israel will make with the Antichrist are all given as a timeline:

Know and understand this: From the time the word goes out to restore and rebuild Jerusalem until the Anointed One, the ruler, comes, there will be seven 'sevens,' and sixty-two 'sevens.' It will be rebuilt with streets and a trench, but in times of trouble. After the sixty-two 'sevens,' the Anointed One will be put to death and will have nothing. The people of the ruler who will come will destroy the city and the sanctuary. The end will come like a flood: War will continue until the end, and desolations have been decreed. He (Antichrist) will confirm a covenant with many for one 'seven.' In the middle of the 'seven' he will put an end to sacrifice and offering. And at the temple he will set up an abomination that causes desolation, until the end that is decreed is poured out on him.[311]

In chapter 13 of Revelation, the apostle John describes a beast that rose up from the sea, possibly a seaport. According to Revelation 13:2, the creature resembled a leopard, but had the feet of a bear and a mouth like a lion. John described it as having "ten horns and *seven* heads, with ten crowns on its horns, and on each head a blasphemous name."[312] This implies a conglomerate of past kingdoms of the earth.

Scripture in Revelation and Daniel refer to the Antichrist as a beast. He will be a man who eventually claims himself god. As Daniel 7:25a prophesied, "He will speak great words against the Most High and shall wear out the saints of the Most High, and think to change times and laws…"[313] He will control the world and the economy. He is in alignment with Satan to rule the world and its people. Revelation 13:4 says, "And they worshiped the dragon (Satan), for he had given his authority to the beast, and they worshiped the beast, saying, 'Who is like the beast, and who can fight against it?'"[314]

According to Scripture, Israel will make a peace treaty with the Antichrist. The treaty will promise peace and safety, but after three and a half years, "the man of lawlessness" (the Antichrist) will break the covenant and attack Israel.[315] "Then he shall confirm a covenant with many for one week; But in the middle of the week he shall bring an end to sacrifice and offering. And on the wing of abominations shall be one who makes desolate, even until the consummation, which is determined, is poured out on the desolate."[316] Isaiah 28:15 describes the disloyalty of the "scoffing rulers of Jerusalem" who said, "We have made a covenant with death, and with Sheol we have made a pact. The gushing flood will not reach us when it passes by, because we have made falsehood our refuge and we have concealed ourselves with deception."[317]

Does the COP28 meeting signify the seven-year covenant made between nations of the world and Israel, and the breaking of the covenant mid-way resulting in the abomination of desolation that leads to the end? Is this the beginning of the revelation of the beast with seven heads? Some may speculate those seven heads represent the G-7? How is Joe Biden contributing?

> DOES THE COP28 MEETING SIGNIFY THE SEVEN-YEAR COVENANT MADE BETWEEN NATIONS OF THE WORLD AND ISRAEL, AND THE BREAKING OF THE COVENANT MID-WAY RESULTING IN THE ABOMINATION OF DESOLATION THAT LEADS TO THE END?

In the US, Joe Biden addressed the need to accelerate "the plan" in his speech at The 2023 Major Economies Forum on Energy and Climate:

Today we have to do more than recognize the climate challenges we face. It seems to me we have to recommit ourselves to action while still — while we still have the time. [...] We have to step up our ambitions. We're going to have to stand together to meet great challenges. And we're going to — we will preserve our planet in the future. That's the question. I think we will, we think we will, but we have to. We're not there yet.

History is going to judge us on how we answer these questions. And today, I hope we all — all answer them loudly and clearly as a "yes." Yes, we're committed to following the science. Yes, we are determined to strengthen our ambition and our actions. And, yes, we're willing to do the hard work to limit global warming to 1.5 degrees Celsius. That's what today is all about: committing together and candidly discussing how we can bridge the gap between our pledge to limit warming to 1.5 degrees and our policies.

You know, over the last two years, I'm proud to say the United States has delivered unprecedented progress here at home. I've signed a thing called the *Inflation Reduction Act* — a piece of legislation we got passed — the single largest *investment in fighting climate change* in history, which will reduce annual carbon emissions by 1 billion tons by 2030. [...]

Finally, I just want to say a few words about the urgent need to scale up *climate finance*. All of you know as well as I do: The impacts of climate change will be felt the most by those who have contributed the least to the problem, including developing nations.

As large economies and large emitters, we must step up and support these economies. So today, I'm pleased to announce the *United States is going to provide $1 billion* to the Green Climate Fund, a fund that that is cri- — fund is a — critical in ways to help developing nations that they can't do now. But it should not be the only way.

Together, we need to strengthen the role of *multilateral development banks* in fighting climate crisis as well, starting with the *World Bank*. Because climate security, energy security, food security, they're all related. They're all related."[318]

It is obvious that there are already in place world plans and a coming climate covenant to change everything over the next seven years, and the Biden administration, with its congressional cronies, are heavily funding it. Every day, our headlines push a climate crisis, climate emergencies. Abortion, touted as women's rights, is promoted as a means to keep "overpopulation" under control. The transgender movement ensures sterilization. Injustice seems to riddle our court system as conservative voices are

IT IS OBVIOUS THAT THERE ARE ALREADY IN PLACE WORLD PLANS AND A COMING CLIMATE COVENANT TO CHANGE EVERYTHING OVER THE NEXT SEVEN YEARS, AND THE BIDEN ADMINISTRATION, WITH ITS CONGRESSIONAL CRONIES, ARE HEAVILY FUNDING IT.

canceled with censorship by legacy media and those who attack our kids and nation and other nations of the world.

Jesus foretold in Matthew 24:7-9 (NIV): "Nation will rise against nation, and kingdom against kingdom. There will be famines and earthquakes in various places. All these are the beginning of birth pains. Then you will be handed over to be persecuted and put to death, and you will be hated by all nations because of me."[319] Christian persecution and martyrdom are happening in nations across the world.

It can be discouraging to think about these events happening. It's almost surreal. But Jesus told us He would not have us ignorant concerning the tribulation time of seven years or of His glorious Return. Jesus' earthly life as a man culminated at His death (and resurrection) during the Roman Empire's occupation of Israel. It was political oppression and religious persecution that crucified Jesus, but it was God's plan to redeem us from the kingdom of darkness. The Roman Empire ruled with an iron fist and the religious leaders of the day were jealous of Jesus and insisted He be put to death. Religion conspiring with an "Emperor god" of Rome came together. At His Return, a similar stage of world players will be set—the Antichrist professing himself to be god and a False Prophet, the religious leader, aligned with Satan in an unholy trinity—but they will be no match for the Kings of Kings. He became our Saviour, but He will return with His saints as our King! "Behold, the Lord comes with tens of thousands of His saints, to execute judgment on all, to convict all who are ungodly among them of all their ungodly deeds which they have committed in an ungodly way, and of all the harsh things which ungodly sinners have spoke against Him."[320]

When you see the things happening like COP28 across the earth, Luke 21:28 tells us to "look up and lift up your heads, because your redemption draws near!" God's Word is an anchor for such times until we see that Day. We have been made victorious. Paul said, "Now thanks *be* to God who always leads us in triumph in Christ,"[321] as "our light affliction, which is but for a moment, is working for us a far more exceeding *and* eternal weight of glory."[322] Paul preached the Gospel, wrote more books of the Bible than any other, and finished his race. We each have a race!

> **WHEN YOU SEE THE THINGS HAPPENING LIKE COP28 ACROSS THE EARTH, LUKE 21:28 TELLS US TO "LOOK UP AND LIFT UP YOUR HEADS, BECAUSE YOUR REDEMPTION DRAWS NEAR!"**

What are we to do? Whatever God tells us to do to play our part in His Kingdom—making a difference in our spheres of influence and, most importantly, in our families. We must recognize and discern the times we are living in. In Matthew 24, Jesus shares how things will look at the end of the age:

> *As he sat on the Mount of Olives, the disciples came to him privately, saying, "Tell us, when will these things be, and what will be the sign of your coming and of the end of the age?" And Jesus answered them, "See that no one leads you astray. For many will come in my name, saying, 'I am the Christ,' and they will lead many astray. And you will hear of wars and rumors of wars. See that you are not alarmed, for this must take place, but the end is not yet. For nation will rise against nation, and kingdom against kingdom, and there will be famines and*

earthquakes in various places. All these are but the beginning of the birth pains.

Then they will deliver you up to tribulation and put you to death, and you will be hated by all nations for my name's sake. And then many will fall away and betray one another and hate one another. And many false prophets will arise and lead many astray. And because lawlessness will be increased, the love of many will grow cold. But the one who endures to the end will be saved. And this gospel of the kingdom will be proclaimed throughout the whole world as a testimony to all nations, and then the end will come.[323]

—Matthew 24:3-14 (ESV)

This good news of the Kingdom will be preached throughout the whole world, and then the end will come. This is a fact, not a fear. We must recognize and resist the spirit of antichrist and bring freedom to the captives! Freedom in Christ! It should not catch us off guard or move us to panic. We are in labor to bring forth the Kingdom of God and bring people into salvation. "The kingdom of heaven has suffered violence, and the violent take it by force."[324] God is calling us to prepare the way and build the Kingdom. There is a great reward ahead, and we only need to believe that we will see the salvation of our God. The harvest is great! The awakening is at the door! The enemy always gets it wrong, but God!

In the words of Isaiah 62:10-12:

Go through, go through the gates. Prepare the way of the people; Build up, build up the highway; clear it of stones; lift up a signal over the peoples. Behold, the Lord has proclaimed to the end of the earth: Say to the Daughter of Zion, "Behold, your salvation comes; behold, His reward is with Him, and His recompense before Him." And they shall be called The Holy People, The Redeemed of the Lord; and you shall be called Sought Out, a City Not Forsaken.[325]

—Isaiah 62:10-12

As for those who do evil, Isaiah 63:1-6 says:

Who is this coming from Edom, from Bozrah, with his garments stained crimson? Who is this, robed in splendor, striding forward in the greatness of his strength? "It is I, proclaiming victory, mighty to save.

Why are your garments red, like those of one treading the winepress? "I have trodden the winepress alone; from the nations no one was with me. I trampled them in my anger and trod them down in my wrath; their blood spattered my garments, and I stained all my clothing. It was for me the day of vengeance; the year for me to redeem had come.

I looked, but there was no one to help, I was appalled that no one gave support; so my own arm achieved salvation for me, and my own wrath sustained me. I trampled the nations in my anger; in my wrath I made them drunk and poured their blood on the ground.[326]

—Isaiah 63:1-6

And what is our response? This: "I will tell of the kindnesses of the LORD, the deeds for which he is to be praised, according to all the LORD has done for us— yes, the many good things he has done ...".[327]

Jesus, our reward, is coming in the twinkling of an eye! As Jesus says in Revelation 3:10-11 , "Because you have kept my word about patient endurance, I will keep you from the hour of trial that is coming on the whole world, to try those who dwell on the earth. I am coming soon. Hold fast what you have, so that no one may seize your crown."[328]

Jesus promised: "And if I go and prepare a place for you, I will come back and take you to be with me that you also may be where I am."[329]

CHAPTER 17

WOE TO CHURCH LEADERS

"Aren't you getting persecuted for speaking out?"That was the question that I was asked as I shared from my *Fight Like Heaven* book at a Christian television station. Since I was scheduled to tape two programs, I politely asked what they wanted me to focus on for each program. I mentioned covering the overall plan of the World Economic Forum's agendas against America for the first one. To my surprise, the host said, "Just say nothing political." I had never appeared on their program and apparently they had not done their homework and had no knowledge of what my book was about. When I mentioned sharing the Transgender movement against kids for the second program, the host responded with, "I wouldn't want to hurt anyone's feelings." Wouldn't want to hurt anyone's feelings? What? I couldn't believe my ears.

> WHILE CHILDREN WERE HAVING THEIR INNOCENCE STOLEN, DECEPTION TAKING THEIR HEARTS AND DESTROYING THEIR BODIES AND POSSIBLY SOULS, A CHRISTIAN MEDIA VOICE WAS MORE CONCERNED ABOUT HURTING THE FEELINGS OF THOSE PERPETRATING THESE AGENDAS.

Surely, I heard wrong. While children were having their innocence stolen, deception taking their hearts and destroying their bodies and possibly souls, a Christian media voice was more concerned about hurting the feelings of those perpetrating these agendas. I was polite but on the inside I felt sick. As the interview began I asked God to give me courage and speak through me with love and truth.

God spoke in my heart, "Did I not give you an assignment?" "Yes, Lord, you did." Then speak what I have shown you and trust me to take care of the rest."

The three women on the set were almost silent as I shared from the book. I would speak, then hesitate, and they sat silent. NO response. Nothing. I would begin to share again until two programs had been completed. It was the hardest interview ever because they said nothing, but in their silence I was able to share completely. When we were finished, two of them asked how they could get my book. One of them said, "You are absolutely right about this. My grandchildren are being told this in school, and I don't know how we stop it. They are even accepting it in our church."

Another said, "Aren't you being attacked?" I said, "Not any more than any follower of Christ has throughout history!" I gave them all a copy of the book, and left as discouraged as I have ever felt, saying, "God, give these platforms to your people who really want to make a difference and not play games entertaining the enemy."

What in the world is going on when the church has not only lost the courage to speak the truth, they are allowing lies to be told to innocent children on their watch? I vented to my husband on the trip home.

Isaiah 28:7b (MEV) says, "The priest and prophet have erred through strong drink, they are confused by wine, they stagger from strong drink; they err while having visions, they stumble when rendering judgment. For all the tables are full of vomit and filthiness so that there is no clean place."[330]

> WHAT IN THE WORLD IS GOING ON WHEN THE CHURCH HAS NOT ONLY LOST THE COURAGE TO SPEAK THE TRUTH, THEY ARE ALLOWING LIES TO BE TOLD TO INNOCENT CHILDREN ON THEIR WATCH?

If churches are not clean places that share God's Holy truth then what will people eat? Regurgitated polluted worldly messaging? How will the people be made clean? If God's leaders drink from the cup of the world, how will they offer the Cup of the Lord? "Among you there must not be even a hint of sexual immorality, or of any kind of impurity, or of greed, because these are improper for God's holy people...Let no one deceive you with empty words, for because of such things God's wrath comes on those who are disobedient."[331]

Isaiah 28:14-16 (MEV) continues:

> *Therefore, hear the word of the Lord, O scoffers, who rule this people who are in Jerusalem, because you have said, "We have made a covenant with death, and with hell we are in agreement. The overflowing scourge shall not come to us when it passes through, for we have made lies our refuge and under falsehood we have hid ourselves.*[332]

This passage goes on to rebuke these leaders, and tell them they will be trodden down because of the covenant they made not with God, but with the world. He calls them to not continue in this way, but rather to receive God's instruction. It stands as a warning to those who are aligning with unholy agendas that harm and bring death and hell.

> **IT STANDS AS A WARNING TO THOSE WHO ARE ALIGNING WITH UNHOLY AGENDAS THAT HARM AND BRING DEATH AND HELL.**

In the book of Jeremiah 23, God rebukes the shepherds, "Woe to the shepherds who destroy and scatter the sheep of My pasture! says the LORD...

I am about to punish you for the evil of your deeds, says the LORD."[333] God's correction begins with leadership and works through His people. But what happens when leaders are no longer receiving the instruction or correction of the Lord and His Word?

In verse 9, Jeremiah under a strong anointed presence of God that made him shake continues:

My heart is broken within me, because of the prophets; all my bones shake; I am like a drunken man, like a man overcome by wine, because of the Lord, and because of His holy words. For the land is full of adulterers; for the land mourns because of the curse. The pleasant places of the wilderness have dried up. And their course is evil and their might is not right. For both prophet and priest are profane, for indeed, in My house I have found their wickedness, says the Lord. Therefore their way will be as slippery ways to them; they shall be driven into the darkness and fall in it; for I will bring disaster upon them, even the year of their punishment.[334]

God does not mince words with the deeds of the people supposed to represent Him and His ways, "I have seen also among the prophets of Jerusalem a horrible thing. They commit adultery and walk in lies. They also strengthen the hands of evildoers, so that no one repents from his wickedness. All of them are as Sodom to Me and her inhabitants as Gomorrah."[335] Because they would not call out evil, it strengthened those who were involved with evil. If there is no righteous standard, there is no means to stop evil. God equated his leaders as Sodom and those who choose to follow them as Gomorrah.

"What was the sin of Sodom and Gomorrah? According to Genesis 19, the sin involved homosexuality. The very name of that ancient city has given us the term sodomy, in the sense of "copulation between two men, whether consensual or forced."[336] Clearly, homosexuality was part of why God destroyed the two cities."[337] In addition we can see the people were full of pride, and unconcerned for the poor and needy. They were self-gratifying homosexuals. Ezekiel 16:50 (NIV) says "they did detestable things."[338] The Hebrew word for detestable is the same word that means "morally disgusting," as seen in Leviticus 18:22 where homosexuality is listed as an abomination to God.[339] Further, Jude 1:7 (NIV) says that Sodom and Gomorrah and the surrounding towns "gave themselves up to sexual immorality and perversion."[340]

After God rebukes the leadership, the Lord instructs the people also through Jeremiah:

> *Do not listen to the words of the prophets who prophesy to you. They lead you into vanity; they speak a vision of their own heart, and not out of the mouth of the Lord. They still say to those who despise me, "The Lord has said, 'You will have peace,' and they say to everyone who walks after the imagination of his own heart, "No evil will come upon you."'* [341]

The ministers were partaking in the lies of the culture, from their drinking strong drink to adulteress affairs. They were prideful, sinful and filled with vanity, so much that they would stroke, appease and reassure the ones who despised the Lord in their sin that all was well and there would be no penalty to pay. They softened the truth until it was not recognizable. The priests who were to set the standard of what the Lord said, were instead involved in sins, and condoned the sin to others with encouragement instead of warning.

God repeatedly warned the so-called, self proclaimed prophets, "voices of God" to stop speaking as if they were an oracle of the Lord, to stop giving their interpretation of what God was saying instead of inquiring of Him and staying with His Word. Jeremiah 23:36 (MEV) says:

"For you have perverted the words of the living God."[342] He further tells them to stop acting as an oracle of God but rather to say what HE the Lord says about the issues. "You shall not say, the oracle of the Lord. Therefore, surely I, even I will utterly forget you and cast you and the city that I gave you and your fathers out of My presence. And I will bring an everlasting reproach upon you and perpetual shame which shall not be forgotten.[343]

As we look across our nation, we can also see this prophecy unfold in many cities that have become sin-filled. "Detroit, in the 1950's was the richest city in the US, and some say it was the richest city in the world."[344] Today, "Sixty percent of all Detroit's children are living in poverty. Fifty percent of the population has been reported to be functionally illiterate, thirty-three percent of Detroit's 140 square miles is vacant or derelict. Eighteen percent of the population is unemployed.[345]" Having one of the highest crime rates in America, Detroit is often called "the murder capital of America."[346]

Churches, ministries, media ministries, prophets, pastors, priests or any other ministry office embracing lies that it is: acceptable to get drunk with wine or do drugs, acceptable to steal and destroy people's property, acceptable to embrace LGBTQ agendas, acceptable to embrace gender ideologies and identities and to change or transition people, especially children, fall into this category of those the Lord will deal with severely for they have perverted the ways of the Lord. Silence is also complicity as we see in Ephesians 5:11 (NIV), "Have nothing to do with the fruitless deeds of darkness but rather expose them."[347] We cannot achieve equality, peace or God's blessing by breaking His ten commandments.

As Jeremiah exposed the wickedness that was being condoned and participated in by spiritual leaders, he became the target of their vehemence. They wanted him to die because he dared to tell God's truth. But God spared Jeremiah's life through a few righteous voices willing to bring up times in the past when prophets had severely warned the people but were not put to death for their speech.

Jeremiah continued to speak to the people about the Babylonian captivity they would fall into because they had forsaken the ways and words of the Lord. But a younger prophet, Hananiah, the son of the prophet Azzur, rescinded the words of Jeremiah, telling the people that instead of living in captivity for 70 years, their slavery to Babylon would be broken apart in two years and the vessels of the Lord would be returned along with their kings. And for dramatic effect, he took Jeremiah's yoke and broke it before the people.

Then the Lord spoke to Jeremiah that Hananiah's word was not the word of the Lord. Jeremiah 28:9 (MEV) says, "As for the prophet who prophesies peace, when the word of the prophet who prophesies comes to pass, then the prophet shall be known as one whom the Lord has truly sent."[348]

We must weigh all prophetic words or approval of behaviors against God's Word and if it is not accurate, it is not the Word of the Lord. "What did God say?" should be our question, not "Did God really say?" spoken by the serpent in the Garden. If God said it, His Word has not changed for He is the same yesterday, today and forever. He does not change nor does what He says is holy or unholy.

Jeremiah turned to Hananiah the prophet and said, "The Lord has not sent you, and you make the people trust in a lie. Therefore says the Lord: I am about to cast you from off the face of the earth. This year you shall die, because you have taught rebellion against the Lord. So Hananiah the prophet died the same year...."[349]

The book of 1 Samuel tells the story of a woman named Hannah who had been unable to conceive and was in deep sorrow. She went to the temple to ask God to give her a baby boy, and told God she would give him to the Lord all the days of His life. The Lord gave her a son and she named him Samuel. He grew up ministering to the Lord before the priest Eli. Eli blessed Hannah and her husband to have more children. "Indeed the LORD visited Hannah, and she conceived and bore three sons and two daughters. And the boy Samuel grew in the presence of the LORD."[350]

Eli grew old and because he had not corrected or attended to his sons, they were wicked, having relationships with the women in the temple and demanding the best for themselves. God rebuked Eli through another man of God because Eli had honored his sons over the Lord. Because Eli had not corrected his sons, they both died instead of fulfilling their priesthood, but God raised up Samuel as a faithful priest to be Eli's successor. In Samuel 3:1 (NIV), it says, "The boy Samuel ministered before the LORD under Eli. In those days the word of the LORD was rare; there were not many visions."[351]

Why was the word of the Lord rare in those days? Because the Lord's house had been a place where Eli's sons had corrupted the temple that was supposed to be upright and holy. It also had removed the vision for the future. If there is no presence of God, there is no vision. The presence of God will not inhabit a place where there is no holy or sacred fear or respect for the Lord or His Word. Sadly, this is the condition of some church leaders and the "temple" or ministry they oversee.

As Samuel was in the house with Eli, he heard a voice from God. The Lord called to Samuel three times, each time he thought it was Eli calling him, and he would go to Eli and say, "Here am I."[352] Eli told Samuel it was not him but rather God speaking. Eli understood that the Lord was calling Samuel, and instructed him to inquire of the Lord. The Lord let Samuel know that He was going to do something in Israel removing wickedness that Eli had allowed. Eli required Samuel to share with him all that God said, and it happened just as the Lord directed. From that day forward, the scripture says, "And the Lord continued to appear at Shiloh (where the temple was), and there he revealed himself to Samuel through his word."[353]

When the Israelites went into battle against the Philistines, the elders declared the Ark of the Covenant be brought into the camp. The people shouted and rejoiced because the glory of God in the Ark was brought out. The Philistine enemy was scared when they heard their shouts and praises. They said:

"God has come into the camp!" And they said, "Woe to us! For such a thing has never happened before. Woe to us! Who will deliver us from the hand of these mighty gods? These are the gods who struck the Egyptians with all the plagues in the wilderness. Be strong and conduct yourselves like men...".[354]

They did beat Israel that day. Eli's sons were defeated in battle and died and the Ark of the Covenant was stolen. Eli fell when hearing the news and broke his neck and died. Eli's daughter-in-law delivered a baby that day and named him, Icabod, meaning the Spirit of the Lord has departed. God's presence could not help Israel because they no longer honored the Lord. A tragic ending to Eli's family lineage, all because he did not honor the Lord by correcting his sons.

The Philistines put the Ark of the Covenant in one of their pagan temples to Dagon, the House of Dagon. Before the Ark the statue of Dagon their god fell over twice and the second time it was decapitated and its hands cut off. The priests of the House of Dagon who ministered there got tumors or died. They recognized that the hand of God was heavy on them and wherever the Ark of God's presence went it brought the wicked doers destruction. They moved it from city to city with the same results until finally deciding it must be returned. They were afraid of this God, the true God!

When this occurred, the people of Israel cried. Samuel spoke to them and said:

If you are returning to the LORD with all your hearts, then rid yourselves of the foreign gods and the Ashtoreths and commit yourselves to the LORD and serve him only, and he will deliver you out of the hand of the Philistines.' So the Israelites put away their Baals and Ashtoreths, and served the LORD only.[355]

Hannah praised God and her prayer over her son can be seen in 1 Samuel 2:1 (NIV). She says, "My heart rejoices in the LORD; in the LORD my horn is lifted high. My mouth boasts over my enemies, for I delight in your deliverance."[356]

Churches and leaders must turn back to God with repentance, and be bold against the enemies. They must lead the people to turn to God with all their hearts, no longer allowing wickedness to control their beliefs. The glory of God will bring blessing when His people are walking upright before Him, but it will bring judgment as it did to the House of Dagon if wickedness abounds. God gives His people victory against the enemy if His people will return to Him and His Word. It's time to lay down foreign gods and commit to the Lord only.

> CHURCHES AND LEADERS MUST TURN BACK TO GOD WITH REPENTANCE, AND BE BOLD AGAINST THE ENEMIES. THEY MUST LEAD THE PEOPLE TO TURN TO GOD WITH ALL THEIR HEARTS, NO LONGER ALLOWING WICKEDNESS TO CONTROL THEIR BELIEFS.

CHAPTER 18

MEN AND A FREE NATION

What happened to manhood and the fight for freedom? On July 4th, 1776, 247 years ago, 56 men put their lives on the line when they signed the Declaration of Independence from King George and England. The Declaration of Independence says,

> We hold these truths to be self-evident, that all men are created equal, that they are endowed by their Creator with certain unalienable Rights, that among these are Life, Liberty and the pursuit of Happiness.—That to secure these rights, Governments are instituted among Men, deriving their just powers from the consent of the governed.[357]

These men listed 27 charges against King George and why they were rebelling.

> And for the support of this Declaration, with a firm reliance on the protection of divine Providence, we mutually pledge to each other our Lives, our Fortunes and our sacred Honor.[358]

Have you ever wondered what happened to the 56 men who were committing treason by signing the Declaration of Independence?

Five signers were captured by the British as traitors and tortured before they died. Twelve had their homes ransacked and burned. Two lost their sons in the Revolutionary War, Nine of the 56 fought and died from wounds or hardships resulting from the Revolutionary War.

Freedom was not free! Freedom has never been free. Why do you love the USA?

FREEDOM HAS NEVER BEEN FREE.

Because of the freedoms you have in this nation. My husband Gary and I started out with no money, but had an opportunity to build a life as God directed and enjoy the benefit of our own labor. That's why so many people are trying to get into the United States. It's not for the scenery, but rather a government that has a Constitution that promises freedom.

There is a night image of North and South Korea that was taken several years ago that perfectly reflects the difference the government makes in a nation. Looking at the image, North Korea, with its communist dictatorship, is almost completely dark compared to neighboring South Korea, with its government that offers freedom and has created a prosperous nation in comparison.[359]

We must always remember that there are evil and greedy people who are inspired by demons and desire to enslave men and women for their own profit or position. We must stand up and ensure freedom for all.

The nation of America was not born free; it was born in blood. More than 1.3 million soldiers have died fighting for America.[360]

Worshipping freely and enjoying my family and my life are the greatest benefits of my freedom as an American. Because of the individual freedom that America embraced, there has never been a nation like the United States of America. The biblical principles from Levitical law and the Ten Commandments of the Mosaic Law formed the foundations of the American Constitution and justice system. Living in the United States is called the American Dream! If you build it, you can enjoy it! "The American economic model of limited government, private initiative, and free enterprise unleashed and helped sustain the dynamism and proactivity of its people. Even today, with rising economic competition across the globe, 45% of start-ups and 50% of unicorns (start-ups valued at $1 billion or more) come from the United States."[361]

Although we hear much about China's productivity today, the US still produces three times the amount that China does, with a population of 332 million versus 1.4 billion, respectively in 2021.[362] What is this difference[363]? GOVERNMENT! "If it were a country, California's $3.1 trillion economy would be the fifth biggest in the world, ranked between Germany and the United Kingdom."[364] Ohio has the 21st largest economy in the world (11.5 million).[365] There are 7.8 billion people on earth today, and yet 2.4 billion make less than $3 a day.[366] The problem is not natural resources, but government.

As Gary and I travel across the world, we cannot help but notice how vastly different America is from other nations. Nonetheless, America has had a profound impact on the world. "Two billion people worldwide speak some form of English, most of them influenced by American English."[367] Throughout the world, American culture, through films, music, fashion, sport and art have "become the world's most widespread and influential today." Today, however, we hear voices telling us that capitalism is bad and socialism is better.[368]

What is capitalism? It is defined as an economic system in which a society's means of production are held by private individuals or organizations, not the government, and where products, prices, and the distribution of goods are determined mainly by competition in a free market.[369] Though imperfect, "free market capitalism as shareholder capitalism has been an incredibly powerful force for good in the world. The combination of liberal democracy and free market economics has lifted billions of people out of poverty and offered more hope to the hopeless than any other economic system in the world."[370] It has caused America to be extremely productive.

America's Major Inventions:

Telephone	Automatic transmission
Man on the moon	Microphones
Hubble telescope	Light switch
Light bulb	Hydraulic brakes
Artificial heart	Power steering
Internet	Car stereo
Personal Computers	Electric guitar
Mobile phones	Richter scale
Email	Fiberglass
Lasers	Teflon
Microchip	Microwave ovens
Light-emitting diodes (LEDs)	Transistor radio
Airplane	Video tapes and video recorders
Smoke detector	Lasers
Dimmer switch	Global Positioning System (GPS)
Radio	Kevlar
Remote control	Compact disc
Semi-automatic guns	Calculator
Hearing aids	Wide-body jet
Mercury vapor lamps	Space shuttle
Air conditioning	

Today, however, America stands at a crossroads. Productivity is falling and an entitlement mentality is growing. Sixty-seven percent of the American population gets a government check every month. Forty-two million families are dependent on food stamps each month. 90% of the manufacturing jobs have left the U.S. We invented the cell phone, and there are expected to be more than 18 billion mobile devices operating worldwide by 2025, but the US manufactures only one slightly obscure brand of phones.[371] Our political system is in chaos! As of July 2023, Congress has an approval rating of only 19%.[372] Of greater concern, is the attitude of young men and women that America is not worth the fight—that socialism may be better than freedom and self-government. Lawlessness has replaced justice in our courts.

Proverbs 29:4 says, "By justice (laws) a king gives a country stability, but those who are greedy for bribes tear it down."[373] We see this when we look at the Biden family, the Clinton Foundation, the Epstein island guests, and more, and wonder, where are the indictments?

But America has deeper problems than the financial issues that confront it and the corrupt politicians that have accrued a 31 plus trillion debt.[374] Families in America are falling apart:

- As of 2021, 40% of babies born in America are born to single moms.[375]
- 50% of couples under 44 live together instead of marriage.[376]
- One third of US children are living without a father in the home.[377]
- The culture has redefined marriage.

- Schools are teaching our children that they may not be the gender they were born with.[378]
- Immorality floods our homes through social media, the internet, TV and video gaming. Children are being inundated with the promotion of sexual sin from the earliest of ages.

> **THE FINANCIAL AND POLITICAL ISSUES FACING AMERICA ARE SYMPTOMS OF A MUCH DEEPER SPIRITUAL ISSUE.**

The financial and political issues facing America are symptoms of a much deeper spiritual issue.

Deuteronomy 28:1 says "If you fully obey the LORD your God and carefully follow all his commands,"[379] you will prosper, and it will go well with you is the bottom line. However, the Bible also warns what will happen if you turn away from God:

> Be careful, or you will be enticed to turn away and worship other gods and bow down to them. Then the LORD's anger will burn against you, and he will shut up the heavens so that it will not rain and the ground will yield no produce, and you will soon perish from the good land the LORD is giving you."

Deuteronomy also gives instructions on how to live out God's best plan for your life:

> Fix these Words of mine in your hearts and minds; tie them as symbols on your hands and bind them on your foreheads. Teach them to your children, talking about them when you sit at home and when you walk along the road, when you lie

down and when you get up. Write them on the doorframes of your houses and on your gates, so that your days and the days of your children may be many in the land the Lord swore to give your ancestors, as many as the days that the heavens are above the earth."

This is clearly more than a Sunday-only event; it is a lifestyle of making God and His ways the center of your life—sitting, walking, sleeping, *everywhere* you are. God's ways and Word are the focus, and this leads you and your children to experience a long life.

Who is training your children and when is the most impactful time to reach them?

"Childhood is when most people find Jesus. No matter who does the survey, one fact is overwhelming. Once a person reaches adulthood, accepting Christ becomes increasingly rare. Evangelism is most effective in the childhood and teenage years. 2/3 of Christians came to faith before the age of 18. 43% came to Christ before the age of 12. Less than 1/4 of current believers came to Christ after the age of 21."[380]

Why? Childhood is the foundation of our lives and training in childhood is the most impactful time, as Proverbs 22:6 says, "Train up a child in the way he should go, Even when he is old he will not depart from it."[381]

Psalm 128:1-4 reminds us our children and families are tender and need a man to lead his family in the fear of the Lord. God's plan is for *family*. He created family and has a design for how our lives will flourish and the blessings that will come when we put God at the center of our lives:

> Blessed are all who fear the Lord, who walk in obedience to him. You will eat the fruit of your labor; blessings and prosperity will be yours. Your wife will be like a fruitful vine within your house; your children will be like olive shoots (tender) around your table. (But tender shoots, turn into hardened trees.) Yes, this will be the blessing for the man who fears the Lord.[382]

The question is, who's "table" are *your* kids sitting around? Who is molding that tender shoot? Who is training your sons and daughters? A secular school system that has outlawed prayer and outlawed the Bible? A culture that has redefined the family and is teaching indoctrination into the Common Core socialist agenda, the LBGTQ lifestyle, and now transgender perversion? Again, I ask you, who is molding your children? What about your grandchildren? Whoever it is, know that they will become hardened into that image over time.

> THE QUESTION IS, WHO'S "TABLE" ARE YOUR KIDS SITTING AROUND? WHO IS MOLDING THAT TENDER SHOOT? WHO IS TRAINING YOUR SONS AND DAUGHTERS?

Children ages 8 to 18 years today spend an average of 6.7 hours a day in school and then 2 hours a day playing video games and 3 or more hours with media[383] (TV and computer). The balance of their time is spent on sports and other activities, and with friends. How much time is left to spend with parents, and more importantly, for pursuing a relationship with God? There is an old saying: if the devil can't make you bad, he'll make you busy. Busy-ness has consumed so much time that there is little left to play, worship together, pray, think, reflect, or build family relationships. The Church can only support what parents are doing at home. An hour and a half in church once a week can't replace the role of parents or the importance of the family structure. Financial purchases that place such a work burden on the family that there is no time left to be together are perhaps better not made.

In Genesis 18:19, God says,

> For I have chosen him (Abraham), so that he may command his children and his household after him to keep the way of the Lord by doing righteousness and justice, so that the Lord may bring upon Abraham what He has spoken about him.[384]

You want to qualify for promotion in God's eyes? Then take training your children as serious business! Fathers have been entrusted by God to lead and protect their families while laying their lives down for their wives, willing to sacrifice their own demands and drives to be men of valor who honor God and the family. This is the foundation of a strong nation, too.

1 Timothy 3:4-5 speaking of a man: "He must manage his own family well and see that his children obey him, and he must do so in a manner worthy of full respect. (If anyone does not know how to manage his own family, how can he take care of God's church?)"[385] Is God going to lead you to a big assignment that you cannot handle?

No! And He is testing you by how you lead your family.

Hitler, influenced by Satan, understood the power of training youth. Hitler said, "'He alone, who owns the youth, gains the future."[386] Hitler stated on November 6, 1933: "When an opponent declares, 'I will not come over to your side,' I calmly say, 'Your child belongs to us already. ... What are you? You will pass on. Your descendants, however, now stand in the new camp. In a short time they will know nothing else but this new community.'"[387]

During the mid-1930s, the Nazis established a party-controlled education system.[388] It began by forming its teachers' union, the Nazi Teachers' League. As the Nazis infiltrated schools, they shaped the curriculum to convey their own values and political beliefs. At the forefront of the Nazi syllabus was their version of racial education, 'enlightening' children about Aryan supremacy, and the despicable traits of subhuman people and races.

**Hitler started the Youth Core
to recruit youth into his cause:**

1933 - 100,000 members

1934 - 3.5 million members

1939 - it was required for ALL youth girls and boys.

Chart:[389]

It was the largest youth movement the world had ever seen. Old history books were destroyed.[390] New history was written of

Germany's past and future. Geometry was taught by plotting the angles of falling bombs. Math was taught figuring how much money could be saved by getting rid of Germany's invalids. Children were taught to turn in their parents. Government became supreme over parents and God.[391]

Joseph John, a former member of Congress and Appellate Judge, wrote:

> The newly adopted Common Core Curriculum erased much of the US History once taught in public schools for over 200 years. That required the revision of the accurate US History textbooks once used in public schools. The revision of US History textbooks was funded by front groups, controlled by George Soros. The new US History textbooks hide the remarkable history of the Republic, portraying Socialism as beneficial for the masses, while stating The Free Enterprise System was unfair; yet The Free Enterprise System has been the most successful economic engine in the history of mankind.[392]

The new US history textbooks eliminated events, misrepresented facts, inserted new individuals who were unimportant, defamed the Founding Fathers, criticized the US Constitution, falsely reported the massive genocide of Native Americans, covered up the fact that the US fought wars to free millions of enslaved people, (600,000 died in the civil war), and invented an inaccurate and wholly negative impression of the Republic as being cruel, racist, oppressive, violent, and discriminatory.

The Common Core Curriculum is re-educating America's youth by misrepresenting the US History of the Republic and by misrepresenting the character of Socialism.[393] American students have never been informed that Socialism has failed miserably in 37 countries over the last 100 years, and that it was responsible for the murder of 60 million formerly free citizens in most of those 37 countries. Students are not taught that the current examples of Socialist governments are Venezuela and Cuba. Venezuela has more oil than Saudi Arabia, yet, as of 2021, 94.5% of the 28 million of the country's residents live in poverty, based on income, and 76.6% lived in extreme poverty.[394][395]

Venezuela's Socialist Government Inflation:	
Characteristic	**Inflation rate compared to previous year**
2023*	**399.98%**
2022*	200.91%
2021	1,588.51%
2020	2,355.15%

Chart:[394][395]

Today multiple generations of students are not taught the importance of, nor do they understand, the Declaration of Independence, US Constitution, Amendments to the US Constitution, the Bill of Rights, how the three branches of government interrelate, why the Electoral College is so important, and/or the Judicial System.[396]

Civics in public schools has been replaced by ethnic studies.[397] Degrading the US history of the Republic, while promoting socialism to America's students since 2008, has resulted in 51% of America's youth preferring socialism to democracy. Now, 72% of voters between the ages of 18 and 34 actually *prefer* to receive basic government free income.

> The first step in liquidating a people is to erase its memory, destroy its books, its culture, and its history. Then have somebody write new books, manufacture a new culture, invent a new history. Before long the nation will begin to forget what it is and what it was. The world around it will forget even faster."[398]

Speaking of the Commandments of God, in Psalm 78:5—8, fathers are commanded to "teach these to their children, that the generation to come might know, even the children to be born. It is a father's calling to teach his children God's commandments and that they should put their confidence in God."

> He decreed statutes for Jacob and established the law in Israel, which he commanded our ancestors to teach their children, so the next generation would know them, even the children yet to be born, and they in turn would tell their children. Then they would put their trust in God and would not forget his deeds but would keep his commands.

> They would not be like their ancestors—a stubborn and rebellious generation, whose hearts were not loyal to God, whose spirits were not faithful to him.[399]

The next generation of men need true men to teach them NOW what it means to be a man and how to be fathers. The absence of masculine role models is creating a crisis in America among male youth. There is a strong influence to try and make men more feminine. Then there are the Andrew Tate's who mix healthy masculinity with unhealthy attitudes toward women, viewing them as property. We need masculine men who also treat women with respect and tenderness. Daughters need

> THE ABSENCE OF MASCULINE ROLE MODELS IS CREATING A CRISIS IN AMERICA AMONG MALE YOUTH.

dads that refute the lies spun about "toxic masculinity" with their caring yet strong example. Sons need to see dads who can be strong and obviously masculine, but not selfish or abusive.

> The true man will recognize that women can bring great happiness to life, and as such, men must seek to win the gift of a woman by having a pure heart and living a clean, guiltless life themselves. If today's young men fail to work on improving themselves —their habits, tendencies, beliefs, and sins— there is no hope for our nation.(The Quest for Masculinity by Annie Holmquist, Epoch Times, August 26, 2023)

What Young Men Must Be:

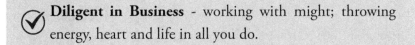

- ✓ **Diligent in Business** - working with might; throwing energy, heart and life in all you do.

- ✓ **Aim High** - Progress and prosperity require improvement; make the best of what's given.

- ✓ **Fight for Right** - fighting for others more than self; correct the evil of lawlessness.

- ✓ **Pursue the Path of Purity** - appreciating passion as a sacred possession; being faithful.

- ✓ **Show Kindness Toward the Fairer Sex** - every true man holds sacred a woman.

- ✓ **Practice Spiritual Disciplines** - a moral and spiritual force that fulfills man's highest needs.

Chart:[400]

Fathers will account to God for their children. Are you showing them how men and women work together so they have a healthy view of masculinity and womanhood? What are your sons learning about marriage and responsibility and how they are to treat a wife? What example are you setting for your children and grandchildren in your faith in God? They will follow your model and take on your priorities, how you live, and what matters to you. They need a relationship with you, and that requires *time* above all else, mixed with love, attention, discipline, and a healthy example to succeed in a woke world full of confusion. If you don't have a good example of fatherhood, God Himself will mentor you and train you to raise your children, if you will commit your time to learn about Him first over sports, games, cars, and other escapes that steal men's hearts and minds away from leading their families. You *can* enjoy these things—as a matter of fact, God wants to bless you and give you good things—but the sorrow that comes when we make these things our top priorities will destroy our lives and families. Faith and family don't *subtract* from a man's life; they are the *greatest win*!

If you have not made a commitment yourself to follow God, your Father, do it now. And then make a commitment to manhood and to raise your children in the Lord, to know righteousness and right from wrong. No, fathers don't always get it right, but if a man will humbly seek God, he will learn how to be a father that protects his daughter in every way from sex-traffickers, evil men and women who want to lead young people into lives of dishonesty, corruption, addiction and brokenness, and who trains his son to honor God and marriage, and to live a life of service, integrity, and blessing.

Leadership in churches is greatly needed as well. Our ministry (Faith Life Now), invests millions each year to give children and young people an opportunity to encounter God and build a relationship with Jesus. One way that we do that is by offering our "Summer Blast" Vacation Bible School program annually, where over 600 children attend. We also reach thousands of youth and young adults through programs every year. We are committed to support the family—to support *your* family. Every week at our church, we teach children about God, His plan for lives, and about Jesus and the Holy Spirit.

America has always been the land of the brave, the strong, and the free because America was founded on Biblical principles of freedom, love and righteousness. God is the only hope for America today. Men are needed to lead the return to His plans and to stand up for our nation, His model for family, and for justice and freedom.

> AMERICA HAS ALWAYS BEEN THE LAND OF THE BRAVE, THE STRONG, AND THE FREE BECAUSE AMERICA WAS FOUNDED ON BIBLICAL PRINCIPLES OF FREEDOM, LOVE AND RIGHTEOUSNESS. GOD IS THE ONLY HOPE FOR AMERICA TODAY.

God said in 2 Chronicles 7:14, "If my people, who are called by my name, will humble themselves and pray and seek my face and turn from their wicked ways, then will I hear from heaven and will forgive their sin and will heal their land."[401]

I believe this invitation is a personal one as well. God can heal your home, your land, and bring prosperity to your life. He did this for us and He will do it for whosoever will call on the name of the Lord. God is our hope, to save our families and our nation. Dads that love their families and who choose to turn from wickedness and obey God, who train their children in right living and with a love for God and country, are the answer.

I love America, and I believe in America

I believe that God is not done with America. We MUST pray for our great nation.

America is made up of her people. Until they are healed, America cannot be healed. If we are to wake up children to who they were created to be, we need fathers in the home to pave the way for their sons and daughters. We need men to lead by example. Women and children will respect a brave, selfless leader—a man of valor and honor. FIght like men. Be strong.

Receive God's gift of life and follow His leadership.

ANOINTED MAMA FOR FAITH, FAMILY, AND CAMP

In the earlier years of our church, we struggled to find a youth leader, with the same family values and maturity to lead youth instead of being one. We had witnessed ministries placing young people in the hands of inexperienced youth leaders who were overseeing youth when they would make some of the most life impacting decisions. Too many times, this goes terribly wrong. My husband turned to me and asked me to lead the youth. I exclaimed, "I don't know how to be a youth leader!" He said, "Just do for them what you do for our children. I thought I can be a mother. I know how to do that (at least sort of). I can love them and guide them in a relationship with the Lord and correct them when they need it and make it fun. I can attest that every week I sought the Lord and gave my best to these young people. I truly loved them like a mother and I was thankful my children (3 were teens at the time) were willing to share my love.

I felt led to do a youth camp. I sought God since it was another learning experience for me. I think I learned as much or more as the youth did and I grew spiritually like no bible school could train me. I prayed our youth camp would be life-changing and prophetic. The first two days were a little bumpy. Worship and teaching in the morning and in the evening each youth team had to take a part of the week's sessions and share the messages, and everyone had to do something. The afternoons were filled with games and activities. I had a few youths who did not want to be there. I prayed for them and believed God that they would have an encounter with Him. By the third morning session, the Holy Spirit came in an unprecedented way. I had never experienced anything like that. The youth were so on fire for God they were praying, prophesying, worshiping and it went on all afternoon into the night, they could care less about "fun." They were experiencing a live, ecstatic love from God. To my excitement, one of the youths that had originally been difficult and did not want to be there, was so filled with God she prayed fervently and prophesied as a powerful voice of the Lord. It was amazing.

I continued to lead the youth for nine years and had the joy of watching these fire-branded youth take that encounter with God to minister in other states and youth groups and bring the fire of God's spirit wherever we went including Albania for a mission's trip and the Ute Indian Reservation. They were bold, danced, praised and brought incredible power when they prayed. Even a Shaman on a reservation could not stop their fire and fervor.

We have had youth camp in our ministry every year since and the youth always come back changed, life-changing and prophetic. This year we were hosting the Flashpoint Truth and Freedom Tour at our ministry headquarters. To prepare, we went to one of their prior tour stops beforehand in Pensacola where revival had previously occurred for years. In the service, revival stirred in me and in prayer, I saw a vision of our tent meeting to occur filled with youth at the altar and God's fire filling the tent. I shared with my husband what I saw and we prayed for this to come to pass. Upon returning home, I discovered our youth camp had been previously scheduled over a year on the same week as Flashpoint's tour. It appeared the vision I saw could not happen, but to my great joy on Friday of the event, the youth returned from camp and most came to the tent meeting that night.

The same anointing that I had experienced at youth camp many times through the years, was there! Recognizing it, I turned to the usher and said, "Do you know if any of the youth are here? If so, have them come join me. He came back and said there's probably 40 or more. I said have them come down. He hesitated and looked at me like what's going on? At that moment, I was called by revivalist Gene Bailey along with two other fire-branded female church leaders to the podium. Gene asked us to pray. I began to intercede for our youth in the nation and repent for our country. As I did, youth filled the altar. I was told by many that prophetically the two generations, Flashpoint's followers, the Flashpoint army and this band of Holy Spirit youth merged together for the glory of God. The youth began to pray for people in wheelchairs and anyone else just like camp. God brought a very significant and prophetic anointing using the leaders as we all prayed. Women began to come down and grab tent poles and pray as the leader, Gene Bailey exhorted them to pray for revival and awakening over our country. It was powerful and life-changing just like youth camp.

This outpouring of God in the tent meeting happened within a couple of miles from the house that Jeffrey Epstein had posed as a "recruiter" for Victoria Secret and committed grievous crimes against young women, where the finances and even the jet that supported the crimes and corruption trafficking children originated.

> **THIS OUTPOURING OF GOD IN THE TENT MEETING HAPPENED WITHIN A COUPLE OF MILES FROM THE HOUSE THAT JEFFREY EPSTEIN HAD POSED AS A "RECRUITER" FOR VICTORIA SECRET AND COMMITTED GRIEVOUS CRIMES AGAINST YOUNG WOMEN, WHERE THE FINANCES AND EVEN THE JET THAT SUPPORTED THE CRIMES AND CORRUPTION TRAFFICKING CHILDREN ORIGINATED.**

God did something very prophetic having anointed mamas pray repentance and cry out for the children of a nation.

I prayed: "I want to exhort all women of God that God has given you the gift to nurture and protect the godly seed, children. Whether you have biological children or not, you are a 'mother,' a mother to the nation. You are an anointed mama and there is power to tear down strongholds and fight against the powers and principalities of darkness that have tried to dominate our nation and destroy the children. Your prophetic voice, prayers, and being a spiritual mother is life-changing to a younger generation of children who are looking for answers and direction. You are needed and God has placed you here for such a time as this."

Recall the story in I Kings 3:17-27 (ESV) in which two prostitutes came before the king to settle a dispute between them concerning their babies.

> *This woman and I live in the same house. I gave birth to a baby while she was with me in the house. Three days later this woman also had a baby. We were alone; there were only two of us in the house." "But her baby died during the night when she rolled over on it. Then she got up in the night and took my son from beside me while I was asleep. She laid her dead child in my arms and took mine to sleep beside her. And in the morning when I tried to nurse my son, he was dead! But when I looked more closely in the morning light, I saw that it wasn't my son at all." Then the other woman interrupted, "It certainly was your son, and the living child is mine." "No," the first woman said, "the living child is mine, and the dead one is yours." And so they argued*

back and forth before the king. Then the king said, "Let's get the facts straight. Both of you claim the living child is yours, and each says that the dead one belongs to the other. All right, bring me a sword." So a sword was brought to the king. Then he said, "Cut the living child in two, and give half to one woman and half to the other!" Then the woman who was the real mother of the living child, and who loved him very much, cried out, "Oh no, my lord! Give her the child—please do not kill him!" But the other woman said, "All right, he will be neither yours nor mine; divide him between us!" Then the king said, "Do not kill the child, but give him to the woman who wants him to live, for she is his mother![402]

—1 Kings 3:17-27 (ESV)

The real mama, even though she had lived herself as a prostitute, loved the child so much, she didn't want any harm to come to him and was willing to cry out on behalf of her child. The real mama cries out, "Do not kill the child!"[403]

Even in nature, mothers care for and protect their offspring at all costs. For example, female octopuses lay an enormous amount of eggs, even thousands, which they fan "with muscular organs called siphons, which keeps the developing babies oxygenated and free of harmful bacteria."[404] While they are guarding their offspring, they do not leave the area or even eat. "A wild deep-sea octopus studied in Monterey Bay, California, watched over her eggs for four

> EVEN IN NATURE, MOTHERS CARE FOR AND PROTECT THEIR OFFSPRING AT ALL COSTS.

and a half years, the longest period ever recorded."[405] When her eggs hatch, she uses her siphon to expel them out into the ocean "and then she dies."[406]

The bond between mother whales and their young is among the strongest of all species on earth. Sperm whales nurse their calves for over two years and watch over them "24/7."[407] When whale calves don't sleep—which lasts for the entire first month after birth— the mothers don't sleep either. "Orca mothers and their children stay together their entire lives, even after they have offspring of their own." Even through adulthood, an orca will only "separate from its mother for a few hours at a time, to forage and mate."[408]

My husband and I were driving our ATV around the yard when a couple of large sandhill cranes came out honking distinctly at us to guard their nest. The mother bird began to fake an injury, dragging her wing along the ground moving into the open field away from her nest to save her babies. She sacrificed herself to protect and move us away from her nest. I was in awe with the maternity instinct God has put in all of creation when it comes to protecting their children. Even in nature, mothers are willing to give up their lives to save their babies.

What we read in the Bible and see in nature stands in stark contrast to the image of women celebrated in modern culture. The marked shift in the value of women and their unique ability to bear children in this country seems to coincide with the birth control and abortion movement started by Margaret Sanger, founder of Planned Parenthood. Sanger said, "The most merciful thing that the large family does to one of its infant members is to kill it."[409] Yes, she said that.

Sanger's ideologies helped spawn second-wave feminism's call for abortion on demand, equating the right to terminate a pregnancy, to kill one's own child, with freedom, liberty and happiness. The left's departed patron saint, Justice Ruth Bader Ginsberg, said that the prohibition of abortion "controls women and denies them full autonomy and full equality with men."[410] She also said that the right to abortion is "central to a woman's life, to her dignity."[411] "It is essential to women's equality with men," she said, and without it, she is "less than a fully adult human."[412]

How humanity has regressed! God created women with what I consider some of His most powerful attributes — the ability to give life, nurture and love their own children. Our very bodies are made for pregnancy, feeding our babies and holding them on our hips. In predictable fashion, the enemy has perverted women's identities, co-opted what is good and called it evil, lying to women that to be equal to men is to be *like* men, stripped of all life-giving capacity. In nature, we have animals faking injuries and laying down their lives to save their offspring, and we humans are fighting for the right to kill ours. Women, mothers, grandmothers, it is time to reject the culture's lies about what it means to have "dignity" and that to be "fully human" means to abandon your nature, instincts, bodies and children.

> GOD CREATED WOMEN WITH WHAT I CONSIDER SOME OF HIS MOST POWERFUL ATTRIBUTES — THE ABILITY TO GIVE LIFE, NURTURE AND LOVE THEIR OWN CHILDREN.

While we were asleep in the night, there were those who slipped a cold, agenda of death into our arms to destroy us and our children.

Now that we have discovered it, we must cry out to the King for justice on behalf of the children. Institutions and social engineers are willing to destroy children's lives, cutting a child in half to exploit for their agendas. If a prostitute was willing to cry out for the child, how much more should women of God, the real mama speak up? The justice system must judge righteously to protect our children from evil and they should hear our loud cries until they do! We can raise the banner of God's Love and justice over the children! Our prayers, love and example do this like no government counterfeit nanny can! Do not kill the child, but give him to the woman who wants him to live for she is his mother!

There is power within the bonds of motherhood. We see it in nature and in ourselves. The culture's demeaning of motherhood and perverse ideologies about women's equality must be sent back to the pit where they originated. Mothers, embrace, protect and unite with your children; be willing to lay your lives down. In the words of Paul Simon, "... On this strange and mournful day, but the mother and child reunion is only a motion away ... Oh, the mother and child reunion Is only a moment away."[413] Mamas, we are anointed. He chose us to give life, feed, nurture and protect our babies. With God's help, the gates of hell will not withstand us.

> THE CULTURE'S DEMEANING OF MOTHERHOOD AND PERVERSE IDEOLOGIES ABOUT WOMEN'S EQUALITY MUST BE SENT BACK TO THE PIT WHERE THEY ORIGINATED.

CHAPTER 19

LET THE LITTLE CHILDREN COME

I was sitting next to a 15-year old girl on a flight who had shaved her head and highlighted her hair in several colors. She was wearing rainbow gear and black and white checkered Vans slides. I struck up a conversation with her about cats since she was looking at a cat picture in her sketchbook. I complimented her creativity and asked her if she liked art. She showed me more designs. She began to tell me all about her cat and I shared about my cat, Louis Douglas, too. I asked her about her trip and parents. She said, "I have no parents," and shared with me that her mother, who had left her when she was just 3 years old for a man and had a family with him, had recently died of cancer. I asked about her father. She said he had gone to prison for doing something very bad to her. She told me she lives with an aunt who will never get married because she's a lesbian. As she talked, she drew circles with an ink pen up and down her arm in a web design. My heart hurt for her. Her identity was of an orphan.

Without hesitation, I instinctively put my hand on her arm like she was one of my children, and said, "You have been through a lot of hurt for someone so young. I want you to know that I believe God had me sit next to you because he wants you to know how much he deeply loves you, and tell you that you are not alone." She said, "Well I don't believe in God. I'm an atheist." I gently said, "He believes in you and He loves you. Anytime you want to talk to Him, He's listening." I prayed for her that she would discover His love and encouraged her that God made her and he cares for her. We had a good conversation. Then she went to sleep. I kept praying silently to myself for her.

Jesus said, "I will not leave you as orphans [comfortless, desolate, bereaved, forlorn, helpless]; I will come [back] to you. Just a little while now, and the world will not see Me anymore, but you will see Me; because I live, you will live also."[414]

There are so many broken children who because of sin, selfishness and trauma, have been damaged by people that were supposed to love them and offer them security and direction. I am not condemning anyone. We have all missed the mark in some way or another. "All have sinned and fall short of the glory of God."[415] To carry the glory of God was His original plan for us in Eden—not separated from Him, but walking alongside Him.

Good parents dream dreams for their children's lives and try to provide a pathway to help them discover their destinies. How much more does God want the best for His children? Jesus said in Matthew 7:11 (ESV), "If you then, who are evil, know how to give good gifts to your children, how much more will your Father who is in heaven give good things to those who ask him!"[416] God intended good for us but sin brought evil, brokenness and pain. The only way to be healed from the pains of this world and hurt is to come to the one who made you and me.

God instructs us as children and refers to us as His children. As a loving Father, His desire is that we come to Him with our pressures and problems. He is always there for us.

> JESUS ESPECIALLY TREASURED CHILDREN. HE ESTEEMED THEM LIKE NO OTHERS.

Jesus especially treasured children. He esteemed them like no others. He said in Matthew 19:13-14 (NIV), "Let the little children come to me, and do not hinder them, for the kingdom of heaven belongs to such as these."[417] His response was in correcting the attitude His followers had that he was too busy for the children. He laid His hands on the children and blessed them. He took the time and we must too. Jesus said in Mark 9:37 (ESV), "Whoever receives one such child in My Name receives me and whoever receives me, receives not me, but Him who sent me."[418]

Children are tender-hearted and want to please their parents. We are all born with a nature to model our parents. Children learn fear, anger, rebellion, neglect and want and become hardened in life. Even though we are born with a nature to do wrong (a sin nature), when a child is handled with love and care, they develop the desire to do right; they will strive to please you. There are foolish mistakes we all make and there will come a time that a child recognizes they have done wrong and want forgiveness. This is a wonderful time to introduce them to God's plan of salvation, and lead them to receive Jesus' sacrifice to take away all their wrong-doing (sin). If this is done in a gentle caring way, most children genuinely want to please and do what is right. Wrong attitudes can occasionally pop up or they may go through stages of testing boundaries or make a foolish mistake, but overall they do not have to become rebellious or go wayward. That's where the loving guidance of encouragement can help children make right choices and turn from the consequences of doing evil so that their soul learns to know God very well as a Father.

Psalm 139:14 (ESV) says, "For you formed my inward parts; you knitted me together in my mother's womb. I praise you, for I am fearfully and wonderfully made. Wonderful are your works; my soul knows it very well."[419]

Teach children from an early age that they are fearfully and wonderfully made by God. He designed them and gave them a special fingerprint, individual DNA, and one-of-a-kind eyes that are unique to only them in all the world. No two people are alike! This is by Father God's design and we accept ourselves because God the Creator specially handcrafted our bodies and identities. We were with Him in spirit and He placed our spirit inside our earth suit, our body.

> TEACH CHILDREN FROM AN EARLY AGE THAT THEY ARE FEARFULLY AND WONDERFULLY MADE BY GOD. HE DESIGNED THEM AND GAVE THEM A SPECIAL FINGERPRINT, INDIVIDUAL DNA, AND ONE-OF-A-KIND EYES THAT ARE UNIQUE TO ONLY THEM IN ALL THE WORLD.

Jeremiah 1:5 (ESV) says, "Before I formed you in the womb I knew you, and before you were born I consecrated you; I appointed you a prophet to the nations."[420] Later in Jeremiah 31:3 (NIV), the Lord said, "I have loved you with an everlasting love; I have drawn you with unfailing kindness.[421] Children need to know that they are loved by Father God. And because we love him back, we want to please Him with our thoughts and actions. Help children know He loves them unconditionally when we have good days and do what is right or days when we make a mistake. God loves us more than anyone else in the world. More than our parents and friends or a future spouse. This secures a child in a world of uncertainties.

Out of love, He also directs us to "turn your ear to [His] word" and "do not let them out of your sight… ; for they are life to those who find them and health to one's whole body."[422] The word of God is a lamp unto [our] feet and a light unto [our] path."[423] Second Timothy 3:16 tells us that "all scripture ... corrects us when we are wrong and teaches us to do what is right."[424] The Father cares that we are full of life, walk in the light and prosper and live in health, and has given us the path to do so— His Word. Help children understand that not only is there a God that loves them, He created a manual to live life by. Since He created them, there is a plan for each of our lives. That manual is the Bible and it is inspired by a loving Father and has instructions that will give them direction on how to discover His love for them and the direction they need to go. If we feel lost, it is a guide and light to show us which way to walk even in a dark world. Teach children when they make a mistake or sin to run to God not hide from God, and that He will help them. We are promised in 1 John 1:9 (AMP), ""If we [freely] admit that we have sinned *and* confess our sins, He is faithful and just [true to His own nature and promises], and will forgive our sins and cleanse us *continually* from all unrighteousness [our wrongdoing, everything not in conformity with His will and purpose]."[425] Impress upon them that they don't have to earn forgiveness because "it is a gift of God."[426]

Just as God is saying to let the little children come, He is calling us to come and sit at His table. Psalm 23:5 (NIV) says, "You prepare a table before me in the presence of my enemies. You anoint my head with oil; my cup overflows."[427] There's goodness and mercy in God's house and it makes us want to spend time with Him! That's the atmosphere of a family table. Families will heal and be strong again if we set aside devices, and get back to sitting at the table together and sharing our hearts with words. When our table is set properly, there is room to invite others who are alone and hurting to join us. When they see we have more than enough of God's love and goodness to share with them, they may ask to sit down.

I encourage families to create a family table where Jesus is the centerpiece. Always keep Him in the center of your family. The four basic pillars or legs to the table are love and discipline, faith and example. Love works with discipline because first we must know how loved we are, and because we are deeply loved, there are standards for that love to stay close. God disciplines the son or daughter He loves not because He is looking to punish us, but rather to separate us from decisions and rebelliousness that will harm us. We must love enough that we do the hard task of confronting. We must care enough to put our immediate desires aside to deal with any issue for which our child needs correction, and to instruct them from a place of love. The scripture tells us to "discipline our son while there is still time, and we will save his soul from death (Proverbs 19:18 LSB)." I don't discipline because my child is a burden; I bear the burden to discipline because I love them.

> I DON'T DISCIPLINE BECAUSE MY CHILD IS A BURDEN; I BEAR THE BURDEN TO DISCIPLINE BECAUSE I LOVE THEM.

Faith and example are the other two legs that also work together. Our children are watching us, our priorities, our passions and pursuits. Some parents often say, "do as I say, not as I do," but children will do as they see us do. If we have outbursts, they will learn from us to shout and lash out at others. They see if our relationship with God is sincere. Do we read our Bible? Go to church service? Worship God in word and deed? Our faith is contagious and the best way for our children to get it is to catch it from us. If we are silent about it, they will not hear. If we say it but don't do it, it is also null. "Faith by itself, if it does not have works, is dead."[428] Paul said, " I will show you my faith by my works."[429] Our faith is not one of legalism, a form of godliness with no power, but it is a vibrant life-producing joyous relationship that calls us to a higher standard than what we see in the world's pursuits.

For us to love and discipline properly, and be the example of faith that can make a difference in our own children's lives, we must first come to God ourselves and look to Him as a Father listening to His instruction and walking with Him daily. We cannot give something we do not possess to another. The broken children in our culture today need to see that there is another way than what they have seen in the world. They need to know there is a God who loves them and He will take them into His arms and love them; though their father and mother forsake them, God will not. Many great men and women of God emerged from dysfunctional families and/or were orphaned or abandoned by their parents. God says He will be a "father to the fatherless."[430] For those who came out of broken homes, God Himself will give you an overflow to heal the hurts of other children, too. Just ask.

CHAPTER 21

WHAT'S LOVE GOT TO DO WITH IT?

There is a vast difference between what is being taunted as "love" and what real love is. We hear the statements like, "Love is Love" and "A person should be able to love who they want to." What if that means a 34-year old male having "love" relations with a child?! That is not love! That is another word; the Bible calls it lust. Lust acts out personal cravings on a victim, taking what it wants no matter the impact on others. It victimizes people and uses them for personal gratification. There are those who learn through these same types of spirits to abuse and to lust after being abused as well.

What we are witnessing in the guise of "love" is really "lust." What the "Love is Love". crowd is really saying is "Lust is Love" instead of Love is Love. Lust is never fulfilled or satisfied. According to Proverbs 27:20 (The Message), *"Hell has a voracious appetite, and lust just never quits."* Instead, it simply craves more perverted means to express itself. These are spirit entities that enter a person and possess their soul, mind, will and emotions. They

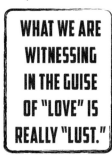

WHAT WE ARE WITNESSING IN THE GUISE OF "LOVE" IS REALLY "LUST."

may "feel" attractions and emotional or sexual appetites for certain fetishes, but this is not "love."

Pornographic images are everywhere: the internet, social media, movies, television and art. Pornography not only exploits imaginations that are already planted in people's thoughts, but it creates appetites for sexual acts that are more debased than most can imagine. A friend of mine who was once an attorney for the porn industry informed me that pornography is available to create and/or satisfy every fetish imaginable, from homosexuality to sex between boys and their step-moms to sadomasochism. She said that among the most popular porn includes men having sex with women who look like teens or post-pubescent children, wearing pig-tails and school uniforms. "Porn is as sick as you want it to be," she said. Of course, there is a market for pedophilia as well, which we frequently hear about on the news (and usually involving someone who works with children).

To be clear, porn is readily-available on any device in your hand or home. Long gone are the days when porn is only found in "dirty magazines" sold in seedy sex shops or secret subscriptions. One can easily access porn through the web of course, but it is also available on apps like Discord, social networking sites like Twitter, and social media platforms, including Facebook.

All of these platforms only require users to be 13-years-old to use their "services." Accordingly, not only are adults now addicted to porn, but so are children. Pornographers specifically target children through gaming platforms by enticing them with clickable anime or other cartoon pornography.[431] There's no depravity too foul or depths to which this industry won't sink.

I will never forget when my husband and I were called to the home of a man who was a part of our congregation. When we arrived, we saw him sobbing hysterically in a corner, completely terrified at what he had just seen in his house—a beautiful woman who transformed before his eyes into a monster. She was literally a demon. He revealed that he was involved in pornography, which was destroying virtually every area of his life. My husband proceeded to cast evil spirits out of him that had entered through porn.

The deliverance team at our church has also ministered to many people, including women and teens, oppressed by spirits of pornography. The spirit of shame is always almost present, which leads to self-hatred, isolation, sickness and disease, and separates them not only from people they love but also God.

Even mainstream entertainment and pop culture are pushing what once would have been considered pornography and perversion. They know if you can control the images, you can control the thoughts. This is where the media becomes the sales agency to buy the real estate. If they can sell transgender ideology or homosexuality in a pretty package of "love and fulfillment" on a big screen coupled with affluence and attention, then the fantasy becomes a reality when it is acted on. Except the only piece of this package that is delivered is the attraction to lust, not real lasting love or fulfillment. Temporary sin brings devastating, life-impacting results and destroys families and lives.

In 2 Samuel 13, there is a story that shows how the power of lust drives a young man named Amnon to sexually violate his half-sister Tamar. "In the course of time, Amnon son of David fell in love with Tamar, the beautiful sister of Absalom son of David. Amnon became so obsessed with his sister Tamar that he made himself ill."[432]

Amnon told his adviser, Jonadab, that he was in love with Tamar. Jonadab "gave him a plan," instructing him, "Go to bed and pretend to be ill,' 'When your father comes to see you, say to him, 'I would like my sister Tamar to come and give me something to eat. Let her prepare the food in my sight so I may watch her and then eat it from her hand.'"[433]

So that's what Amnon did, and King David sent Tamar to take care of her half-brother while he was sick.

> *"Go to the house of your brother Amnon and prepare some food for him." So Tamar went to the house of her brother Amnon, who was lying down. She took some dough, kneaded it, made the bread in his sight and baked it. Then she took the pan and served him the bread, but he refused to eat.*

> *"Send everyone out of here," Amnon said. So everyone left him. Then Amnon said to Tamar, "Bring the food here into my bedroom so I may eat from your hand." And Tamar took the bread she had prepared and brought it to her brother Amnon in his bedroom. But when she took it to him to eat, he grabbed her and said, "Come to bed with me, my sister."*

> *"No, my brother!" she said to him. "Don't force me! Such a thing should not be done in Israel! Don't do this wicked thing. What about me? Where could I get rid of my disgrace? And what about you? You would be like one of the wicked fools in Israel. Please speak to the king; he will not keep me from being married to you." But he refused to listen to her, and since he was stronger than she, he raped her.*

> *Then Amnon hated her with intense hatred. In fact, he hated her more than he had loved her. Amnon said to her, "Get up and get out!"* [434]

Notice after Amnon sinned against her, he hated her. This is the result of lust. Lust takes, manipulates for itself. An evil spirit of lust drives the person to perpetrate its demonic compulsion and plan upon another. Spirit activity is involved and overwhelms the person possessed by lust. Once Amnon had her, he now hated her. He actually never loved her. He simply lusted to take her as his own. Then he sent her away.

> *"No!" she said to him. "Sending me away would be a greater wrong than what you have already done to me." But he refused to listen to her. He called his personal servant and said, "Get this woman out of my sight and bolt the door after her." So his servant put her out and bolted the door after her. She was wearing an ornate robe, for this was the kind of garment the virgin daughters of the king wore. Tamar put ashes on her head and tore the ornate robe she was wearing. She put her hands on her head and went away, weeping aloud as she went.*[435]

Amnon's violation of Tamar brought a spirit of rejection and shame upon her. To put ashes on her head was an act of mourning and deep sorrow, even repentance. She was left in a state of misery and unhappiness. Lust broke her heart and left her empty. Sexual immorality results in pain, abuse, and brokenness.

> *Her brother Absalom said to her, "Has that Amnon, your brother, been with you? Be quiet for now, my sister; he is your brother. Don't take this thing to heart." And Tamar lived in her brother Absalom's house, a desolate woman. When King David heard all this, he was furious. And Absalom never said a word to Amnon, either good or bad; he hated Amnon because he had disgraced his sister Tamar.*[436]

Amnon's supposed love, turned hatred, created brokenness in Tamar, and then hatred in her brother. Two years later, he avenged her, ordering his men, "Listen! When Amnon is in high spirits from drinking wine and I say to you, 'Strike Amnon down,' then kill him. Don't be afraid. Haven't I given you this order?"[437] Absalom's men killed Amnon. Regardless of the vengeance, Absalom remained bitter toward his father, King David, and eventually tried to take his throne by tearing his leadership down throughout the Kingdom. In the end, Absalom died too. He was caught by his long thick hair in an oak tree during battle. When King David's servant, Joab heard this, he plunged three swords into Absalom and then his men beat him to death. At this news, David wept bitterly for days, until a rebellion arose because his men believed he cared more for his wayward son than the men who fought to save him from Absalom's rebellion and treason. In his grief, King David sent away his many concubines and never had relations with them again.

David's household was torn apart because he did not honor his own family relations or marriage as sacred, possessing 8 wives and 18 kids, as many kings chose to do in that time. However, the relations that resulted between his step-children and the generational lust that was part of his family, brought ruin. Rape, death, rebellion, and the death of 20,000 soldiers were the result of the infidelity and the spirit of lust. King David's son, Solomon, repeated the family sin and had over 700 wives and 300 concubines! Like his father, his son increased his sin. Eventually, the family strife broke the nation in two.[438]

As we look across our world today, we can see our nation broken in two, the spirit of lust and addiction being seeded everywhere. Marriage and family are no longer considered holy or sacred.

Pornography, infidelity, adultery, fornication, and sexual perversion are destroying lives. Children's lives being destroyed are the results of sexual immorality.

Jesus warned, *"And if your eye causes you to stumble, gouge it out and throw it away. It is better for you to enter life with one eye than to have two eyes and be thrown into the fire of hell."*[439]

> **PORNOGRAPHY, INFIDELITY, ADULTERY, FORNICATION, AND SEXUAL PERVERSION ARE DESTROYING LIVES.**

First Corinthians 6:12-20 (NIV) says,

> *The body, however, is not meant for sexual immorality but for the Lord, and the Lord for the body. By his power God raised the Lord from the dead, and he will raise us also. Do you not know that your bodies are members of Christ himself? Shall I then take the members of Christ and unite them with a prostitute? Never! Do you not know that he who unites himself with a prostitute is one with her in body? For it is said, "The two will become one flesh." But whoever is united with the Lord is one with him in spirit.*

> *Flee from sexual immorality. All other sins a person commits are outside the body, but whoever sins sexually, sins against their own body. Do you not know that your bodies are temples of the Holy Spirit, who is in you, whom you have received from God? You are not your own; you were bought at a price. Therefore honor God with your bodies.*

Sex is more than a physical act. It is spiritual. When evil spirits are involved (spirits of lust, fear, pride, vanity, and other bondages), sexual involvement unites or binds a person to those spirits. That's how sexual sin causes us to sin against our own body. We become one with that person and the spirits they carry. This is why we see tremendous confusion, self-hatred, suicidal thoughts, self-harm, and addictions ravaging lives.

> **SEX IS MORE THAN A PHYSICAL ACT. IT IS SPIRITUAL.**

What is true love then? Love is to care more for a person than to desire to exploit them, take from them, use them, or abuse them. Love is willing to give itself for the other person, to lay down one's own needs, or want to do what is best for the other person. *"Greater love has no man than to lay down his life for his friends."*[440] Jesus demonstrated real love in that while we were yet sinners, He died for us. God is love and there is no greater example of this love. It is called *agape* love, a love that seeks the other's best and highest.

Those who practice deviant sexual behaviors are not trying to protect, love, help, or better the person who is the object of their lust. They will seek to use the person in ways that destroy them, spirit, soul, and body.

Once a person has been violated by evil spirits operating through another person, even though the victim may hate what was done to them, they are most often drawn to the same perverse thoughts, actions, and curses. These spirits now have a new body to possess and control, harass and torment. This is why those who are abused often turn and become abusers. Without spiritual freedom, they will likely repeat what has been done to traumatize them, suffering shame, guilt and deep, painful wounds. This trauma is driven by evil spiritual entities that hate people and desire to control them.

There is hope and help because perfect love, God's love, casts out all fear and heals wounded souls. Scientific studies confirm what the Bible has already taught us about how the brain and appetites change when pornography or sexual perversion is viewed or acted upon. Strongholds and patterns develop, and without God, sins are passed to the third and fourth generations.

Exodus 34:7 (KJV), referring to God, says,

> *Keeping mercy for thousands, forgiving iniquity and transgression and sin, and that will by no means clear the guilty; visiting the iniquity of the fathers upon the children, and upon the children's children, unto the third and to the fourth generation.*
>
> —Exodus 34:7 (KJV)

God is merciful and will forgive us, but our choices to sin trouble our lives and our families to even the third and fourth generation. This is why certain family weaknesses seem to continue in a lineage. Sin forms a pattern and opens people to spiritual activity that is familiar to families. These patterns must be broken by the love and power of Christ Jesus. He is our deliverer. His death and sacrificial blood was given to justify us and cleanse us from all sin—ours and those carried out against us—whether in our families or other abusers and trauma.

Romans 8:31-39 (NIV) assures us:

> *What, then, shall we say in response to these things? If God is for us, who can be against us? He who did not spare his own Son, but gave him up for us all—how will he not also, along with him, graciously give us all things? Who will bring any charge against those whom God has chosen? It is God who justifies. Who then is the one who condemns? No one. Christ Jesus who died—more than that, who was raised to life—is at the right hand of God and is also interceding for us. Who shall separate us from the love of Christ? Shall trouble or hardship or persecution or famine or nakedness or danger or sword? As it is written:"For your sake we face death all day long; we are considered as sheep to be slaughtered." No, in all these things we are more than conquerors through him who loved us. For I am convinced that neither death nor life, neither angels nor demons, neither the present nor the future, nor any powers, neither height nor depth, nor anything else in all creation, will be able to separate us from the love of God that is in Christ Jesus our Lord.*
>
> —Romans 8:31-39 (NIV)

> **JESUS CAME TO HEAL THE BROKENHEARTED; HIS LOVE AND POWER TO DELIVER IS THE ONLY ANSWER FOR THE SIN-SICKENED SOUL AND A WORLD SPEEDING TOWARD SEXUAL IDOLATRY AND SELF-DESTRUCTION.**

Jesus came to heal the brokenhearted; His love and power to deliver is the only answer for the sin-sickened soul and a world speeding toward sexual idolatry and self-destruction. When God's people were sinning in sexual perversion, God gave them this command in Leviticus 17:7 (KJV), "And they shall no more offer their sacrifices unto devils, after whom they have gone a whoring. This shall be a statute for ever unto them throughout their generations." Our bodies are temples of the Holy Spirit, and we must choose to not offer them as sacrifices to demonic spirits.

The world is trying to entice people, especially youth into sin and lust. "The lust of the flesh, the lust of the eyes, and the pride of life—comes not from the Father but from the world."[441] If we are not preaching a gospel that requires God to accomplish it, we are not preaching the gospel. We are called to live His standard. He said, ""Be holy, because I am holy."[442] And on another occasion He said, ""Why do you call me, 'Lord, Lord,' and do not do what I say?[443] He calls us to obey Him if we love Him. That is the reason He sent the Holy Spirit, to give us the ability to be like Him.

In ourselves, we cannot be free from sin or lust but with God all things are possible. Ephesians 5:6-9 (NLT) says:

> Don't be fooled by those who try to excuse these sins for the anger of God will fall on all who disobey Him. Do not participate in the things these people do, for once you were full of darkness but now you have light from the Lord so live as people of light. For this light within you produces only what is good and right and true.
>
> —Ephesians 5:6-9 (NLT)

We must become fully persuaded in God and His Word, and when we are, we will believe we are free from the sin that bound us, and by His grace, His power, the Holy Spirit gives us power over sin, lust and every stronghold from the past. If we continue down the road of sin excusing these actions the love of the Father is not in us. "Those who say they live in God should live their lives as Jesus did."[444] We died with Christ and so did our sins so we must "[l]et the Spirit renew your thoughts and attitudes. Put on your new nature, created to be like God, truly righteous and holy."[445]

CHAPTER 22

SAVING OUR CHILDREN AND FAMILIES

They're loud, and proud about their agendas that bring destruction to your children! Can we not be loud and proud to protect our children and grandchildren? Are we not proud of our children, our nation, enough to stand up to these bullies and take back our kids?

The fear mongering directed toward our kids—COVID scares, vaccination mandates, school closings, social-distancing, lockdowns, "climate emergency," and gaming violence—is enough to send any healthy child into mental distress and arrested development. Nearly adult-aged youth are now seen in broad daylight wearing their pajamas and slippers in the store, carrying stuffed animals as if they were small kids. This has never been a typical activity for youth who in past times would have already been working their first side jobs.

Our big scary future is made up of a lot of things: the uncertainty of the future, the dropping value of the dollar, monopolies in tech and medical companies that control narratives and peer acceptance, and AI replacing many entry level jobs traditionally supplied by young persons. That's enough to make anyone want to stay in their pajamas and check out emotionally. One mother told me she is so scared for her 10-year-old daughter. She said to me, "My daughter is out of control. If we don't give her everything she wants, she becomes outraged. She can't accept any correction, and we have already had to put her in counseling." In past times, counselors may have coached families on communication, discipline, anger management, and cooperation, but today's counselor may be more likely to lead the child to question their sexual identity and possibly side with the child against parental authority.

This delayed development in youth is a symptom of the breakdown in family, a failure to instruct children in basic principles of life and previously accepted social-norms. Parents should help their children form a sense of identity, confidence and optimism toward a brighter future. Our root problem is a spiritual problem. God created life. When we stop honoring God as our Creator and the life that He created, we lose our way. The principles He gave us are the only answers to life's complex problems. The answers are quite simple, even

> **OUR ROOT PROBLEM IS A SPIRITUAL PROBLEM. GOD CREATED LIFE. WHEN WE STOP HONORING GOD AS OUR CREATOR AND THE LIFE THAT HE CREATED, WE LOSE OUR WAY.**

basic, but God never intended for His ways to be complex. People have made them difficult, and sometimes (if not all the time), they have done so to make themselves more important and God less so.

Parents are overwhelmed, frustrated and feel defeated. The same symptoms children are dealing with—fear, insecurity, identity and low confidence— plagues parents too. After working in a stress-filled environment, they are tired and have little money or time left to give their children. In addition to working two and three jobs to make ends meet, some parents fear doing their job of parenting. They don't know how to lead their families and take the time to do so, causing them to check out and hand their children over to the social engineers that profit from a mother and father's absence. Parents are intentionally made to feel inadequate and the last to "need to know" about important issues and decisions involving their child. The school system makes it easy to hand children over, and let them assume that responsibility. At first it may seem a good solution to give the burden to someone else (kind of like letting ChatGPT think for you), but the outcome has devastating life consequences. Here's a fathers story:

Actor, writer and attorney, Ben Stein tells their story in a letter about the tragic end of his adopted son's life, after they tried to have children for years without success, they cherished this son. Ben shares the difficulties in raising his son, Tommy, that resulted in him and his wife placing him in a private school called Cardington Mountain.[446] He said his son resisted at first but eventually learned to love the school and his friends, even crying upon graduation to leave it behind. But Ben says, "He discovered drugs there, and after that it was all downhill. Don't tell me marijuana is harmless. From pot he went into a downward spiral. Thrown out of school for drunkenness and vandalism. Then back to Los Angeles, to hang out with horrible drug addicts."[447]

The Steins then got their son into Presbyterian College where he fell in love with a girl. He married her and they moved into an apartment in L.A. where he says they mostly smoked dope and drank. They quarreled and eventually divorced. From that marriage, he and his first wife had what Ben describes as the most gorgeous daughter on earth. "Coco was what we called her."[448] They had quarrels over custody battles and he eventually met another girl he met in a café.

Tommy kept drinking and tried to work but he couldn't. Ben says, "He had a psychiatrist, but she seemingly only gave him an even wider, ever more powerful range of psychotropic meds. As far as I know he never met his shrink in person. Only over the internet. Tommy grew so upset about the custody battles over Coco and on July 4, 2023, he committed suicide with one of his guns."[449]

Ben shared, "My wife and I are deeply upset about his death. Deeply to the point that my wife can barely get out of bed. I wish I had known how many drugs my boy was taking. I would have taken him out of South Carolina and brought him here, where a good shrink would have treated him differently. Maybe with love, instead of prescriptions. I loved him so much. I cried when his name came up on my screen. Now for my wife and I, every day is trying to wade through quicksand. Be careful about pot. Be careful about doctors."[450]

Sadly, this heart-wrenching story is no longer an anomaly but rather has become more normal. Fentanyl deaths and drug overdoses are shockingly taking more young lives than imaginable.[451] Many heartbroken parents struggle, thinking, "What could we have done differently?" Obviously, the culture has changed drastically as covered previously, but how do we get back to healthy childhoods and restore purpose for the next generations?

> THE AMERICAN DREAM IS NOT A LOT OF STUFF, IN SPITE OF WHAT MANY THINK. IT NEVER WAS. STUFF CAN BECOME A COUNTERFEIT FOR WHAT REALLY MATTERS.

How do we raise healthy well-adjusted children who honor their parents, respect life themselves and others, and possess character, integrity, work ethic and discipline in their lives? We must get back to the basics, what is really important, prioritize that and tell hell to take their hands off our most precious relationship—our family! How many more things can we buy? Cars to drive or houses? They will not be satisfying when our relationships turn to a wreck. The American dream is not a lot of stuff, in spite of what many think. It never was.

Stuff can become a counterfeit for what really matters. We must stop following the pleasures, distractions, and side bars, and focus on what really matters. Simplicity and priorities. Character and Integrity. Truth and what is right (righteousness). Purpose and destiny. That will bring us real joy and happiness. None of this comes without Christ. We need a Jesus Revolution.

Kids need God, a relationship with the one that created them. Kids need security. They need love and discipline. They need examples and faith to work together. And they need God at the center of every relationship, decision, and all they do. The greatest of these is love. First and foremost, a child needs to know you love them, accept them (not always their behavior, but them) as a person who is deeply loved by God and you. Secondly, we must love them enough to have boundaries that protect them, and others from harm, which sometimes requires justice and discipline. We discipline the child we love. If we don't care enough to confront and correct, then our love is not love, it's convenience. Our lack of discipline of our child, will cause them to stand before more threatening repercussions. Better to have consequences that are small compared to life-altering ones.

Sometimes that discipline is removing privileges or teaching work ethic; sometimes in younger children, it is a swat on the back-side with loving redirection. We also teach our children faith: faith in God, themselves, His Word, and the future because God is in the future too! The Bible has every answer. Our children must learn to trust this. Lastly, your example speaks louder than words. You model for them in your everyday life, your priorities, your marriage, your church attendance, your integrity, and character. These are simple, but will require a daily walk with God to accomplish. God will train you as His child as you train your children. You will both grow together in wisdom, and they will grow in stature into a person you will one day enjoy as a friend. But you'll never truly be their friend, if you weren't first their parent while they were growing up.

In the '60s, Dr. Benjamin Spock tried to get parents to abdicate their parenting to be a friend when kids were at home growing up. It does not work that way. How insecure is life without a parent, an authority that has walked already down a path and knows the right way to go? How insecure is life if that person who gave you life is not there when you need direction, correction, and affection? Parents correct and discipline because they love and care. There is a difference when children are small; they need to obey without explanation. When they're older, they need to understand the why behind what you say. But if you are not the established authority, they will learn nothing. We do not learn from those we do not honor. That is why the Bible says, *"Honor your father and mother.... If you honor your father and mother, 'things will go well for you, and you will have a long life on the earth.'"*[452] (Ephesians 6:2a-3, NLT). This is a promise. If a child doesn't learn honor, their life will be cut short. This could be in years or in blessing, but it will fall short.

There is a place for education, recreation, finances, possessions, entertainment, and social engagement, but if we put these above honoring God and what is right, we cut our lives short too. Our children will do what they see us do. Honor what we honor not with our lips only, but in our actions. Our priorities will show up in our lives, and in our children.

There are time-tested principles that work in life, family, and in any generation. Everything can be screaming against your children, but if you drown out the screamers and choose for your family who you will serve and how you will live, you can succeed beyond your wildest imagination and build the happy, satisfying life that God promised you in His Word. It won't always be easy, but it will be worth it. And remember, it's much harder to deal with the breakdown from neglect than making the investment in the long run. Anything worthwhile takes a solid effort, a commitment. I used these principles raising our five children with success, not perfection, but success. These principles are the foundation of what built America into a prosperous nation with entrepreneurship, small business, respect for one another, and a love of freedom.

Youth and children need:

- ☑ Boundaries
- ☑ Respect
- ☑ Consequences
- ☑ Down time to think, pray
- ☑ Bible - in hand not online
- ☑ Great outdoors adventures
- ☑ Physical activity
- ☑ Parents and right mentors
- ☑ Cut off negative influences
- ☑ Understanding Ministry vs. friendships

The globalists are banking on you and I taking their convenient, hand-over-our-responsibility pathway and losing America, our families, and our honor for God and nation. Tyrants always underestimate God and His people. Where are we? Are we going to speak up or cower? Where is our courage? Will we keep taking the short-cut with a dead-end, the road that leads to destruction, or instead, the road that leads to life. I pray we rise up with a courageous love that shouts louder and prouder, "You'll not have my children, my livelihood, my nation!"

Olivia came from a larger family, and her parents were heavy drinkers, physically and emotionally abusive toward her and other children. In fifth grade, the principal took her and her siblings out of class and asked questions that she answered. She had no idea what was happening but later, children's services took her father away. A year later, her mom had a stroke. Life was so hard as a kid; she blocked a lot of it out and doesn't remember mostly. Because her parents weren't around, she and her siblings did what they wanted. She could walk the streets at midnight or spend the night at a boy's house, and no one would question it or ask her where she was. She got involved in drugs and sleeping with whoever she could find. She just wanted attention. She was drinking alcohol underage, using a lot of illegal drugs.

Realizing she wanted something different, Olivia moved to Columbus, Ohio, to visit an organization she read about that offered help. It was all about positivity, self-help, and how it could change your life. She thought, "I could use a life change." She picked up and went, but later found out it was a cult. She met a guy there who she dated for three years, and he brought her to our church. She said it was weird; they would do all sorts of occult ceremonies living together and attending that organization, and then go to church. At one point, she moved in with a witch she met in the organization. She didn't understand at the time it was really witchcraft and that it was bad. She had made a commitment to the Lord asking Him to be her Savior when she was in 8th grade, but with lack of understanding, she didn't have teaching to know what it meant for Him to be her Lord or to live for Him.

Olivia read my husband's book, *Your Financial Revolution*, and it intrigued her. She knew she was doing wrong, but needed money, had no way to stop living this way or to move out from her boyfriend. She wanted out, but as hard as she wanted to get out, sin was dragging her in. She wanted to live free and live the life God wanted for her. She cried out to God and said, "I need Your help. I'm one lost kid, and I need you to help me, 'cause if not, I don't want to live. I don't want to live because I have no one or nothing."

"I cried out to God, and on a Saturday night, I answered an altar call for the baptism of the Holy Spirit," Olivia said. A few weeks later in worship at church, she began to pray in the Spirit. Then she woke up her boyfriend in the bed another night praying in the Spirit. In shock, she said, "I am really filled with power." It took a bit, but that gave her the power, the strength to get out of sin, and helped her get out of the relationship. Once she did, she had to keep learning her authority over satanic thoughts. She said, "I learned I could actually use my spiritual authority, and use my mouth and tell Satan to get off, and it would work." She started seeing good fruit in her life, actually taking spiritual warfare seriously.

When Olivia was driving in the car and heard evil voices or thoughts, she said, "No, I have a renewed mind. I think the thoughts of God, which are good and pure." She rolled down the window, and said, "Get out of my car, Satan!" and forced the enemy away. She noticed her mind was more clear. She also was delivered from witchcraft in our ministry.

"People don't realize when they've been involved with something like that, they are dealing with the spirit realm. Olivia stated, "For the longest time, I was living a double life. I wanted to be free, but I just didn't know how. I finally got more breakthrough meeting my husband at church." She was still vacillating back and forth but once she met him, she said, her love for the Lord and his love for the Lord came together. "He didn't judge me but loved me. I had a revelation that I could be free. We got married and our lives totally exploded in a great way. I learned gradually to understand what was right and wrong. I got free, joined the worship team, joined small groups, and had friends that encouraged me in the church."

Olivia said her pastors, small group leaders, and all these people helped her get free. She encourages anyone who will listen, "Jesus paid for our freedom. When you've been in that condition and God still loves you, takes you, and forgives you and frees you, and turns you into a successful person, you're like, me? You'd do this for me?" She said she's learned to put the Word of God in her, and it continues to renew her mind. She is reminded about what God says about her and the world. Olivia knows that the Word fights for her, so she speaks God's Word out loud. "The cross means freedom. I'm a new creation. Jesus paid for me to become a new creation. I died with Christ, but I have risen with Him. And I am a new person. I'm a whole new person. I'm never going back." Olivia and her husband just had their first baby together.

Olivia was one of those kids who did not have an example, parents who are there for them, and it caused great pain, guilt, and low esteem, but God's love broke through.

> **THE KIDS WHO ARE MOST AT RISK ARE THOSE WHO LIVE ON THE EDGE AND ARE VERY CREATIVE, GIFTED BUT ALSO TARGETS OF THE ENEMY BECAUSE OF THEIR TALENT.**

The kids who are most at risk are those who live on the edge and are very creative, gifted but also targets of the enemy because of their talent. Our son Tom plays the drums, writes music, books, productions, documentaries, and can create anything. I shudder to think what would have happened had we put him in the traditional school system, forcing his wiggles, curiosity, and creativity into a desk for seven hours a day. He would have likely been diagnosed with ADD, placed on Ritalin (a path leading boy's into drug addiction), and pushed down a dangerous road. Thank you, God, we refused to allow that! There were people who helped me see early the value of home education. It's one reason I am such an advocate for parents. Here is a story that parents of creative or adventurous children must read. Tom shared the following passage in my book, *New Vintage Family: A Vintage Look for The Modern-Day Family*:

> Tom, get away from the edge!" I remember my father's words as though they were yesterday. His face was tense with stress, his grip firm on my arm.

In front of me lay a vast panorama filled with rolling mountains peppered with tall sky-stretching trees. The only thing between that invoking view and me was a sharp three-hundred-foot plummet to the bottom—the reason my father was sweating on this cool Colorado morning.

It was day six of our Keesee family vacation that consisted of our family renting an RV and blitzing through the West like a bandit on the run. It was not a normal family vacation, but our family was anything but average. We homeschooled, ran our own company, and pastored a church. My parents actually cared about each other, and we kids really got along, most of the time. Looking back on those days, I have to wonder how my parents stayed sane. I certainly didn't help to make their life less hectic or stressful. Then again, an RV trip across America with five kids bouncing off the walls wasn't a great help either.

Our family of seven had spent the better part of an hour making the trek, each of us alerted to the hopelessness of the climb by the continuous rain of complaints fired off by my younger sister Polly. With each melodic "I hate hiking!" I became more determined that I was better than the average human. I would run ahead and prove that this was nothing to me. If I was lucky, my speed and prowess would challenge my older brother, Tim, to an unspoken race to the top. Like many other days, my attempts were to no avail. He gated with consistent strides, his face more than annoyed by the teasing of his kid brother.

My mother was somewhere in the center of the group, talking about how awesome it was that we were all finally on our trip across America and making us all slow down to take family pictures in front of every rock and tree (if you think I'm joking, just ask my siblings). My father had the task of carrying the littlest of the clan, Kirsten. She was rather partial to riding on her daddy's shoulders and letting us all know that she was living the good life, broadcasting her smug expression atop her kingly tower.

That left my oldest sister, Amy, who didn't stray far from the adults. This was not because she was afraid. It was simply because she was born an adult, or so I had surmised during my summers of detective work. She enjoyed conversing with Mom and Dad about church and the complexities of going to college at an age much younger than pretty much anyone else had ever gone. She was the reason much of my adolescent life was spent getting in trouble. I could swear that I had seen her and my mother "Vulcan mind meld" (pardon my Star Trek reference). Amy could always tell if I had done any wrong, was doing wrong, or planned on doing wrong in the near future. The bottom line? My older sister helped to guard us convicts when Mom and Dad were busy with their priestly duties. This may be a great time to let you know that I tease about my family as a means of protecting my super sensitive and boyish heart. It's true . . . I would do absolutely anything for them. Just don't let them know I'm such a softy.

My role in the family was simple, really. I had the task of ensuring that life was never boring or simple for the other siblings or Mom and Dad. If there was danger, I found it. If there was something to be conquered, I was Napoleon. If everyone was too silent, I stirred up some chaos. I wasn't trying to be rebellious. I was just so darn curious and handsome.

I should have seen the signs that there was no place on the mountain for curiosity that day. There weren't many cats in the Colorado Rockies—let me put it that way. There was a plethora of danger hiding around every bend, and my dad was getting tired of being a cat herder.

"Tom, I said stay away from the edge!"

"I'm not even that close."

"It just takes one slip."

I was like every other full-blooded American middle child. I knew precisely what I was doing. I was fifteen after all, which might as well have been fifty when my accrued knowledge of everything the world had to offer was taken into account. I could stand close to the edge of danger and walk away unscathed with the best of them. Besides, leaning over the edge was the only way I could catch a glimpse of the rocks that I was throwing down upon unsuspecting wildlife below. There my father was, guarding his young ward from sudden death as a true father should. There I was, the young gallivanting youth who needed to assert his fearlessness at the edge of every mountain in Colorado; Lumberjack Batman and skater Robin.

It would have been fine if this were the first time that I heard those firm and commanding words, but it wasn't. My father pulled me away.

I've always been one to push the boundaries of what was both safe and humanly possible. I was born with a disease that many young men are born with . . . it's called stupidity. Every now and again, I just do dumb things. Those of you who are parents of boys are either laughing or crying by now. This is because you have man-children. Boys are not intentionally dumb; they just are, without even trying. Throwing firecrackers out of house windows, jumping motorcycles into trees, running on ice—all symptoms of stupidity. Don't worry, though, your child can get healing. There's a wonderful thing that fixes this illness. It's a little thing called *discipline*.

Don't let your parenting become religious. Don't keep the amazing panorama of life from your children. Don't keep them from reaching for their dreams because you're afraid of the edge. Instead, be right there with them.

That morning I was particularly dumb. I don't think I had an ounce of sense in my lanky body. If I fell from that ledge,

> DON'T LET YOUR PARENTING BECOME RELIGIOUS. DON'T KEEP THE AMAZING PANORAMA OF LIFE FROM YOUR CHILDREN. DON'T KEEP THEM FROM REACHING FOR THEIR DREAMS BECAUSE YOU'RE AFRAID OF THE EDGE. INSTEAD, BE RIGHT THERE WITH THEM.

there was no breaking my descent. I would be met with the choice of either rocks or the tops of evergreen Yosemite pines—both were sure to be fatal to a mortal. If I did survive, the forest creatures would exact their vengeance on my rock-tossing terrorist hindquarters. Now that I've experienced much more discipline, I realize how foolish I was. I'd love to say that was the only time I did something foolish. I've had scores of learning opportunities that life has dealt me by way of my decisions. The only thing I can tell you is that my family is the reason I'm not a monument.

I thank God for my family every day and for my amazing parents. I could write a library of books about their heroism in the face of danger and still not encompass their outlandish deeds. My father is a true hero to me and will forever be that way no matter his age or strength. My mother will always be among the most beautiful women whom I've ever seen, because that is who my father told me she was every day I was raised. These ideals and words are not written in textbooks and can't be learned from Rosetta Stone in thirty days or less. They are instilled in your child from the day they are born to the day they march into the world.

The thing is, there's a danger that is always calling your children closer to the edge. They may think they know best. They may be curious or just lack some discipline. This is why you are the parent. The day my father grabbed my arm wasn't about him trying to shove his life values on me or to keep me from having fun. It was to protect me from myself. My father has since "grabbed my arm" on more than one occasion, which

I am more than grateful for. But even more important than those moments of protection is the learning of how to follow the voice of our heavenly Father when He says, "Don't get too close to the edge."

"But I'm not even that close, God."

"It just takes one slip."

You see, going to the top of the mountain isn't wrong to do. How else can you see and experience many of the great things that life has? Don't let your parenting become religious. Don't keep the amazing panorama of life from your children. Don't keep them from reaching for their dreams because you're afraid of the edge. Instead, be right there with them. Guide them. Show them that God wants them to live a life full of adventure. But keep a watchful eye. What are your kids watching and playing? With whom are they spending time? Are you journeying with them or have you stopped somewhere down the hill? They need you in their life. And don't allow yourself to lose hope for that one in your family who may go too close to the edge by nature. He or she just may be made with that fearlessness because they are going to pull others away from the edge. Instead, keep a hold of their arm, spiritually. Some kids are going to take a bit more prayer and a bit more work. But you know, those kids just might be the ones who keep everyone's lives interesting and adventurous in the long run."[453]

Tom is right.

CHAPTER 23

DEATH?
DECEPTION?
NO! DELIVERANCE!

Many think there is no hope for the evil around us and spend their time only focused on all that is wrong. They think and speak that this generation is hopeless. It is crucial to *"have nothing to do with the fruitless deeds of darkness, but rather expose them,"* but we don't stop there![454] We have to ask, "What is God's solution? Why is there such evil in this time?" The target on youth in this hour is greater than ever, but there is a reason the enemy targets a generation. Certainly, he wants to discourage and hurt them, parents, and grandparents, but even more than that he fears who they are and what they may become if they discover what their mission is and the authority they have over darkness.

When Moses the deliverer was born, eventually freeing the Hebrew slaves from Egypt, the targeting of children happened, but it later backfired on Pharaoh.[455] At the coming of the Savior Jesus' birth, the enemy targeted children and had all the baby boys under two years old killed by Herod's evil government.[456] Satan knows his time is short and fears the great destiny and deliverance of this generation's youth, just as great as the deliverance of Israel out of Egypt and as the first coming of Jesus as Savior. This current generation will usher in Jesus' return as King! Just as when Jesus came the first time, those sitting in darkness have seen a great light. This generation will see the light of His love and power! Sin will be brought into the light so it can be dealt with so they can be freed and be catalysts to free others!

Psalm 50:15 says, "And call upon me in the day of trouble; I will deliver you, and you shall glorify me."[457]

For people to be delivered, they must call on Jesus. Bringing sin into the light exposes it and destroys its power. James 5:16 (ESV) instructs us, *"Therefore, confess your sins to one another and pray for one another, that you may be healed. The prayer of a righteous person has great power as it is working."* In Acts 2:17 when the Spirit of God was poured out in such a mighty and powerful way, Peter got up to address the crowd and explain this unprecedented scene. Peter said:

> *In the last days, God says, I will pour out my Spirit on all people. Your sons and daughters will prophesy, your young men will see visions, your old men will dream dreams. Even on my servants, both men and women, I will pour out my Spirit in those days, and they will prophesy. I will show wonders in the heavens above and signs on the earth below, blood and fire and billows of smoke. The sun will be turned to darkness and the moon to blood before the coming of the great and glorious day of the Lord. And everyone who calls on the name of the Lord will be saved.*
>
> —Acts 2:17-20 (NIV)

> THIS GENERATION OF YOUNG PEOPLE WILL EXPERIENCE THE SPIRIT OF THE LORD AND PROPHESY THE COMING OF JESUS, BUT WE MUST FIRST SEE THEM FREED FROM THEIR OPPRESSION, DELIVERED BY THE POWER OF GOD, AND FILLED WITH HIS SPIRIT TO BE WHO THEY WERE CREATED TO BE.

This generation of young people will experience the Spirit of the Lord and prophesy the coming of Jesus, but we must first see them freed from their oppression, delivered by the power of God, and filled with His Spirit to be who they were created to be. Truth is the foundation of freedom. *"And you shall know the truth, and the truth shall make you free."* [458]

There is a story of a boy who threw himself into the fire. His self-destructive actions were motivated by a demonic spirit. His father asked Jesus for help. We see this story in Mark 9:20-27:

> So they brought him. When the spirit saw Jesus, it immediately threw the boy into a convulsion. He fell to the ground and rolled around, foaming at the mouth. Jesus asked the boy's father, "How long has he been like this?" "From childhood," he answered. "It has often thrown him into fire or water to kill him. But if you can do anything, take pity on us and help us." "'If you can'?" said Jesus. "Everything is possible for one who believes." Immediately the boy's father exclaimed, "I do believe; help me overcome my unbelief!" When Jesus saw that a crowd was running to the scene, he rebuked the impure spirit. "You deaf and mute spirit," he said, "I command you, come out of him and never enter him again." The spirit shrieked, convulsed him violently and came out. The boy looked so much like a corpse that many said, "He's dead." But Jesus took him by the hand and lifted him to his feet, and he stood up.
>
> —Mark 9:20-27 (NIV)

This is a perfect example of deliverance. As our ministry has asked God to pour out His Spirit and help us reach people outside the church, we have witnessed dynamic unprecedented services. Months back, there was a very strong presence of God during worship. I remember thinking, "Jesus is here walking among us." At the first of the year in prayer, I heard, "Make more room for the Holy Spirit." As service ended, we invited people who wanted prayer. A young woman came to the altar and handed my husband the visitor card. It said, "Can you help me? Demons are tormenting me and my family." As I started to talk to her and asked to pray for her, immediately, she began to shriek, yell, and fell forward on the floor. She was in a violent warfare, and I kept praying with authority and commanding evil spirits to leave in the Name of Jesus. She foamed at the mouth and great anguish was on her face as an unseen fight was clearly happening, a spiritual battle.

I instructed her, "I'm going to take authority over evil spirits that are harassing you. I'm not talking strongly to you, I'm commanding them to Go!" Then I commanded the evil spirits to get out of her in Jesus' name, and stood firm against them. Occasionally, I would gently speak to her as a person and check on her as the fight pursued. "Are you alright?" She nodded her head, yes, and I kept working with the Holy Spirit to see her fully delivered. And just as the Bible says, they "came out [of her] with a shriek."[459] Her body was rigid, and I kept telling spirits to go, different ones, for at least 45 minutes–until her tense body finally relaxed.

Then I heard strongly the Lord say, "Lead her to the baptism of the Holy Spirit." At first, I argued mentally with him. I said, "We normally give people a book first." He said, "And where do you see that in the Bible?" (I know it sounds ridiculous that I questioned, but I wasn't accustomed to seeing someone manifest demonic spirits, lead them from there to receive Jesus, and get baptized with the Holy Spirit all in one take.) Then the Lord said to me, "You have cleansed the house but if you don't fill it with the Holy Spirit now, she won't make it." When I heard that, I immediately shared with her the free gift that Jesus told the disciples not to leave Jerusalem without. *"Do not leave Jerusalem, but wait for the gift my Father promised, which you have heard me speak about. For John baptized with water, but in a few days you will be baptized with the Holy Spirit"* (Acts 1 :4-5 NIV).

I let her know that Jesus would give her this gift to help her stay free and hear His direction. It is a secret weapon against the enemy. When you pray in the Spirit, you pray mysteries, 1 Corinthians 14:2 says. I instructed her, "I will lay my hands on you and say, 'Jesus, baptize her in the Holy Spirit.' You say, 'I receive the Holy Spirit.' And you will pray in the Holy Spirit. I laid my hands on her and she did receive. To my almost shock, she began to pray boldly in the Holy Spirit in tongues. I had never seen someone go from the bondage of demonic spirits to praying with such joy and boldness.

Soon after, I learned that she had contacted our deliverance ministry team because she was again experiencing demonic oppression. Heaven only knows, but something must have opened the door for more attacks after she left church. They ministered to her for hours in which a multitude of demons manifested and were expelled in the name of Jesus. The major entry points for these demons were family members (with whom she lived as a child) who were actively engaged in satanism, and rejection from her mother in the womb. One spirit even boasted that it "has blinded her." By the end of her session, she put on her prescription glasses and couldn't see through them. Her eyesight had been completely restored, and she was truly free! That very evening, she attended our Saturday evening service, then the next week she was back, and the next and the next. Her children got born again, and on Mother's Day, she assisted our pastoral team in water baptizing her children. Her husband started coming, and after a while, we led him to Jesus too. As she continued to attend, she would stay with me at the altar to see others set free and experience what she had received. I believe this is how the early church turned the world upside down.

A few weeks after this young woman's deliverance, she would show me pictures of her after leaving church that day, and she physically had bruises on her face. I said, "You know I didn't do that to you but devils did." She agreed with a nod. I had not physically touched her face, but spirits were trying to harm her, and their warfare may have left a few bruises, but freedom came! We are in a spiritual fight with wickedness in heavenly places! I said, "There was intense warfare over you. Those spirits did not want you free, but they lost! Now stay clean. Go and sin no more!"

The Holy Spirit is the power of God that overcomes the world, its lies, and evil luciferian spirits that are oppressing and possessing lives. The scripture says, *"He who dwells in the secret place of the Most High Shall abide under the shadow of the Almighty."* [460]

When we dwell in God, He is our fortress protecting our soul from evil that seeks to penetrate our person. When spiritual darkness has entered into people's lives through sin, hurts, trauma, abusiveness, and familiar spirits (spirits familiar with the surroundings or people accustomed to them), the enemy violates the fortress of their soul and enters in the secret place of their thoughts, meditations, and eventually actions, if not stopped. This is why we must guard our hearts because apart from our spirit, everything in our person comes from our soul (mind, will and emotions), and they affect the body's health. Only by dwelling in God's secret place can we keep our soul free. He is shadowing over us as we

> **ONLY BY DWELLING IN GOD'S SECRET PLACE CAN WE KEEP OUR SOUL FREE.**

stay under His protection. In His shadow, we have a refuge from darkness. He is the impenetrable fortress standing over us to protect us. *"I will say of the LORD, "He is my refuge and my fortress, my God, in whom I trust."* [461]

Many times parents will say, "I had no idea my child was looking at pornography or struggling with an area in their life, like that." Satanic activity is all around us, more than ever, and even children in strong church families are targets of lies, secret sin, and strongholds that can develop when these areas are not addressed. That's why it's important that parents have a relationship that's very open and close to their children. It's why we must protect them. And it's why they need the baptism of the Holy Spirit to do the spiritual warfare that they must do to stay on fire for God. We will not always be there to protect them but God's Spirit will.

God's Word gives us a picture of how life is to be lived. God's Spirit, the Holy Spirit, gives us the power to live it. We must have the picture and the power to be free and resist the temptations and lies all around us. Jude 1:20 says, *"Building yourselves up in your most holy faith and praying in the Holy Spirit."*

Ephesians 6:18 says as a final addition to the armor of God, *"and praying in the Spirit at all times"* (KJV), or *"on all occasions"* (NIV). Ephesians 6:17 instructs, *"Take the helmet of salvation and the sword of the Spirit, which is the word of God. And pray in the Spirit on all occasions with all kinds of prayers and requests"* (NIV). We hear the armor taught, but rarely is the final instruction included "to pray in the Spirit!"

The same weekend that the young mother came forward and was freed, I would learn that we had multiple similar situations happening in the building! I ministered to another young woman whom I had never seen who wanted to hurt her newborn baby. Again, I looked her in the face and said, "Look at me." She began to twitch and said, "No." This was the evil spirit talking, not her. This time I held her cheeks gently and began to tell every evil spirit to leave her in the Name of Jesus. She also fell to the ground and began to shriek. The spirit of murder was on her, but she was freed after a brief spiritual wrestling match. Again, this time I learned quickly; I led her to receive the Holy Spirit. By 3:00 in the afternoon we were finished. I realized I was supposed to have lunch with my daughter-in-law and mentioned to our assistant, she must have left by now. My assistant said, "No, she's in the ministry room with others, ministering to a girl who began to growl and shriek at the back of service." Later I found out that several of our team had helped her, and two more people were free. In the Saturday service, another was delivered and freed from evil spirits. At our very late Sunday lunch, the family was more excited about all God had done than eating. We were already hours past lunch. This must be what Jesus was experiencing when he said in John 4:34 (NIV), *"My food' said Jesus, 'is to do the will of Him who sent Me and to finish His work.'"* [462]

I know this is uncomfortable for "church as usual," but these are not comfortable times. When I asked God was it alright that these deliverances happened at the end of service in front of some members, He said, "How will my people know how to cast out devils if they've never seen it happen at church?" We are either going to do what the Bible says, or lose a generation to the devil. Which will it be? This is the time we are living in, and the church must know how to do what Jesus did. He cast out devils consistently in His ministry. Mark 16:17 (NIV) says, *"And these signs will accompany those who believe: In my name they will cast out demons; they will speak in new tongues."* [463] Casting out devils is the sign of a believer, according to Jesus Himself.

Evil spirits are operating as never before in the lives of people, and Jesus commanded us to do the same works he did. This generation needs freedom and power, and then they will usher in the greatest awakening and revival the world has seen. We are not to be afraid to deal with spirits. Jesus said he has given us all authority to cast out devils. Praying in the Spirit will bring the boldness and direction of how to minister to someone. Every situation has its direction by the Spirit because people are all unique. God and His Spirit know what their hurts, issues, and pains are and how to deal with them, uniquely.

People ask me, "How do you know someone has spirits tormenting them?" One evidence is that there are often physical signs in their appearance. Depending on the degree of spiritual activity, it can be mild or extreme. A demonized person can certainly go undetected when it comes to appearance. Some of the most demonically oppressed people come to church in their Sunday best, pray the most eloquent prayers and serve whenever the lights are on. However, there are outward indicators of severe cases of demonization, which include the following: a change in appearance for the worse; neglect of personal care; an intense or angry glare in their eyes as if something/someone else is looking through; strange or unusual behavior or dress; and provocative or otherwise revealing clothing.

> THIS GENERATION NEEDS FREEDOM AND POWER, AND THEN THEY WILL USHER IN THE GREATEST AWAKENING AND REVIVAL THE WORLD HAS SEEN. WE ARE NOT TO BE AFRAID TO DEAL WITH SPIRITS. JESUS SAID HE HAS GIVEN US ALL AUTHORITY TO CAST OUT DEVILS.

Other signs can be emotional manifestations of anger, abusive language, destructive behavior, self-harm, cutting, picking at or scratching one's skin and making themselves bleed, or dangerous, often spontaneous actions, like trying to jump out of a car or off a high place. Signs can also include thoughts to do evil that won't go away, lustful thoughts to abuse another or self. Basically any action that steals, kills, destroys is from Satan's demonic horde. Evil spirits hate people because we are made in the likeness and image of God. They want to assault God by harming His creation and children.

The enemy has influenced the world to use tactics to lure people, especially children, into traps of bondage. God's love and the Holy Spirit are the only answers to their search but alcohol, drugs, sex, vanity, and pride, masked as an angel of enlightenment, trick unsuspecting souls. The counterfeit is never the real deal. When young people get filled with God's Spirit, they don't need to hang with the enemy's crowd to get high.

Ephesians 5:18 says, *"Do not get drunk with wine, for that is wickedness (corruption, stupidity), but be filled with the [Holy] Spirit and constantly guided by Him."* [464]

Oftentimes a person needs to be delivered from these spirits in order to have the right mind to receive Jesus as Savior. Those spirits have controlled their thoughts, then actions, and eventually oppressed them to the place where they no longer have the ability to maintain control over their own lives. Evil spirits can torment them, drive them to sin and will eventually try to destroy their lives. That is why we cannot follow the world's "solutions!" What is often deemed mental illness in young people or adults is spirit activity. The world's institution's encourage them further down a path of spirit activity by offering more perversion, transition surgeries, and drugs, while normalizing sinful behavior which gives Satan greater authority to destroy their lives. I'm often asked, "Can a Christian be possessed by devils?" Their soul (mind, will, and emotions) can be tormented or oppressed by devils although not possessed. A person becomes possessed when demonic spirits take control of their human spirit. In either case, deliverance is needed.

Deliverance ministry takes time and a deep compassion for people. Jesus was moved with compassion and healed the sick. He spoke to demons, and they left people. In Matthew 8:28, Jesus ministered to men who were violently possessed by devils.

> *When Jesus arrived on the other side of the lake, in the region of the Gadarenes, two men who were possessed by demons met him. They came out of the tombs and were so violent that no one could go through that area. They began screaming at him, "Why are you interfering with us, Son of God? Have you come here to torture us before God's appointed time?" There happened to be a large herd of pigs feeding in the distance. So the demons begged, "If you cast us out, send us into that herd of pigs." "All right, go!" Jesus commanded them. So the demons came out of the men and entered the pigs, and the whole herd plunged down the steep hillside into the lake and drowned in the water. The herdsmen fled to the nearby town, telling everyone what happened to the demon-possessed men. Then the entire town came out to meet Jesus, but they begged him to go away and leave them alone.*[465]
> —Matthew 8:28-34 (NLT)

Sadly, the people were like many churches today who want Jesus to leave if it messes up their normal. They actually begged Jesus to go from them, which makes me think they were living in either religion or a sinful town. Religion has a form of godliness but no power to free people. Sinful leaders and cities want to remain in their filth as someone is profiting from the wickedness. I am disgusted to see how evil governmental policies that promote drugs, sexual perversion, abortion, and lawlessness have destroyed lives and broken children's hearts. Those who do such things will go to hell if they do not repent. These actions invite demonic activity, and we cannot help people if we are not willing to do what Jesus did. Cast out evil spirits!

Jesus is the word made flesh, and the word anchors our soul, our mind, will, and emotions. But we also must have a move of the spirit. There's an old saying we used to hear, "All Word, you dry up. All spirit, you blow up. Word and Spirit, you grow up." That's where we are at in the body of Christ. It's time to discern the time you're living in, what you're doing, why you're doing it, whatever piece and part you have to play in this. Every person is indispensable according to 1 Corinthians 12:22. We rise up, *"held up by every supporting ligament,"* to grow and build up the *"whole body"* together.[466] God's reward is worth every bit of it.

> **"ALL WORD, YOU DRY UP. ALL SPIRIT, YOU BLOW UP. WORD AND SPIRIT, YOU GROW UP."**

Luke 10:17 (NKJV) says:

> *Then the seventy returned with joy, saying "Lord, even the*

demons are subject to us in Your name." And He said to them, "I saw Satan fall like lightning from heaven. Behold, I give you authority to trample on serpents and scorpions, and over all the power of the enemy, and nothing shall by any means hurt you. Nevertheless do not rejoice in this, that the spirits are subject to you, but rather rejoice because your names are written in heaven."

—Luke 10:17 (NKJV)

It's exciting to let God use you to bring freedom and deliverance to people, and even as great as that is, it's even greater that we have an eternity in God's presence, because our names are written in His Kingdom in heaven.

Any born again, Holy Spirit-filled believer who walks in integrity with the Word of God, doing what He says, can learn to drive out evil spirits. Every church should have people who are trained and seasoned to train up others to minister deliverance. People from all over our city, states across the country, and even countries as far away as New Zealand have sought out our church seeking deliverance because their own churches don't and won't do it! If churches do not have this ministry operating, they better, as we will see more demonic activity as our nation has invited strongholds and spirits into government, medicine, education, arts, music, media, and homes. God is pouring out His Spirit. Let's get in step with Him and set the captives free.

When we minister deliverance, we must counsel those who receive it that returning to sin, ungodly relationships, and old thought patterns may reopen the door for demons to return. Jesus warned:

When an impure spirit comes out of a person, it goes through arid places seeking rest and does not find it. Then it says, 'I will return to the house I left.' When it arrives, it finds the house swept clean and put in order. Then it goes and takes seven other spirits more wicked than itself, and they go in and live there. And the final condition of that person is worse than the first.[467]

—Luke 11:24-26 (NIV) (emphasis added)

Unfortunately, I have seen this happen numerous times.

During one of the deliverances in our ministry, a demon spoke through the person, saying "I'll go, but I'll be right around the corner." The demon, although a liar, was stating a fact. This is why it is so important for those who receive freedom to stand on their deliverance. This means getting into the Word, spending time in worship and prayer, being established in a Kingdom-teaching local church, cultivating Jesus-centered friendships and accountability partners through small groups, and cutting off unholy ties to people and behaviors. This way, when a demon comes around the corner, there's no door for it to enter.

> THIS IS WHY IT IS SO IMPORTANT FOR THOSE WHO RECEIVE FREEDOM TO STAND ON THEIR DELIVERANCE. THIS MEANS GETTING INTO THE WORD, SPENDING TIME IN WORSHIP AND PRAYER, BEING ESTABLISHED IN A KINGDOM-TEACHING LOCAL CHURCH, CULTIVATING JESUS-CENTERED FRIENDSHIPS AND ACCOUNTABILITY PARTNERS THROUGH SMALL GROUPS, AND CUTTING OFF UNHOLY TIES TO PEOPLE AND BEHAVIORS.

How to minister Jesus/Salvation:

God loves you. We have all sinned and made mistakes. God sent Jesus to pay for our sins by His death so we would not have to go to hell with Satan. Would you like to receive God's gift of Jesus? Just ask and you will receive. "Call on the Lord Jesus and you will be saved." Repeat after me: Jesus, help me. Be my Savior. I give you my life.

How to minister the Holy Spirit:

1) Share that Jesus commanded us to receive the gift in Acts 1 to help us. It's a gift you receive. You don't work for it. One only needs to be born again to receive it.

2) Encourage the person that Jesus is the one who will baptize them in the Holy Spirit.

3) "I will lay my hands on you and say "Receive the Holy Spirit."

4) You say, "Jesus, I receive the Holy Spirit."

5) Tell them: "You will be able to pray in the Spirit. Say whatever comes out, but not in English. You cannot pray in the Spirit in tongues and English at the same time, just like you can't speak French and English at exactly the same time."

6) Ready? Relax and receive. Raise your hands. Shut your eyes and focus on Jesus.

7) Then begin. "Jesus, baptize her/him in the Holy Spirit now." Touch their hands. Tell them to say, "Jesus, I receive the Holy Spirit."

And just as he promised:

> *When the day of Pentecost came, they were all together in one place. Suddenly a sound like the blowing of a violent wind came from heaven and filled the whole house where they were sitting. They saw what seemed to be tongues of fire that separated and came to rest on each of them. All of them were filled with the Holy Spirit and began to speak in other tongues as the Spirit enabled them.*[468]

—Acts 2:1-4 (NIV)

There is nothing quite like receiving the Holy Spirit and His anointing. Reading the scroll of Isaiah, Luke writes, *"The Spirit of the Lord is upon me, because he has anointed me to proclaim good news to the poor. He has sent me to proclaim liberty to the captives and recovering of sight to the blind, to set at liberty those who are oppressed."* [469] When the Spirit comes upon us, we are empowered to be His witnesses!

How to minister deliverance:

While Jesus said that casting out demons is a sign that *"will follow those who believe,"* [470] it is **not** for the spiritually immature, those engaged in habitual sin, those who are in spiritual bondage themselves, or anyone who operates in fear. This is front-line spiritual warfare. Like a soldier, you must be *called* and *trained* before going into battle. Jesus did this when *"he called the twelve and began to send them out two by two, and gave them authority over the unclean spirits."* [471]

Everyone on our ministry's deliverance team is to be vetted, trained, and undergo deliverance themselves before they're ever released to minister to others.[472] Those who are in training or in active deliverance ministry must *"be prepared in season and out of season."*[473] This means studying and reading the Word each day, praying in the Spirit consistently, and spending time with Jesus daily. If not, a demon will be the first to call you out on it or worse. Remember the seven sons of Sceva? Witnessing the miracles and power of Paul, they essentially used the name of Jesus, not to further the gospel, but for their own glory and gain. The demons knew this, saying to them, *"'Jesus I know, and Paul I know about, but who are you?'* Then the man who had the evil spirit jumped on them and overpowered them all. He gave them such a beating that they ran out of the house naked and bleeding."*[474]

Once you've been trained, including observing, supporting, and interceding for a more experienced person, you may proceed with ministering deliverance with at least one other person. (Jesus sent them out two by two, remember?) While every deliverance experience is unique and there is no formula for handling, an *ideal* general model to follow would include:[475]

1. Have the person affirm his or her faith in Jesus and profess Him as Lord. The most important thing we can minister is salvation; the most important factor in staying delivered is the gift of the Holy Spirit through salvation and baptism;

2. Encourage the person to confess and repent of any known sin. This is how we strip demons of any legal rights to stay;

3. Lead the person to forgive all people and offenses they may be harboring. Again, this is a legal issue about authority;

4. Command the demons to go in Jesus' name! Sometimes this may involve calling them by name or function as the Holy Spirit leads or commanding them to identify themselves as Jesus did with Legion. Maintaining eye contact with the person and speaking with authority (not yelling) are effective keys to bring the demon to attention and expel it.

5. Send the demons to the pit or abyss never to return!

Of course, there are instances in which the first three steps are not possible given the unclean spirit (or spirits) control of the person. In this case, expel the demons and then proceed with steps 1 through 3.

However, deliverance is not just about expelling demons. It is a ministry to the entire person. Part of it is helping the person identify and understand the doors in which darkness entered and how to avoid succumbing to faulty thought patterns and snares. We can help them do this by identifying sinful behaviors and ungodly thoughts and sharing scriptures that they can stand on. As always, we encourage those who've been through deliverance to join small groups and find accountability partners to help them walk out their freedom.

> **DELIVERANCE IS NOT JUST ABOUT EXPELLING DEMONS. IT IS A MINISTRY TO THE ENTIRE PERSON. PART OF IT IS HELPING THE PERSON IDENTIFY AND UNDERSTAND THE DOORS IN WHICH DARKNESS ENTERED AND HOW TO AVOID SUCCUMBING TO FAULTY THOUGHT PATTERNS AND SNARES.**

I also recommend *The Truth About You: Overcoming Seven Lies You Believe About Yourself* by Amy Freudiger to minister to the soul and help bring freedom from Satan's lies. This book can help in the areas of identity and staying free once delivered to renew the mind and spirit. It is excellent especially as a Bible study for young people and anyone struggling with rejection, fear, unworthiness, and guilt.

My book, *Better Than You Feel,* can help you overcome guilt, rejection, fear, and recognize how to forgive and be set free.

Every person needs a pathway of restoration from the sin they have previously lived with. Getting delivered from spirit activity, born again, and filled with the Spirit is the beginning of a walk with Jesus Christ. We need to renew our mind with the Word of God, studying a new way of living and not returning to the habits and patterns of this world and the sin that had us bound.[476] God will rebuild lives and give us beauty instead of all the pain and sorrow we used to live in when sin was our master and we followed the world's dictates and plans. Isaiah 61:3 says He gives us *"a beautiful headdress instead of ashes, the oil of gladness instead of mourning, the garment of praise instead of a faint spirit; that they may be called oaks of righteousness, the planting of the Lord, that he may be glorified."*[477]

CHAPTER 24

COURAGEOUS LOVE: A CALL

"Go woke, go broke!" This was my warning to corporations almost two years ago in my book, *Fight Like Heaven! A Cultural Guide to Living on Guard.* I meant what I said then, and I mean it now. When corporate giants push the LGBTQ agenda to sexualize our children, we must push back with our dollars. As I predicted, the bigger they are, the harder they fall.

This especially applies to the Walt Disney Company, which has sustained a nine-year low in its stock price as of September 2023. "Disney, which became a symbol for wokeism after protesting Florida's parental rights law in March 2022, hit a stock price low of $83.53 on Monday. The company's market cap has fallen from $350.09 billion on March 22, 2022, to $154.04 billion. That's a decline of $196.05 billion — or a 56% drop in market cap."[478]

The most obvious example was Bud Light, "but the revolution is escalating and extending and hitting brands that were once beloved, but clearly are in bed with ruling elites. These companies proved useless in defending commercial rights during the lockdowns and now want to shove anti-scientific political symbolism down all our throats. They might not get away with it this time."[479]

We have seen one of the most notorious offenders, Target, lose $12 billion in market capitalization in two weeks after it revealed its 2,000+ products for Pride month in mid-May.[480] While the new adult collection included one surprising element even for Target—a woman's swimsuit with a "tuck friendly" feature for males—it was the line for children that finally triggered backlash from Americans. The message was clear: *don't mess with our children*!

> **DISCOURAGEMENT IS NOT OUR DEFAULT. WE CAN WIN THIS FIGHT!**

Discouragement is not our default. We can win this fight! There are great strides being made, but we must continue to put pressure on woke companies. We are witnessing the impact our willingness to engage the fight is having on corporations.

By boycotting woke companies, we can continue to band together and exalt true capitalism. If they fall, we break up corporate monopolies along with their woke ideologies that wreak havoc on citizens and children. And when they want you to "think" they've pulled back, don't cave in; fight harder! It takes courage, but you are called to be bold and courageous.

While boycotting is one powerful action we can take, we must fight this battle on multiple fronts. It will take courage.

Many of us don't consider ourselves courageous! Most of us, myself included. When our love for someone or something ignites a passion so great we can't hold back, our fear is cast out by love, and we become courageous. It's not so much that we don't struggle with fear; we simply have more passion to engage than retreat. We don't feel strong in ourselves or better equipped than another; our love burns brighter than fear with a desire to fight for a heavenly cause infusing us with the power to overcome fear, and act. In that moment, it looks like courage, but the power behind it is love. Courageous love causes our faith to work by love.

Faith also takes courage! For our families, we must have the courage to believe what God says and act on it. Likewise, so do our children.

What we say to them and about them impacts their belief system. What we believe in our heart, what we speak about, and we act on determines our outcome.

As Proverbs 18:21 (NKJV) warns, *"Death and life are in the power of the tongue,"* the words we speak. We see negative pictures around us, and we have been raised with negative words that can operate like a curse over our lives. We could repeat these words over our children, continuing to live under a curse or we could choose God's Word, His deliverance, and change our family and our legacy to God's picture! We can speak what God says and release His power over our children. Or we can repeat the negative words we heard growing up over our children and bring negative outcomes. This is a trick of the enemy to tempt us to come into agreement with Satan's lies and expectations over our children in thought and word. We must fervently guard the picture of what God says as our promise over our children and life. We can pray and speak the promises of God about our children and their future.

One of my favorite verses that I have continually spoken over my children is Isaiah 54:13-14:

> *All your children shall be taught by the Lord, And great shall be the peace of your children. In righteousness you shall be established; You shall be far from oppression, for you shall not fear; And from terror, for it shall not come near you.*
> — Isaiah 54:13-14 (NKJV)

When we speak God's Word over our children and pray His Words, we are agreeing with what He says about our family. When a situation appears that attempts to get us to believe a wrong picture, we must reject the enemy's picture and continue to speak what God says. The shield of faith will quench every fiery dart from the enemy. That doesn't mean everything goes perfectly all the time, but the outcome of the battle will be God's promise. Of course, we must mix faith and our words with our corresponding actions. Faith without works (action) doesn't produce the promise. Actions could include changing our child's school, deciding to homeschool, changing influences, ridding our lives of certain games, devices, negative input, and refocusing our attention on investing in the right picture from God's promises. He is faithful to keep His promise. We must be courageous to believe, speak, and act on what God says. We must be courageous to contend for the faith of our kids!

Outside of our home and in the world, we must have a courageous love for our country that incites us to stand up to tyranny, bribery, and corruption, and fight the forces of darkness to restore our Constitutional Republic and the Judeo-Christian principles that favored our nation through a covenant with God in its inception.

> **WE MUST HAVE A COURAGEOUS LOVE FOR GOD AND HIS WORD IF WE ARE TO UPHOLD THE BANNER OF CHRIST AND WAKE UP A WOKE WORLD AND RETURN TO GOD AND HIS WAYS INSTEAD OF DESTRUCTION.**

We must have such courageous love that we will fight for the children of our nation and the world who are the commodities of a system that manipulates their souls to take their bodies, steal their destiny, and destroy their spirit from following the living God.

THEY ARE COMING FOR YOUR CHILDREN
THE FIGHT WE MUST WIN!

We must have a courageous love for God and His Word if we are to uphold the banner of Christ and wake up a woke world and return to God and His ways instead of destruction.

We must have a courageous love that says, "Whatever it takes, I will fight the good fight of faith and lay hold of that for which Christ Jesus laid hold of me!"

For every tyrant God has…

- A David, to take down giants mocking our nation and families.

- A Deborah to be a mother to stand up for our nation, against the evil-doers in our cities and towns.

- An Elijah, with a miraculous deliverance bringing down tyrants and thugs.

- A Josiah to destroy the works of darkness and deliver children from sacrifice.

- An Esther, saving her people from wickedness that seeks God's people to destroy.

- A Samuel to pour out the power of God's anointing oil.

- A Mary who says, "Let it be done to me according to Your Word."

- And a Jesus who sacrifices His life for us all.

Let the little children come and do not forbid them, for such is the Kingdom of God.

Will you join me? Together let's stand, arms linked for our children and grandchildren and pray:

> *Father, We commit to Your cause and Your Kingdom. This is our time to do what You have called each of us to do to engage the battle. We choose to fight the fight of faith. We choose to believe Your promises concerning our nation, our children and our destiny. We ask you to pour out Your Spirit on our sons and daughters, a Great Awakening, an epic raising of the sword of the Lord that would shudder darkness, free God's children and usher in the return of our Lord, Jesus Christ. Your Kingdom is here, and it is within us. We are Yours to command. We choose You first, not governments, not tyrants. We receive the boldness of a lion, and a tenacious faith that will not be denied. The gates of hell will not prevail against Your church! We are Your church.*

> **FOR THE CHILDREN'S SAKE, FOR FREEDOM'S SAKE, WE WILL NOT BE SILENT ANYMORE.**

For the children's sake, for freedom's sake, we will not be silent anymore.

JOIN THE FIGHT!

Enough is enough!

Are you tired of being lied to? What if everything you watch, hear, read, and search for is being filtered, censored, and manipulated to present a false narrative? How would you find the truth?

I have spent countless hours uncovering the web of lies and deceit that has infiltrated everything that we know. **I can clearly say there ARE powers controlling EVERY area of influence in the world!** We must be GUARDIANS OF THE TRUTH , and the only way to do that is to UNITE! From the media to the medical field, there are players in key positions who are trained and empowered to influence and attempt to control your life. So, what can you do when it seems Hell is being unleashed?

You need to **Fight Like Heaven** and kick Hell out!

> Ephesians 6:12 says, "*For we wrestle not against flesh and blood, but against principalities, against powers, against the rulers of the darkness of this world, against spiritual wickedness in high places.*"

YOU have the power to make a difference!

God is calling men and women from all walks of life to take up their spiritual swords and fight the evil that is infiltrating our communities, families, and this nation! You can bring change to your local church and school. **You can take back your family!** You can take a stand for what is right. You have a voice, and it needs to be heard!

Let's stand together!

Join the *Drenda on Guard* movement and stay up to date on current and spiritual events and find out how you can let your voice be known. The fight for what's right is on, and you are called to be a GUARDIAN OF TRUTH! **Join the Fight Club today at DrendasFightClub.com!**

When you join today, you will receive a FREE digital copy of *A Call To Arms: Your Quick Start To Fight Like Heaven*! Not only will this book quickly uncover the systems of control and who is pulling the strings, but it will also equip you to fight like heaven!

You're here because you no longer want to be a bystander, so get in the fight! Sign up now at **DrendasFightClub.com**!

Welcome to the Fight Club!

WE'RE UNSTOPPABLE WHEN WE'RE UNITED!

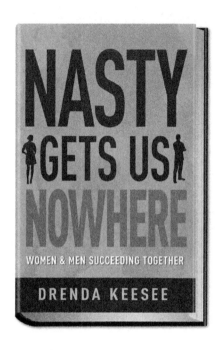

Men and women were never meant to compete with each other. We were designed to complement each other. Women and men both succeed when they're working together.

We *need* each other.

But there aren't many voices in today's culture war of feminism, sexual fluidity, and confused gender roles that want to talk about that.

Enter Drenda Keesee.

Exposed to the feminist message while in high school, Drenda became a strong supporter of the feminist movement, abandoning the idea of marriage and children...until everything changed.

Nasty Gets Us Nowhere: Women and Men Succeeding Together is more than Drenda's story; this groundbreaking book uncovers and confronts the lies that are invading our culture at an accelerated pace and tells the true story that no one wants to talk about—we can't fulfill our God-ordained destiny without working *together*, and we MUST start working together in our marriages and families or we will never be able to impact our nation and our world.

Read real-life stories of women and men succeeding together in business, relationships, and leadership, and gain valuable insight and answers on these topics:

- What happened to the family?
- Men and women - whose fault is it?
- The science behind our differences
- What men *really* want from women and vice versa
- Tools for better communication
- The cheat sheet everyone needs to resolve conflict
- The new "S" word that's critical to relationship success
- Is there *ever* a time you should be nasty?
- And more!

Be a part of the movement toward a future where women and men succeed together for the Kingdom of God! Get your copy of *Nasty Gets Us Nowhere: Women and Men Succeeding Together* by scanning the QR code or visiting Drenda.com.

IT'S TIME TO FIGHT LIKE HEAVEN!

There's no doubt warfare is happening in our culture.

How should you handle warfare?

How can you know the right decisions to make for your family, freedom, country, and faith?

What is your purpose for being here at this time, and what can you do?

Are we really living in the last days?

Get the answers to these urgent questions and much more in Drenda Keesee's powerful, best-selling book, *Fight Like Heaven! A Cultural Guide to Living on Guard.*

Join Drenda as she identifies the Seven Mountains of Influence that the Antichrist spirit has invaded—family, government, church, education, media, arts, and health. She leaves no stone unturned as she uncovers and exposes the enemy's shocking last days' agendas to deceive, enslave, impoverish, and kill God's most prized creation—people—while taking particular aim at destroying our children from the inside out.

Discover how you can stand up and fight the "war on God" as a believer and find peace and provision above this world's chaotic systems.

Get equipped to fight like heaven, kick hell out, and take back these mountains for the Kingdom of God!

Get your copy of *Fight Like Heaven! A Cultural Guide to Living on Guard* today by scanning the QR code, or by going to FightingLikeHeaven.com or Drenda.com.

This is what the LORD says: "Stand at the crossroads and look; ask for the ancient paths, ask where the good way is, and walk in it, and you will find rest for your souls.

—Jeremiah 6:16

Our culture is at a crossroads. We're living in prophetic times, with so many things rapidly changing in our world. We've made so many advancements in our world in the last 50-60 years, but in our pursuits, we've lost many of the things we thought we were gaining.

Now, we're in a pivotal season of decision between throwing the family model out altogether, or fighting to get back to ground zero…to the "vintage" model—to God's design for family and marriage.

Jeremiah 6:16 tells us to look for the ancient paths. But we can't just *look* for the path to doing family God's way; we have to *FIGHT* for it. We must not sit by and watch God's plan for our most important relationships get cast aside.

With Jesus in us, we are the answer. We're here for such a time as this. We need to act now. It's time for us to bravely, boldly, and beautifully rise up and bring our families, our marriages, our homes, and our culture together. To do so, we must learn how to simplify and focus on what really matters, and we must understand how to build on the right foundation, with principles that work.

We must build our lives and our families on timeless truths.

But how?

Find out in *The New Vintage Family: Vintage Values for Your Modern-Day Family*, by Drenda Keesee!

Drenda combines her wit, humorous stories, and the principles that will give you the tools to change your family life and equip you to build a family that can outlast the culture. You'll learn to use the four pillars of family, to effectively communicate, and to fit the pieces of family mentorship, business, and home life together for success, as well as discover how to navigate every stage of parenting well, including parenting grown-up kids.

Are you ready to have a family that shines in the darkness? Order your copy of *The New Vintage Family: Vintage Values for Your Modern-Day Family* by scanning the QR code or by visiting Drenda.com.

Discover the joy of childbirth, God's way!

Are you expecting a new addition to your family or considering starting one? Packed with natural wisdom and supernatural principles for bringing your baby into this world, *The Know How Book on Birth: The Miracle of New Life, From Pregnancy to Delivery* is your go-to resource for answers.

Does labor have to be a painful, traumatic experience?

What can you do now to prepare for becoming a mommy?

What should you really expect when you're expecting and after the baby arrives?

Drenda Keesee and her oldest daughter Amy Freudiger answer these questions and many more in this comprehensive guide written to encourage and empower you with the knowledge and confidence you need for a safe and fulfilling childbirth experience. As a mom of five and someone who has been present at and assisted with hundreds of births, Drenda shares tried-and-true tips, powerful faith-building scriptures, medical insight, miracle stories, age-old wisdom, and encouragement to help coach you through conception, pregnancy, delivery, and postpartum.

Embark on the miraculous journey of birth with wisdom, courage, and peace of mind. *The Know How Book on Birth* is your trusted companion every step of the way.

This book is a must-have resource for expectant parents, midwives, and anyone interested in the miracle of childbirth. Are you ready to embrace the beauty and wonder of bringing new life into the world, armed with the knowledge and confidence to make it an unforgettable experience? Get your copy today by scanning the QR code or visiting Drenda.com

ENDNOTES

1   Robin D. Bullock, https://www.youtube.com/watch?v=TC2Bv_hCVTM&ab_channel=VoiceofRevival, June 20, 2023

2   Ty Gibson, "Frederick's Experiment," *Signs of the Times*, https://signsofthetimes.org.au/2018/08/fredericks-experiment, August 23, 2018

3   Judges 5:6b-7 (NIV)

4   Judges 4:6b-9 (NIV)

5   Judges 4:14 (NIV)

6   Judges 4:16 (NIV)

7   Judges 4:19 (NIV)

8   Judges 4:21, 23-24 (NIV)

9   Judges 5:20-24 (NIV)

10   Jonathan Allen, "New Study Estimates 1.6 Million in U.S. Identify as Transgender," https://www.reuters.com/world/us/new-study-estimates-16-million-us-identify-transgender-2022-06-10/, June 10, 2022

11   Anna Brown, "About 5% of Young Adults in the U.S. Say Their Gender Is Different from Their Sex Assigned at Birth," https://www.pewresearch.org/short-reads/2022/06/07/about-5-of-young-adults-in-the-u-s-say-their-gender-is-different-from-their-sex-assigned-at-birth/, June 7, 2022

12   Ibid.

13   Sean Salai, "Queer Young Adults Report More Emotional, Mental, Physical Problems Than Straight Peers," https://links.truthsocial.com/link/110628238833677029, June 29, 2023

14   Isaiah 53:2 (NIV)

15   Jonathan Richie, "Target Criticized for LGBTQ Kids' Clothes," https://dallasexpress.com/business-markets/target-criticized-for-lgbtq-kids-clothes/, May 13, 2023

16   Lewis Pennock, "Target Selling Bathing Suits with a Section to 'Tuck' Private Parts in New Pride Collection," https://www.dailymail.co.uk/news/article-12103015/Target-selling-bathing-suits-section-tuck-private-parts-new-Pride-collection.html, May 19, 2023

17   Ibid.

18   Nicole Wells, "Target Offers 'Tuck-Friendly' Bathing Suits in Pride Line," https://www.newsmax.com/us/target-pride-lgbtq/2023/05/19/id/1120536/, May 19, 2023

19   Helen Reid, "Target Pride Backlash Exposes 'Rainbow Capitalism' Problem, Designer Says," https://www.reuters.com/business/retail-consumer/target-pride-backlash-exposes-rainbow-capitalism-problem-designer-says-2023-05-31/, May 31, 2023

20   "Dodgers Re-invite Drag Nuns to Pride Night after Cutting Them," https://www.theguardian.com/us-news/2023/may/23/los-angeles-dodgers-queer-drag-nuns, May 23, 2023

21   Rachel Barclay, "Do Video Games Make Kids Saints or Psychopaths (and Why Is It So Hard to Find Out)?" https://www.healthline.com/health-news/video-games-saints-or-psychopaths-082814, October 20, 2018

22   Ibid.

23   Ellie Kaufman, "Fact Check: Are Violent Video Games Connected to Mass Shootings?" https://www.cnn.com/2019/08/05/politics/violent-video-game-shooting-fact-check/index.html, August 6, 2019

24   Ibid.

25   Ibid.

26   Ibid.

27   Ibid.

28   Ibid.

29   J. Clement, "Video Game Industry - Statistics & Facts," Statista, https://www.statista.com/topics/868/video-games/#topicOverview, August 11, 2023

30   Wallace Witkowski, "Video games Are a Bigger Industry Than Movies and North American Sports Combined, Thanks to the Pandemic," https://www.marketwatch.com/story/videogames-are-a-bigger-industry-than-sports-and-movies-combined-thanks-to-the-pandemic-11608654990, January 20, 2021

31   Zara Abrams, "Why Young Brains Are Especially Vulnerable to Social Media," https://www.apa.org/news/apa/2022/social-media-children-teens, August 25, 2022

32   Rachel Brown, "Sex Trafficking of Youth in the United States," https://ballardbrief.byu.edu/issue-briefs/sex-trafficking-of-youth-in-the-united-states, Fall 2021

33   Ibid.

34   Nicole Wells, "Report: Instagram Connects Pedophile Accounts," https://www.newsmax.com/us/instagram-pedophiles-algorithm/2023/06/07/id/1122718/, June 7, 2023

35   Ibid.

36   Angela An, "Children Being Exposed to Pornography Through Parents' Internet Searches," https://www.10tv.com/article/news/crime/crime-tracker/children-being-exposed-pornography-through-parents-internet-searches-2019-jul/530-b462f3c2-2c34-4f74-a686-717fba720fa9, July 19, 2019

37   Ibid.

38   Ibid.

39   Ibid.

40   Leon Wolf, "Doctor Groups Warn of 'Astronomical' Rise of Children Seeking Mental Health Help in Emergency Rooms," https://www.theblaze.com/news/doctor-groups-warn-of-astronomical-rise-of-children-seeking-mental-health-help-in-emergency-rooms, August 19, 2023

41   Ibid.

42   Ibid.

43   Amy Furr, "We're Coming for Your Children': NYC Drag Marchers Chant Ominous Message at Pride Event," https://www.breitbart.com/social-justice/2023/06/25/watch-were-coming-your-children-nyc-drag-marchers-chant-ominous-message-pride-event/, June 25, 2023

44   Samuel A. Nigro, "The Homosexual Manifesto—as to Congress in 1987 and Implemented by the Entropic U. S. Supreme Court in 2015," *Journal of Psychology & Clinical Psychiatry*, No. 1, MedCrave Group, LLC, June 2016, *Crossref*, doi:10.15406/jpcpy.2016.06.00341.

45   Amy Furr, "'We're Coming for Your Children': NYC Drag Marchers Chant Ominous Message at Pride Event," https://www.breitbart.com/social-justice/2023/06/25/watch-were-coming-your-children-nyc-drag-marchers-chant-ominous-message-pride-event/, June 25, 2023

46   Michael Knowles, *Speechless: Controlling Words, Controlling Minds*, (Regenery Publishing, Washington, D.C., 2021), 179-181

47   David Ng, "'RuPaul's Drag Race' Star Jinkx Monsoon Accuses Conservatives of Using Children as 'Shields': 'What the GOP Is Doing Is Objectively Evil,'" https://www.breitbart.com/entertainment/2023/06/16/rupauls-drag-race-star-jinkx-monsoon-accuses-conservatives-of-using-children-as-shields-what-the-gop-is-doing-is-objectively-evil/, June 16, 2023

48   Dale Chamberlain, "Jesus 'Had Two Dads'—Church Recitation of 'Sparkle Creed' Draws Criticism," https://churchleaders.com/news/453937-church-recitation-of-sparkle-creed-draws-criticism.html, June 28, 2023

49   Ibid.

50   2 Thessalonians 2

51   Brooke Mallory, "Study: Screen Time for Toddlers Linked to Developmental Delays," https://www.oann.com/newsroom/study-screen-time-for-toddlers-linked-to-developmental-delays/, August 22, 2023

52   Ibid.

53   "Harari: What Do We Do with the Useless Eaters?," https://www.youtube.com/watch?v=Ex3_brOUdpA.

54   Matthew Benninger, "Sheriff: Johnson City Middle School Principal Tried Having Sex with Minor," https://www.wbng.com/2023/07/10/sheriff-johnson-city-middle-school-principal-tried-having-sex-with-minor/, July 10, 2023

55   Kelly Hessedal, "Push to Hire 10,000 Mental Health Clinicians in California Schools amid the Pandemic," https://www.cbs8.com/article/news/education/hire-10000-mental-health-clinicians-california-schools/509-ace17e03-395f-4e02-bee0-e5b9ee31d549, March 8, 2022

56   "Is Adoption the New Cool for Hollywood's Millionaire Elite?," *Glasgow Times*, https://www.glasgowtimes.co.uk/news/12823286.is-adoption-the-new-cool-for-hollywoods-millionaire-elite/, March 18, 2007.

57   Eric L. Pinckney, "I'm a Drag Queen Who Loves Reading to Kids. Those Protesting Me Are the Real Danger," https://www.usatoday.com/story/opinion/voices/2023/07/03/anti-drag-laws-harm-kids-lgbtq-community/70347476007/, July 3, 2023.

58   Elaine Mallon, "NJ Drag Queen: Banning Drag Queen Shows for Children a 'Disservice to Their Young Minds,'"
https://www.breitbart.com/entertainment/2023/07/03/nj-drag-queen-banning-drag-queen-shows-children-disservice-to-their-young-minds/, July 3, 2023

59   Rikki Schlott, "'Fastest girl in Connecticut' Chelsea Mitchell Suing State after Losing to Trans Athletes," https://nypost.com/2023/05/31/runner-chelsea-mitchell-who-lost-to-trans-athletes-this-is-about-fairness/, May 31, 2023

60   Warner Todd Huston, "Riley Gaines Destroys Dem Witness Who Said Men Can't beat Serena Williams," https://www.breitbart.com/sports/2023/06/21/watch-riley-gaines-destroys-dem-witness-who-said-men-cant-beat-serena-williams/, June 21, 2023

61   Paul Bois, "Riley Gaines Torches Letter 'Emotionally Blackmailing' Harvard Swim Team on Lia Thomas," https://www.breitbart.com/sports/2023/06/21/riley-gaines-torches-letter-emotionally-blackmailing-harvard-swim-team-on-lia-thomas/, June 21, 2023

62   https://www.psychologytoday.com/us/basics/gaslighting

63   Paul Bois, "Riley Gaines Torches Letter 'Emotionally Blackmailing' Harvard Swim Team on Lia Thomas," https://www.breitbart.com/sports/2023/06/21/riley-gaines-torches-letter-emotionally-blackmailing-harvard-swim-team-on-lia-thomas/, June 21, 2023

64   https://twitter.com/Riley_Gaines

65   Paul Bois, "Riley Gaines Torches Letter 'Emotionally Blackmailing' Harvard Swim Team on Lia Thomas," https://www.breitbart.com/sports/2023/06/21/riley-gaines-torches-letter-emotionally-blackmailing-harvard-swim-team-on-lia-thomas/, June 21, 2023

66   Ibid.

67   National Center for Transgender Equality, https://transequality.org/press/releases/ncaa-swimmer-lia-thomas-speaks-out-for-trans-inclusion-in-title-ix, May 8, 2023

68   "Y Chromosome: MedlinePlus Genetics," *MedlinePlus - Health Information from the National Library of Medicine*, https://medlineplus.gov/genetics/chromosome/

69   Oliver Haug, "Over 450 Celebrities Sign onto Letter Condemning TERFs, Supporting Trans Equality," https://www.them.us/story/celebrities-sign-letter-condemning-terfs-and-supporting-trans-equality-laverne-cox-janelle-monae, March 3, 2021

70   Alia E. Dastagir, "Marsha Blackburn Asked Ketanji Brown Jackson to Define 'Woman.' Science Says There's No Simple Answer," https://www.usatoday.com/story/life/health-wellness/2022/03/24/marsha-blackburn-asked-ketanji-jackson-define-woman-science/7152439001/, March 27, 2022

71   For more about men and women succeeding together, see my book *Nasty Gets Us Nowhere: Women and Men Succeeding Together.*

72   Excerpts and story taken from: The Daily Signal Podcast: "Interview/ She Saved Her Daughter from Transgenderism. Mother Erin Friday Explains How," https://shows.acast.com/thedailysignal/episodes/tds013023int, January 30, 2023.

73   AB-957 Family Law: Gender Identity. California Legislative Information, https://leginfo.legislature.ca.gov/faces/billTextClient.xhtml?bill_id=202320240AB957, Accessed August 31, 2023

74   Jamie Joseph, "Minors May Get Sex Changes Without Parental Consent, If California's Teachers Union Has Its Way," *The Epoch Times*, https://www.theepochtimes.com/us/minors-may-get-sex-changes-without-parental-consent-if-californias-teachers-union-has-its-way-3243361, February 19, 2020, updated February 20, 2020

75   Jon Michael Raasch, "California bill That Could Punish Parents Who Don't 'Affirm' Children's Gender Is 'Reckless': Psychotherapist," *Fox News*, https://www.foxnews.com/us/california-bill-punish-parents-affirm-childrens-gender-reckless-psychotherapist, June 13, 2023

76   "Health Insurance FAQ - Gender Health," UCLA Health: Center for High Quality Health Care Services, https://www.uclahealth.org/medical-services/gender-health/patient-resources/health-insurance-faq#, accessed August 27, 2023

77   https://www.cdc.gov/healthyyouth/mental-health/index.htm

78   Daniel Jackson, "Suicide-Related Outcomes Following Gender-Affirming Treatment: A Review," National Library of Medicine, https://www.ncbi.nlm.nih.gov/pmc/articles/PMC10027312, March 20, 2023.

79   "Five Reasons Why Role Play Is Important for Early Years!," Playground Design & Equipment for Schools - Outdoor Learning Environments, https://newbyleisure.com/blog/2020-02-17-five-reasons-why-role-play-is-important-for-early-years#, February 17, 2020.

80   Ryan T. Anderson, Ph.D., "Sex Reassignment Doesn't Work. Here Is the Evidence," The Heritage Foundation, https://www.heritage.org/gender/commentary/sex-reassignment-doesnt-work-here-the-evidence, March 9, 2018, accessed August 27, 2023.

81   "Abuse and Neglect: How Broken Children Become Broken Women," Regain - Relationship Therapy, https://www.regain.us/advice/general/abuse-and-neglect-how-broken-children-become-broken-women/, updated August 15, 2023.

82   "Emotional Intelligence EQ vs. IQ: Why Do Some Smart People Keep Making the Same Dumb Mistakes?," Serenity Online Therapy, http://serenityonlinetherapy.com/iq-eq.htm, Accessed August 27, 2023.

83   https://www.edweek.org/about/

84   Eesha Pendharkar, "The Evolution of the Anti-CRT Movement: A Timeline," https://www.edweek.org/leadership/the-evolution-of-the-anti-crt-movement-a-timeline/2022/12, December 13, 2022

85   Melissa Moschella, Ph.D., "Critical Race Theory, Public Schools, and Parental Rights, The Heritage Foundation, https://www.heritage.org/education/commentary/critical-race-theory-public-schools-and-parental-rights, March 24, 2022

86   Eesha Pendharkar, "The Evolution of the Anti-CRT Movement: A Timeline," https://www.edweek.org/leadership/the-evolution-of-the-anti-crt-movement-a-timeline/2022/12, December 13, 2022

87   Ken Paulson, "Divisive Concepts," https://mtsu.edu/first-amendment/article/2178/divisive-concepts, December 4, 2022

88   "Executive Order 13950 | U.S. Department of Labor." *DOL*, https://www.dol.gov/agencies/ofccp/executive-order-13950#:~:text=On%20January%2020%2C%202021%2C%20as,things%2C%20prohibited%20federal%20contractors%20and

89   Ken Paulson, "Divisive Concepts," https://mtsu.edu/first-amendment/article/2178/divisive-concepts, December 4, 2022

90   "Combating Race and Sex Stereotyping, A Presidential Document by the Executive Office of the President, https://www.federalregister.gov/documents/2020/09/28/2020-21534/combating-race-and-sex-stereotyping, September 28, 2020

91   Eesha Pendharkar, "The Evolution of the Anti-CRT Movement: A Timeline," https://www.edweek.org/leadership/the-evolution-of-the-anti-crt-movement-a-timeline/2022/12, December 13, 2022

92   Ibid.

93   Eesha Pendharkar, "Here's What Florida's 'Don't Say Gay' and Anti-'Woke' Bills Actually Say, Education Week, https://www.edweek.org/policy-politics/heres-what-floridas-dont-say-gay-and-anti-woke-bills-actually-say/2022/03, March 18, 2022

94   Ibid.

95   Eric Lendrum, "Gallup Poll: Over Two-thirds of Americans Oppose Trans-
      gender Participation in Sports," https://amgreatness.com/2023/06/13/
      gallup-poll-over-two-thirds-of-americans-oppose-transgender-participa-
      tion-in-sports/, June 13, 2023

96   Eesah Pendharkar, "Two Okla. Districts Get Downgraded Accreditations
      for Violating State's Anti-CRT Law," Education Week, https://www.
      edweek.org/leadership/two-okla-districts-get-downgraded-accredita-
      tions-for-violating-states-anti-crt-law/2022/08, August 2022

97   Sarah Rankin, "Virginia Finalizes Guidance on Transgender Students, In-
      cluding Rolling Back Some Accommodations," AP News, https://apnews.
      com/article/virginia-transgender-students-schools-youngkin-ba073a1e8a9
      286456a7509688f40115b, July 18, 2023

98   Eesah Pendharkar, "Two Okla. Districts Get Downgraded Accreditations
      for Violating State's Anti-CRT Law," Education Week, https://www.
      edweek.org/leadership/two-okla-districts-get-downgraded-accredita-
      tions-for-violating-states-anti-crt-law/2022/08, August 2022

99   Joshu Klein, "Arizona Launches Hotline to Report CRT, Gender Ide-
      ology Lessons in Schools," Brietbart, https://www.breitbart.com/poli-
      tics/2023/03/13/arizona-launches-hotline-report-crt-gender-ideology-les-
      sons-schools/, March 13, 2023

100   Nick Gilbertson, "Trump Vows to Cut Federal Funding to Schools Push-
      ing CRT, Gender Ideology if Elected," Breitbart, https://www.breitbart.
      com/politics/2023/06/30/trump-vows-to-cut-federal-funding-to-schools-
      pushing-crt-gender-ideology-if-elected/, June , 30, 2023

101   Ibid.

102   Lawrence Wilson, "The Great Dropout: Why 1.4 Million Children
      Left Public Schools in 2020 and Where They Went," The Epoch Times,
      https://www.theepochtimes.com/article/the-great-dropout-why-1-4-mil-
      lion-children-left-public-schools-in-2020-and-where-they-went-4991654,
      January 25, 2023

103   Beth E. Schueler and Luke C. Miller, "Post-Pandemic Onset Public
      School Enrollment and Mobility: Evidence From Virginia," National
      Library of Medicine, PubMed Central (PMC), https://www.ncbi.nlm.nih.
      gov/pmc/articles/PMC10333555/, July 3, 2023

104   "Answers to Your Most Pressing Homeschooling Questions, HSLDA,
      https://hslda.org/post/answers-to-your-most-pressing-homeschool-
      ing-questions, January 10, 2020

105   Ibid.

106   "Harari: What Do We Do with the Useless Eaters?," https://www.youtube.
      com/watch?v=Ex3_brOUdpA

107   Vivian Bricker, "What Should Christians Know about the Dangers of Cultural Marxism?," https://www.christianity.com/wiki/cults-and-other-religions/what-should-christians-know-about-the-dangers-of-cultural-marxism.html, March 17, 2022

108   Lance D. Johnson, "World Economic Forum Believes People Are 'Useless Eaters,' and Views Their 'Brains and Bodies' as Product that Can Be Hacked, Controlled, and Discarded," Collapse News, https://www.collapse.news/2022-05-02-world-economic-forum-believes-people-useless-eaters.html?utm_source=ground.news&utm_medium=referral, May 2, 2022

109   Mike Gonzalez and Katharine Gorka, "How Cultural Marxism Threatens the United States—and How Americans Can Fight It," The Heritage Foundation, https://www.heritage.org/progressivism/report/how-cultural-marxism-threatens-the-united-states-and-how-americans-can-fight, November 14, 2022.

110   Kim Stanley Robinson, "Empty Half the Earth of Its Humans. It's the Only Way to Save the Planet," The Guardian, https://www.theguardian.com/cities/2018/mar/20/save-the-planet-half-earth-kim-stanley-robinson, March 20, 2018

111   Rob Toews, "Artificial Intelligence and the End of Work," Forbes, https://www.forbes.com/sites/robtoews/2021/02/15/artificial-intelligence-and-the-end-of-work/?sh=b3682b856e3b, February 15, 2021

112   "Artificial Intelligence: Can It Replace Human Intelligence?," MIT Centre for Future Skills Excellence, https://mitfutureskills.org/blog/artificial-intelligence-can-it-replace-human-intelligence/, August 23, 2021

113   Brian Gibby, "World Economic Forum Admits That Depopulation Is Their Goal," Intelligible Noise, https://intelligiblenoise.substack.com/p/world-economic-forum-admits-that, August 21, 2022

114   Jon Miller, "Great Reset: Why LGBT+ Inclusion Is the Secret to Cities' Post-Pandemic Success," World Economic Forum, https://www.weforum.org/agenda/2020/06/lgbt-inclusion-cities-post-covid-reset-recovery/, June 3, 2020

115   Bianca Salvetti, "Talking to Your Child about What It Means to Identify as Lesbian, Gay, Bisexual or Transgender (LGBT)," Children's Hospital, Los Angeles, https://www.chla.org/blog/advice-experts/talking-your-child-about-what-it-means-identify-lesbian-gay-bisexual-or, March 28, 2016

116   Norman Cohn, "Apocalypticism Explained: Nazism & Marxism," Frontline, PBS: Public Broadcasting Service, https://www.pbs.org/wgbh/pages/frontline/shows/apocalypse/explanation/marxism.html. Accessed September 1, 2023

117   Kyle Morris and Sam Dorman, "Over 63 Million Abortions Have Occurred in the US Since Roe v. Wade Decision in 1973," Fox News, https://www.foxnews.com/politics/abortions-since-roe-v-wade, May 4, 2022

118 "Child Abuse and Neglect Fatalities 2019: Statistics and Interventions," U.S. Department of Human Services, https://www.childwelfare.gov/pub-pdfs/fatality.pdf, March 2021

119 A case in point is the recent Supreme Court ruling involving a web designer, 303 Creative v. Elenis,600 U.S. ____ (2023), No. 21—476, in which a business owner challenged a Colorado law that prohibits business owners from discriminating against LGBTQ+ customers. In this case, the designer sought to expand her business to offer wedding websites, but not for same-sex couples. In a 6-3 decision, the high court held the First Amendment prohibits Colorado from compelling a website designer to create content that violated her religious freedom or deeply held beliefs.

120 "Child Abuse and Neglect Fatalities 2019: Statistics and Interventions," U.S. Department of Human Services, https://www.childwelfare.gov/pub-pdfs/fatality.pdf, March 2021

121 A case in point is the recent Supreme Court ruling involving a web designer, 303 Creative v. Elenis,600 U. S. _____ (2023), No. 21—476, in which a business owner challenged a Colorado law that prohibits business owners from discriminating against LGBTQ+ customers. In this case the designer sought to expand her business to offer wedding websites, but not for same-sex couples. In a 6-3 decision, the high court held the First Amendment prohibits Colorado from compelling a website designer to create content that violated her religious freedom or deeply held beliefs.

122 316th Wing Historian, "The History of Pride Month," Joint Base Andrews, https://www.jba.af.mil/News/Article-Display/Article/2669499/the-history-of-pride-month/, June 23, 2021

123 https://en.wikipedia.org/wiki/Marina_Abramovic

124 Ibid.

125 Ibid.

126 Ibid.

127 Ibid.

128 Ibid.

129 Ibid.

130 Ben Davis, "Some Believe Marina Abramovic Is the Satanic Ringleader of a Global Political Conspiracy. That's Ludicrous. But Here's What They Get Right," Artnet News, https://news.artnet.com/opinion/marina-abramovic-new-world-order-explainer-1838223, April 20, 2020

131 Ashley Overbeek, "Screen Time: How Nadya Tolokonnikova and UnicornDAO are Warming the Web3 World," https://gagosian.com/quarterly/2022/11/28/essay-screen-time-how-nadya-tolokonnikova-and-unicorn-dao-are-warming-the-web3-world/, November 28, 2022

132 Ibid.

133 Ibid.

134 Rugmini Dinu, "NFT Use Cases, NFT Marketplaces, Legal Issues with NFTs," Vakilsearch, Blog 18, https://vakilsearch.com/blog/nft-use-cases-marketplaces-legal-issues/, August 8, 2023

135 Ibid.

136 Rai Ling, "Anarchism and Cryptocurrency," The Anarchist Library, https://theanarchistlibrary.org/library/rai-ling-anarchism-and-cryptocurrency, October 20, 2022

137 Ashley Overbeek, "Screen Time: How Nadya Tolokonnikova and UnicornDAO are Warming the Web3 World," https://gagosian.com/quarterly/2022/11/28/essay-screen-time-how-nadya-tolokonnikova-and-unicorn-dao-are-warming-the-web3-world/, November 28, 2022

138 Ibid.

139 Ibid.

140 *Gagaosian Quarterly,* https://gagosian.com/quarterly/issues/spring-2023/, page 76, Spring 2023

141 Claire Selvin, "Jeffrey Epstein's Art World Connections: A Guide," https://www.artnews.com/art-news/news/jeffrey-epstein-art-connections-13147/#!, August 27, 2019

142 Ibid.

143 Ibid.

144 Ibid.

145 Emma Parry and Chris White, "Pedo's Lair: First Pictures of Jeffrey Epstein's Ohio Guesthouse Where He Abused Girls & Which Hosted Concerts Starring Ariana Grande," The U.S. Sun, https://www.the-sun.com/news/2299525/jeffrey-epstein-ohio-guesthouse-abused-girls-pictures/, February 10, 2021

146 "What Is the Meaning of the Greek Word 'Charis' in the Bible?," CompellingTruth, https://www.compellingtruth.org/charis-in-the-Bible.html, accessed September 5, 2023

147 Ben Feuerherd and Kenneth Garger, "Jeffrey Epstein Hosted Bill Clinton on Private Island: Court Docs," *New York Post,* https://nypost.com/2020/07/31/jeffrey-epstein-hosted-bill-clinton-on-private-island-court-docs/, July 31, 2020

148 Shawn McCreesh, "Creating Jeffrey Epstein," *New York Magazine,* https://nymag.com/intelligencer/2022/06/how-leslie-wexner-helped-create-jeffrey-epstein.html, June 29, 2022.

149 Dave Ghose, "What the Jeffrey Epstein Scandal Means to Columbus and Retail Magnate Les Wexner," *Columbus Monthly,* https://www.columbusmonthly.com/story/lifestyle/features/2022/10/25/what-jeffrey-epstein-scandal-means-to-columbus-and-les-wexner/69589703007/, October 25, 2022

150 Brynley Louise, "Jeffrey Epstein Island logs: Everyone Who Allegedly Flew on 'Lolita Express,'" Film Daily, https://filmdaily.co/news/epstein-island/, July 14, 2022

151 Lee Brown, "Ex-US Virgin Islands First Lady Helped Get Epstein Victims' Visas: Court Docs," *New York Post*, https://nypost.com/2023/06/16/ex-us-virgin-islands-first-lady-helped-get-epstein-victims-visas-court-docs/, June 16, 2023

152 Ibid.

153 Ibid.

154 Ibid.

155 Emily Flitter and James B. Stewart, "Bill Gates Met with Jeffrey Epstein Many Times, Despite His Past," *The New York Times*, https://www.nytimes.com/2019/10/12/business/jeffrey-epstein-bill-gates.html, July 12, 2022

156 Brittany Bernstein, "Jeffrey Epstein Visited Bill Clinton's White House at Least 17 Times from 1993 to 1995, Visitor Logs Show," National Review, https://www.nationalreview.com/news/jeffrey-epstein-visited-bill-clintons-white-house-at-least-17-times-from-1993-to-1995-visitor-logs-show/, December 3, 2021

157 Jack Crowe, "Epstein's Lawyer Claimed the Alleged Pedophile Helped Devise the Clinton Global Initiative," National Review, https://www.nationalreview.com/news/jeffrey-epstein-lawyer-claimed-alleged-pedo-phile-helped-devise-clinton-global-initiative/, July 8, 2019

158 Ibid.

159 Priscilla DeGregory and Aaron Feis, "Trump Barred Jeffrey Epstein from Mar-a-Lago Over Sex Assault: Court Docs," *New York Post*, https://nypost.com/2019/07/09/trump-barred-jeffrey-epstein-from-mar-a-lago-over-sex-assault-court-docs/, July 9, 2019

160 "Southern District of New York | Ghislaine Maxwell Sentenced to 20 Years in Prison for Conspiring with Jeffrey Epstein to Sexually Abuse Minors," United States Department of Justice, https://www.justice.gov/usao-sdny/pr/ghislaine-maxwell-sentenced-20-years-prison-conspiring-jeffrey-epstein-sexually-abuse, June 28, 2022

161 Joachim Hagopian, "The Latest Epstein Revelations Expose the Crumbling Rothschild Khazarian Mafia Pedo-Empire, Part 1," https://jameshfetzer.org/2023/05/joachim-hagopian-the-latest-epstein-revelations-expose-the-crumbling-rothschild-khazarian-mafia-pedo-empire-part-1/, May 21, 2023

162 Ibid.

163 David Ng, "Exclusive: Inside Trump's 'Sound of Freedom' Screening with Jim Caviezel and Tim Ballard—'A Great Movie' and 'Incredible Inspiration,'" Brietbart, https://www.breitbart.com/entertainment/2023/07/20/exclusive-inside-trumps-sound-of-freedom-screening-with-jim-caviezel-and-tim-ballard-a-great-movie-and-incredible-inspiration/, July 20, 2023

164 Ephesians 5:11 (NIV)

165   Virginia Allen, "Biden Administration Official Unclear on Location of 85,000 Migrant Kids," https://www.dailysignal.com/2023/04/18/biden-administration-official-unable-answer-whereabouts-85000-migrant-children/, April 18, 2023

166   Hannah Blue, "Tim Ballard: Thousands of Children 'Disappearing' into U.S. Interior," Breitbart, https://www.breitbart.com/politics/2023/07/25/exclusive-tim-ballard-thousands-of-unaccompanied-children-disappearing-into-u-s-interior/ July 23, 2023

167   Benjamin VanHoose, "'Sound of Freedom' Has Now Made More Money in U.S. Than Latest 'Indiana Jones' and 'Mission: Impossible,'" *People,* https://people.com/sound-of-freedom-passes-indiana-jones-mission-impossible-domestic-box-office-7644230, August 16, 2023

168   Miles Klee, "'Sound of Freedom': Box Office Triumph for QAnon Believers," https://www.rollingstone.com/tv-movies/tv-, July 7, 2023,

169   Sam Adams, "Sound of Freedom movie: In a crowded theater, I saw what this movie is really all about," https://slate.com/culture/2023/07/sound-of-freedom-movie-jim-caviezel-trafficking-qanon.html, July 10, 2023

170   Ibid.

171   Hannah Blue, "Tim Ballard: Thousands of Children 'Disappearing' into U.S. Interior," https://www.breitbart.com/politics/2023/07/25/exclusive-tim-ballard-thousands-of-unaccompanied-children-disappearing-into-u-s-interior/ July 23, 2023

172   Ibid.

173   Ibid.

174   Ibid.

175   Proverbs 24:11-12a (NIV)

176   "Coronavirus (COVID-19) Vaccinations," Our World in Data, https://ourworldindata.org/covid-vaccinations, accessed 27 Aug. 2023

177   Tiffany Nguyen, "Is a Transgender Woman Still Genetically Male after Surgery?," https://www.thetech.org/ask-a-geneticist/articles/2020/transgender-genetics/, March 18, 2020

178   Ibid.

179   Ibid.

180   https://medlineplus.gov/genetics/condition/androgen-insensitivity-syndrome/#frequency

181   Brandy Schillace, "The Forgotten History of the World's First Trans Clinic," https://www.scientificamerican.com/article/the-forgotten-history-of-the-worlds-first-trans-clinic/, May 10, 2021

182   Ibid.

183   Ibid.

184   Ibid.

185   Ibid.
186   Ibid.
187   Ibid.
188   Ibid.
189   Ibid.
190   Alison Flood, "Richard Dawkins Loses 'Humanist of the Year' Title over Trans Comments," https://www.theguardian.com/books/2021/apr/20/richard-dawkins-loses-humanist-of-the-year-trans-comments, April 20, 2021
191   Dr. R. Albert Mohler, Jr., "The End of Parental Rights? A Chilling Case From Canada," https://albertmohler.com/2019/03/04/end-parental-rights-chilling-case-canada, March 4, 2019
192   Brooke Mallory, "American Medical Association Suggests Taxpayers Fund $300K Uterus Transplants For Trans Women," https://www.oann.com/newsroom/american-medical-association-suggests-taxpayers-fund-300k-uterus-transplants-for-trans-women/, August 7, 2023
193   Timothy F. Murphy, PhD and Kelsey Mumford, "Should Uterus Transplantation for Transwomen and Transmen Be Subsidized?," AMA *Journal of Ethics*, https://journalofethics.ama-assn.org/article/should-uterus-transplantation-transwomen-and-transmen-be-subsidized/2023-06#, June 2023
194   Brooke Mallory, "American Medical Association Suggests Taxpayers Fund $300K Uterus Transplants For Trans Women," OAN, https://www.oann.com/newsroom/american-medical-association-suggests-taxpayers-fund-300k-uterus-transplants-for-trans-women/, August 7, 2023
195   https://thebodyhealthcare.com/
196   https://ourduty.group/education/transition-regret-numbers-and-reasons/
197   Stephen C. Meyer, "How Science Stopped Backing Atheists and Started Pointing Back to God," Newsweek, https://www.newsweek.com/how-science-stopped-backing-atheists-started-pointing-back-god-opinion-1724448#, July 14, 2022
198   Ibid.
199   Ibid.
200   Ibid.
201   Dickens Olewe, "Stella Immanuel - the Doctor Behind Unproven Coronavirus Cure Claim," BBC News," https://www.bbc.com/news/world-africa-53579773, July 29, 2020
202   Nick Robins-Early, et al, "How Quack Doctors and Powerful GOP Operatives Spread Misinformation to Millions," Huff Post, https://www.huffpost.com/entry/how-quack-doctors-and-powerful-gop-operatives-spread-misinformation-to-millions_n_5f208048c5b66859f1f33148, July 28, 2020

203   Charles Horton, M.D., "The Problem with America's Frontline Doctors: Examining the Questionable Claims of an Alternative Medical Organization," World, https://wng.org/roundups/the-problem-with-americas-frontline-doctors-1627736816, July 31, 2021

204   Hannah Grossman, "Feminist medical school professor says trans kids identifying as 'minotaurs' are part of 'gender revolution,'" Fox News, https://www.foxnews.com/media/feminist-medical-school-professor-says-trans-kids-identifying-minotaurs-part-gender-revolution, August 16, 2023

205   Ibid.

206   Ibid.

207   Ibid.

208   *Caring for LGBTQ+ Patients and Families in Pediatric Settings Reference Manual for Staff 2022*, Nationwide Children's Hospital, 2022

209   Ibid.

210   Ibid.

211   John Christenson, "COVID Scientists Downplayed Lab Leak in Fear of China: Panel," *New York Post*, https://nypost.com/2023/07/11/covid-scientists-before-house-panel-downplayed-lab-leak-in-fear-of-china/, June 19, 2023.

212   Ibid.

213   Ibid.

214   Ibid.

215   Ibid.

216   *Caring for LGBTQ+ Patients and Families in Pediatric Settings Reference Manual for Staff 2022*, Nationwide Children's Hospital, 2022

217   Chad Terhune, Robin Respaut, and Michelle Conin, "As Children Line Up at Gender Clinics, Families Confront Many Unknowns, " Reuters Investigates Youth in Transition: Part 1 of a Dearth of Science," https://www.reuters.com/investigates/special-report/usa-transyouth-care/, October 6, 2022

218   Christina Buttons, "BREAKING: Second Lawsuit Filed in US Against Medical Transition of Minors," Reality's Last Stand, https://www.realityslaststand.com/p/breaking-second-lawsuit-filed-in, June 14, 2023

219   Ibid (Buttons)

220   Christina Buttons, "Detransitioner Chloe Cole Announces Official Lawsuit Against Kaiser Permanente for 'Medical Negligence,'" Daily Wire, https://www.dailywire.com/news/detransitioner-chloe-cole-announces-official-lawsuit-against-kaiser-permanente-for-medical-negligence, February 23, 2023

221   Christina Buttons, "BREAKING: Second Lawsuit Filed in US Against Medical Transition of Minors (realityslaststand.com)" https://www.realityslaststand.com/p/breaking-second-lawsuit-filed-in, June 14, 2023

222   "Transgender Health Care Access," McLean Clinic, https://www.topsurgery.ca/blog/transgender-health-care-access#:~:text=Presently%2C%20Canadian%20provinces%20and%20territories,confirming%20procedures%20for%20transgender%20people, accessed August 27, 2023

223   Susan Cornwell, "From 'Hillarycare' Debacle in 1990s, Clinton Emerged More Cautious," Reuters U.S., https://www.reuters.com/article/usa-election-hillarycare/from-hillarycare-debacle-in-1990s-clinton-emerged-more-cautious-idINKCN0YS0X7, June 6, 2016

224   Tim Mullaney, "Work Health Insurance, Obamacare Coverage Spur Sex Change Surgery Boom," CNBC, https://www.cnbc.com/2018/03/27/work-health-insurance-obamacare-coverage-spur-sex-change-surgery-boom.html, March 27, 2018

225   Ann Gorman, "Obamacare Now Pays for Gender Reassignment: The Nation's Health Law Opens the Door for Transgender People to Gain Coverage for Gender Reassignment Surgeries They Previously Could Not Afford, *The Daily Beast*, https://www.thedailybeast.com/obamacare-now-pays-for-gender-reassignment, August 25, 2014, updated July 12, 2017

226   Chad Terhune, Robin Respaut, and Michelle Conlin "As Children Line Up at Gender Clinics, Families Confront Many Unknowns," Reuters, https://www.reuters.com/investigates/special-report/usa-transyouth-care/, October 6, 2022.

227   Ibid.

228   Ibid.

229   Ibid.

230   Ibid.

231   Ronnie Sandroff and Eric Estevez, "Does Insurance Cover Gender-Affirming Care?," https://www.investopedia.com/paying-for-transgender-surgeries-5184794, June 26, 2023

232   Dave Muoio, "Transgender Patients: Calculating the Actual Cost," https://www.managedhealthcareconnect.com/article/transgender-patients-calculating-actual-cost, September 2017

233   Valerie A. Flores and Hugh S. Taylor, "The Effect of Menopausal Hormone Therapies on Breast Cancer: Avoiding the Risk," PubMed Central (PMC), https://www.ncbi.nlm.nih.gov/pmc/articles/PMC4555991/, June 23, 2015

234   FETAL TISSUE: IS IT BEING SOLD IN VIOLATION OF FEDERAL LAW,?" U.S. Government Publishing Office, https://www.govinfo.gov/content/pkg/CHRG-106hhrg63102/html/CHRG-106hhrg63102.htm, accessed August 27, 2023

235   "Fentanyl Flow to the United States." *DEA Intelligence Report*, https://www.dea.gov/sites/default/files/2020-03/DEA_GOV_DIR-008-20%20Fentanyl%20Flow%20in%20the%20United%20States_0.pdf, Jan. 2020

236   Marina Caparini, "Transnational organized crime: A threat to global public goods," Stockholm International Research Institute, https://www.sipri.org/commentary/topical-backgrounder/2022/transnational-organized-crime-threat-global-public-goods#:~:text=Transnational%20organized%20crime%20occurs%20when,are%20often%20used%20for%20others September 2, 2022

237   United Nations Office on Drugs and Crime, "UNODC Organized Crime," https://www.unodc.org/unodc/en/organized-crime/intro.html

238   Britannica, The Editors of Encyclopaedia. "oligarchy." *Encyclopedia Britannica*, https://www.britannica.com/topic/oligarchy, June 22, 2023

239   James B. Stewart, *Deep State, Trump, the FBI and the Rule of Law* (2019)

240   Ebony Bowden, "'Oh s--t': The moment the FBI found Clinton emails on Weiner's laptop," *New York Post*, https://nypost.com/2019/10/08/oh-s-t-the-moment-fbi-agents-found-hillary-clinton-emails-on-anthony-weiners-laptop/, Oct. 8, 2019

241   "Strzok's 'Weiner Timeline' Shows Gap between Clinton Email Discovery and Search Warrant, Judicial Watch, https://www.judicialwatch.org/judicial-watch-strzoks-weiner-timeline-shows-gap-between-clinton-email-discovery-and-search-warrant/, March 26, 2020

242   Nancy Cordes, "Clinton had emails on server more classified than top secret," Hillary Clinton had emails on server more classified than top secret," CBS News, January 20, 2016

243   Nate Ashworth, "Named and Shamed: The 51 Intel Officials Who Lied About the Hunter Biden Laptop Emails," Election Central, https://www.uspresidentialelectionnews.com/2022/03/named-and-shamed-the-51-intel-officials-who-lied-about-the-hunter-biden-laptop-emails/, March 21, 2022

244   GAI's Bruner: FBI Corruption 'Goes All the Way to the Top'" Breitbart, https://www.breitbart.com/politics/2023/07/18/gais-bruner-fbi-corruption-goes-all-the-way-to-the-top/, July 18, 2023

245   Ibid.

246   John Miltimore, "8 Cases That Show the FBI and CIA Were Out of Control Long Before Russiagate" Foundation for Economic Education, https://fee.org/articles/8-historic-cases-that-show-the-fbi-and-cia-were-out-of-control-long-before-russiagate/, March 25, 2019

247   Ibid.

248   Ibid.

249   James Hill and Aaron Katersky "US Attorney Alex Acosta showed 'poor judgment' when giving Jeffrey Epstein state-based plea deal in 2008: DOJ," ABC News, https://abcnews.go.com/US/us-attorney-alex-acosta-showed-poor-judgment-giving/story?id=74178029, November 12, 2020

250   Addison Aloian, "Where Is Epstein Island? What To Know About Little Saint James," *Women's Health*, https://www.womenshealthmag.com/life/a40603323/jeffrey-epstein-island/, July 13, 2022

251 Neal Baker, "Jeffrey Epstein listed 301 Brit associates including Mick Jagger and Tony Blair in pervert's 'little black book' found by FBI," *The Sun*, https://www.thesun.co.uk/news/9709564/jeffrey-epstein-british-contacts-mick-jagger-tony-blair/, August 13, 2019

252 Malia Zimmerman, "Flight logs show Bill Clinton flew on sex offender's jet much more than previously known," FOX News, https://www.foxnews.com/us/flight-logs-show-bill-clinton-flew-on-sex-offenders-jet-much-more-than-previously-known, May 13, 2016

253 Ibid.

254 Daniel Bates, "New Jeffrey Epstein book 'explains' Clinton-Lewinsky scandal," Daily Mail Online, https://www.dailymail.co.uk/news/article-8362601/Bill-Clinton-confessed-Jeffrey-Epstein-slept-Monica-Lewinsky.html, May 27, 2020

255 Rothschild Foundation, "Spencer House," https://rothschildfoundation.org.uk/spencer-house/

256 "Signs You May Have Climate Anxiety," Cleveland Clinic, https://health.clevelandclinic.org/climate-anxiety/

257 Rodney Howard-Brown and Paul Williams, *Killing The Planet: How The Financial Cartel Doomed Mankind* (2019), page 498.

258 Ibid.

259 Ibid.

260 Ibid.

261 Ibid. pgs. 475-476

262 Ibid. p. 499

263 Ibid. p. 500

264 Steve Friess, Hacking the Vote: It's Easier Than You Think," Alumni Association of the University of Michigan, https://alumni.umich.edu/michigan-alum/hacking-the-vote/, Fall 2018

265 https://www.mcusercontent.com/cc1fad182b6d6f8b1e352e206/files/5b-cd9811-ee15-e7a3-0a00-923a9b327aa7/BlackRock_Letter.pdf

266 Dana Kennedy, "Inside the CEI System Pushing Brands to Endorse Celebs Like Dylan Mulvaney," *New York Post* https://nypost.com/2023/04/07/inside-the-woke-scoring-system-guiding-american-companies/, April 7, 2023

267 "Corporate Equality Index: About the Survey," Human Rights Campaign Foundation, https://www.thehrcfoundation.org/professional-resources/corporate-equality-index-about-the-survey, April 6, 2021

268 "Sexual Behaviour In Children & Young People," KidsHealth NZ, https://www.kidshealth.org.nz/sexual-behaviour-children-young-people

269 "In conversation with Prime Minister Jacinda Ardern," Chathamhouse, https://www.chathamhouse.org/events/all/members-event/conversation-prime-minister-jacinda-ardern, July 1, 2022

270   Edward Felsenthal. "The World Economic Forum's Klaus Schwab on What Lies Ahead," *Time*, https://time.com/6245704/klaus-schwab-interview-davos-2023/, January 17, 2023

271   "Remarks by Vice President Harris on Combatting Climate Change and Building a Clean Energy Economy," The White House, https://www.whitehouse.gov/briefing-room/speeches-remarks/2023/07/14/remarks-by-vice-president-harris-on-combatting-climate-change-and-building-a-clean-energy-economy/, July 14, 2023

272   "Patent Application 060606 Does Not Mention Inserting Microchips Into the Body," Full Fact, https://fullfact.org/online/bill-gates-patent-microchips/, May 28, 2020

273   Tiffany Fourment, "What Is The Conference Of Parties Of The United Nations Framework Convention On Climate Change?" World Meteorological Organization, https://youth.wmo.int/en/content/what-conference-parties-united-nations-framework-convention-climate-change#:~:text=The%20Conference%20of%20Parties%2C%20known%20as%20COP%2C%20is,Convention.%20The%20COP%20has%20met%20annually%20since%201995

274   United Nations Climate Change, "COP28 Presidency | Bringing The World Together," https://www.cop28.com/en/cop28-presidency

275   Remarks by President Trump to the World Economic Forum — The White House (archives.gov)

276   United States Department of State, "The United States Officially Rejoins the Paris Agreement," https://www.state.gov/the-united-states-officially-rejoins-the-paris-agreement/

277   United Nations Sustainable Development, "Climate Action," https://www.un.org/sustainabledevelopment/climate-action/#:~:text=The%20Paris%20Agreement%20was%20adopted%20by%20all%20196,grave%20risks%2C%20to%20strive%20for%201.5%20degrees%20Celsius.

278   Ibid.

279   Sustainable Markets Initiative, "Terra Carta," https://www.sustainable-markets.org/terra-carta/

280   "Green & Just Transition," C40, https://www.c40.org/what-we-do/green-just-transition/

281   Ibid.

282   "Global Covenant of Mayors for Climate and Energy (GCoM)," C40, https://www.c40knowledgehub.org/s/article/Global-Covenant-of-Mayors-for-Climate-and-Energy-GCoM?language=en_US

283   "2023 Sustainable Markets Initiative Terra Carta Accelerator Press Release," https://a.storyblok.com/f/109506/x/a1f8a94069/2023-smi-terra-carta-accelerator-press-release.pdf

284   C40, "15-minute city initiatives explorer," https://www.c40knowledgehub.org/s/article/15-minute-city-initiatives-explorer?language=en_US

285   Janie DuVall, "*END TIME ALERT* 40 Weeks Until Everything Changes...," https://www.youtube.com/watch?v=6kslvS5lLdo&ab_channel=JanieDuVall, August 12, 2023

286   Romans 1:25 (NIV)

287   Courtney Mares, "Pope Francis launches 7-year Laudato si' action plan," Catholic News Agency, "https://www.catholicnewsagency.com/news/247777/pope-francis-launches-7-year-laudato-si-action-plan, May 25, 2021

288   Ibid.

289   Ibid.

290   Janie DuVall, "*END TIME ALERT* 40 Weeks Until Everything Changes...," https://www.youtube.com/watch?v=6kslvS5lLdo&ab_channel=JanieDuVall, August 12, 2023

291   Ibid.

292   Ibid.

293   Ibid.

294   "Religious leaders join UN in praying for peace — 'our most precious goal'," United Nations, https://news.un.org/en/story/2023/04/1135672, April 14, 2023

295   " About the UN," United Nations, https://reform.un.org/content/about-the-un#:~:text=Due%20to%20the%20powers%20vested%20in%20its%20Charter,emergencies%2C%20gender%20equality%2C%20governance%2C%20food%20production%2C%20and%20more

296   Associated Press, "King Charles III Addresses German Parliament, Meets Scholz" *US News & World Report*, https://www.usnews.com/news/entertainment/articles/2023-03-30/king-charles-iii-to-speak-to-german-parliament-meet-scholz#:~:text=%22Together%20we%20must%20be%20vigilant%20against%20threats%20to,security%2C%20prosperity%20and%20well-being%20that%20our%20people%20deserve.%22, March 30, 2023

297   "UN Security Council Members UAE, Malta, Mozambique, and Switzerland Announce Sweeping New Climate, Peace and Security Pledges" UAE Ministry of Foreign Affairs, https://www.mofa.gov.ae/en/mediahub/news/2023/3/22/22-03-2023-uae-un, March 22, 2023

298   Paul Carey, "Cop28 President-designate meets King Charles to discuss climate change solutions," The National News, https://www.thenationalnews.com/climate/cop28/2023/02/17/cop28-president-designate-meets-king-charles-to-discuss-climate-plans/, February 17, 2023

299   Ibid.

300   1 Thessalonians 5:3 (KJV)

301   Terry Eagleton, "Harmony: A New Way of Looking at Our World by HRH The Prince of Wales," *The Guardian*, https://www.theguardian.com/books/2010/nov/06/harmony-prince-charles-review, November 5, 2010

302   The U.S. National Archives and Records Administration, https://www.archives.gov/exhibits/featured-documents/magna-carta

303   "Memorandum of Understanding between the Ministry of Foreign Affairs of Israel and the UK Foreign, Commonwealth & Development Office on the UK-Israel Strategic Partnership," GOV.UK, https://www.gov.uk/government/publications/uk-israel-strategic-partnership-memorandum-of-understanding-2021, November 29, 2021

304   Ibid.

305   "Climate Change 2023: Synthesis Report," UNEP - UN Environment Programme, https://www.unep.org/resources/report/climate-change-2023-synthesis-report

306   "Climate Change 2023 Synthesis Report," IPCC, https://www.ipcc.ch/report/ar6/syr/downloads/report/IPCC_AR6_SYR_LongerReport.pdf

307   Deena Kamel, "World has 'small window' of opportunity for major course correction on climate change," The National, https://www.thenationalnews.com/business/energy/2023/03/29/world-has-small-window-of-opportunity-for-massive-course-correction-on-climate-change/, March 29, 2023

308   "Prince Charles Delivers Remarks to G7 Leaders: CSPAN: June 12, 2021," https://archive.org/details/CSPAN_20210612_063800_Prince_Charles_Delivers_Remarks_to_G7_Leaders

309   Deena Kamel, "World has 'small window' of opportunity for major course correction on climate change," The National, https://www.thenationalnews.com/business/energy/2023/03/29/world-has-small-window-of-opportunity-for-massive-course-correction-on-climate-change/, March 29, 2023

310   "World Bank Launches 2022 Funding Year with New 7 Year GBP Benchmark," The World Bank, https://www.worldbank.org/en/news/press-release/2021/07/08/world-bank-launches-2022-funding-year-with-new-7-year-gbp-benchmark, July 8, 2021

311   Daniel 9:25-27 (NIV) (emphasis added)

312   Revelation 13:1 (NIV) (emphasis added)

313   Daniel 7:25a (KJV)

314   Revelation 13:4 (ESV)

315   2 Thessalonians 2:3 (NIV)

316   Daniel 9:27 (NKJV)

317   Isaiah 28:14-15 (NASB)

318   "Remarks by President Biden at the 2023 Major Economies Forum on Energy and Climate," https://www.whitehouse.gov/briefing-room/speeches-remarks/2023/04/20/remarks-by-president-biden-at-the-2023-major-economies-forum-on-energy-and-climate/

319   Matthew 24:7-9 (NIV)

320   Jude 1:14-15 (NKJV)

321   2 Corinthians 2:14 (NKJV)

322   2 Corinthians 4:17 (NKJV)

323   Matthew 24:3-14 (ESV)

324   Matthew 11:12   (ESV)

325   Isaiah 62:10 12 (ESV)

326   Isaiah 63:1-6 (NIV)

327   Isaiah 63:7 (NIV)

328   Revelation 3:10-11 (ESV)

329   John 14:3 (NIV)

330   Isaiah 29:7b (MEV)

331   Ephesians 5:3 (NIV)

332   Isaiah 28:14-16 (MEV)

333   Jeremiah 23:1-2 (MEV)

334   Jeremiah 23:9-12 (MEV)

335   Jeremiah 23:14 (MEV)

336   "What was the sin of Sodom and Gomorrah?" https://www.gotquestions. org/Sodom-and-Gomorrah.html

337   Ibid.

338   Ezekiel 16:50 (NIV)

339   Ibid.

340   Jude 1:7 (NIV)

341   Jeremiah 23:16-1 (MEV)

342   Jeremiah 23:36 (MEV)

343   Jeremiah 23:38-40 (MEV)

344   Sunil mehrotra, "Detroit was once the richest city in America, what happened and why?" Medium, https://smehro.medium.com/detroit-was-once-the-richest-city-in-america-what-happened-and-why-509d564a190, October 4, 2020

345   Ibid.

346   Ibid.

347   Ephesians 5:11 (NIV)

348   Jeremiah 28:9 (MEV)

349   Jeremiah 28:15-17 (MEV)

350   1 Samuel 2:21 (ESV)

351   1 Samuel 3:1 (NIV)

352   1 Samuel 3:5-6,8 (NIV)

353   1 Samuel 3:21 (NIV)

354   1 Samuel 4:7-9 (NKJV)

355   1 Samuel 7:3-4 (NIV)

356   1 Samuel 2:1 (NIV)

357   The Declaration of Independence, July 4, 1776

358   Ibid.

359   "The Koreas at Night," NASA, https://earthobservatory.nasa.gov/imag-

es/83182/the-koreas-at-night, January 30, 2014

360 Jim SergentVeronica Bravo, "Memorial Day facts: Remembering the 1.3M US soldiers killed at war," *USA Today*, https://www.usatoday.com/in-depth/graphics/2023/05/28/memorial-day-how-many-soldiers-died-fighting/70247875007/, May 28, 2023

361 Christopher Barnard & Kai Weiss, "Don't Give Up on America," *National Affairs*, https://www.nationalaffairs.com/publications/detail/dont-give-up-on-america, Spring 2023

362 Denise-Marie Ordway, "Using the term 'per capita' to describe data: 4 things for journalists to know," The Journalist's Resource, https://journalistsresource.org/economics/per-capita-right-wrong-journalists-tips/, June 16, 2023

363 Samantha Masunaga, "We're No. 8: California near Top of World's Largest Economies," *Los Angeles Times*, Los Angeles Times, 2 July 2015, https://www.latimes.com/business/la-fi-california-world-economy-20150702-story.html.

364 "California," Forbes, https://www.forbes.com/places/ca/?sh=9a0b10e3fefc, December 2019

365 "Ohio Economy," Ohio Ventures, https://www.ohioventure.org/ohio-economy/

366 "Poverty Overview: Development News, Research, Data" World Bank, https://www.worldbank.org/en/topic/poverty/overview, November 30, 2022

367 "America's Cultural Role in the World Today," Access International, https://access-internationalvg2.cappelendamm.no/c951212/artikkel/vis.html?tid=385685

368 Ibid.

369 "Capitalism Definition & Meaning," *Merriam-Webster*, https://www.merriam-webster.com/dictionary/capitalism#:~:text=Capitalism%20refers%20to%20an%20economic,competition%20in%20a%20free%20market

370 Christ Stewart, "Capitalism is worth defending," Deseret News, https://www.deseret.com/opinion/2020/9/28/21456892/chris-stewart-capitalism-isnt-perfect-but-it-is-worth-defending, September 28, 2020

371 "Forecast number of mobile devices worldwide from 2020 to 2025 (in billions)," Statista, https://www.statista.com/statistics/245501/multiple-mobile-device-ownership-worldwide/#:~:text=In%202021%2C%20the%20number%20of,devices%20compared%20to%202020%20levels, March 10, 2023

372 "Do you approve or disapprove of the way Congress is handling its job?" Statista, https://www.statista.com/statistics/207579/public-approval-rating-of-the-us-congress/, August 17, 2023

373 Proverbs 29:4 (NIV)

374   "The National Debt Is Now More than $32 Trillion. What Does That
      Mean?" Peter G. Peterson Foundation, https://www.pgpf.org/infographic/
      the-national-debt-is-now-more-than-32-trillion-what-does-that-mean,
      June 16, 2023

375   "Percent of Babies Born to Unmarried Mothers by State," Centers for
      Disease Control and Prevention, https://www.cdc.gov/nchs/pressroom/
      sosmap/unmarried/unmarried.htm

376   "Key Findings on Marriage and Cohabitation in the U.S.," Pew Research
      Center, https://www.pewresearch.org/social-trends/2019/11/06/mar-
      riage-and-cohabitation-in-the-u-s/, November 6, 2019

377   "About One-Third of U.S. Children Are Living with an Unmarried
      Parent," Pew Research Center, https://www.pewresearch.org/short-
      reads/2018/04/27/about-one-third-of-u-s-children-are-living-with-an-un-
      married-parent/, April 27, 2018

378   Laura Meckler, "Gender Identity Lessons: What Schools Are Teaching
      Students," *The Washington Post*, https://www.washingtonpost.com/edu-
      cation/2022/06/03/schools-gender-identity-transgender-lessons/, June 3,
      2022

379   Deuteronomy 28:1 (NIV)

380   Tony Kumer, "Children's Ministry Statistics (2019): How Do Kids Come
      to Christ?" https://www.ministry-to-children.com, February 17, 2022

381   Proverbs 22:6 (NIV)

382   Psalm 128:1-4 (NIV), *notes added*

383   "Evaluation of Video Game Playing Status in School-Age Children with
      Various Variables," PubMed Central (PMC), https://www.ncbi.nlm.nih.
      gov/pmc/articles/PMC8269944/, January 6, 2021

384   Genesis 18:19 (NASB)

385   1 Timothy 3:4-5 (NIV)

386   "Adolf Hitler: He Alone, Who Owns the Youth, Gains the Future,"
      Quotes, https://www.quotes.net/mquote/1131636

387   Bill Federer, "Hitler: 'Your child belongs to us already'" WND, https://
      www.wnd.com/2015/03/hitler-your-child-belongs-to-us-already/, March
      21, 2015

388   "Indoctrinating Youth," *Holocaust Encyclopedia*, United States Holocaust
      Memorial Museum, Washington, DC, https://encyclopedia.ushmm.org/
      content/en/article/indoctrinating-youth.

389   Krista Conrad, "The Story Of World War II's Nazi Youth Indoctrination
      Camps," WorldAtlas, https://www.worldatlas.com/articles/the-story-of-
      world-war-ii-s-nazi-youth-indoctrination-camps.html, August 17, 2020

390   "Book Burning," *Holocaust Encyclopedia*, United States Holocaust Me-
      morial Museum, https://encyclopedia.ushmm.org/content/en/article/
      book-burning

391   "NAZI Curriculum: Mathematics." Historical Clothing, https://histclo. com/schun/country/ger/era/tr/cur/nedc-math.html

392   Vincent F. Shapanu, "The True Agenda of Common Core Standards," Delmarva Parent Teacher Coalition, https://www.delmarvaptc.org/post/ the-true-agenda-of-common-core-standards, July 19, 2020

393   Joseph R. John, "The Indoctrination of American Students in Socialism," Sonoran News, https://sonorannews.com/2019/10/07/the-indoctrina- tion-of-american-students-in-socialism, / October 7, 2019

394   Aaron O'Neill, "Venezuela - Inflation Rate 2024," Statista, https://www. statista.com/statistics/371895/inflation-rate-in-venezuela/, August 29, 2023

395   Sarah Kinosian, "Extreme poverty in Venezuela rises to 76.6% - study," Reuters, https://www.reuters.com/world/americas/extreme-poverty-vene- zuela-rises-766-study-2021-09-29/, September 29, 2019

396   Tom Lindsay, "Will U.S. Education Remedy A Half-Century Of Neglecting Civics Education?" Forbes, https://www.forbes.com/sites/ tomlindsay/2020/02/21/will-us-education-remedy-a-half-century-of-neg- lecting-civics-education/?sh=55f102075fb9, February 21, 2020

397   Keri D. Ingraham, "Students Exit the K-12 System With an Anti-Amer- ican Worldview," American Center for Transforming Education, https:// www.discovery.org/education/2022/09/28/students-exit-the-k-12-system- with-an-anti-american-worldview/, September 28, 2022

398   Joseph R. John, "The Indoctrination of American Students in Socialism," Sonoran News, https://sonorannews.com/2019/10/07/the-indoctrina- tion-of-american-students-in-socialism, / October 7, 2019

399   Psalms 78:5-8 (NIV)

400   Conwell, Joseph Alfred. Manhood's Morning. Philadelphia : Vir Publish- ing ; Toronto : Wm. Briggs, 1903

401   2 Chronicles 7:14 (NIV)

402   1 Kings 3:17-27 (ESV)

403   1 Kings 3:27 (NLT)

404   Liz Langley, "6 Fierce Animal Moms That Go to Extremes For Their Young," *National Geographic*, https://www.nationalgeographic.com/ani- mals/article/animals-mothers-pandas-spiders-octopus, May 13, 2017

405   Ibid.

406   Ibid.

407   Channing Sargent, "Maternal instinct in the animal kingdom," One Earth, https://www.oneearth.org/maternal-instinct-in-the-animal-king- dom/, September 7, 2022

408   Ibid.

409   Margaret Sanger, *Woman and the New Race*, p. 63. (1920)

410   Olivia B. Waxman, "What Ruth Bader Ginsburg Said About Abortion and Roe v. Wade," *Time*, https://time.com/5354490/ruth-bader-ginsburg-

roe-v-wade/, June 4, 2022

411   Chloe Mayer, "Ruth Bader Ginsburg's Abortion Comments During 1993 Confirmation Go Viral," *Newsweek*, https://www.newsweek.com/ruth-bader-ginsburg-abortion-video-viral-1719429, June 27, 2022

412   Ibid.

413   Paul Simon, "Mother and Child Reunion," Columbia Records (1972).

414   John 14:18-26 (AMP)

415   Romans 3:23 (NIV)

416   Matthew 7:11 (ESV)

417   Matthew 19:14 (NIV)

418   Mark 9:37 (ESV)

419   Psalm 139:13-14 (ESV)

420   Jeremiah 1:5 (ESV)

421   Jeremiah 31:3 (NIV)

422   Proverbs 4:20 - 22 (NIV)

423   Psalm 119:105 (KJV)

424   2 Timothy 3:16 (NLT)

425   I John 1:9 AMP

426   Ephesians 2:8-9 (NIV)

427   Psalm 23:5 (NIV)

428   James 2:17 (ESV)

429   James 2:18 (ESV)

430   Psalm 68:5 (NIV)

431   "FBI warns of online gaming dangers for kids, launches public service campaign," ABC7 New York (abc7ny.com), https://abc7ny.com/online-gaming-dangers-fbi-sexual-predators/10843464/, June 29, 2021

432   2 Samuel 13:1-2 (NIV)

433   2 Samuel 13:5 (NIV)

434   2 Samuel 13:7-15

435   2 Samuel 13:16-19 (NIV)

436   2 Samuel 13:7-21 (NIV)

437   2 Samuel 13:28 (NIV)

438   1 Kings 11:3

439   Matthew 18:9 (NIV)

440   John 15:13 (NIV)

441   1 John 2:16 (NIV)

442   1 Peter 1:16 (NIV)

443   Luke 6:46 (NIV)

444   I John 2:6 (NLT)

445   Ephesians 4:23-24 (NLT)

446   Ben Stein, "Tragic End to Trouble Life," *Newsmax Magazine*, September 2023, pg. 32.

447   Ibid.

448   Ibid.

449   Ibid.

450   Ibid.

451   "Drug Overdose Death Rates," National Institute on Drug Abuse, https://nida.nih.gov/research-topics/trends-statistics/overdose-death-rates, 30 June 2023

452   Ephesians 6:2a-3 (NLT)

453   Drenda Keesee, *The New Vintage Family: A Vintage Look for a Modern-Day Family*, (Free Indeed Publishers, 2015), pp. 32-37

454   Ephesians 5:11 (NIV)

455   Exodus 1:15-22

456   Matthew 2:26-18

457   Psalm 50:15 (ESV)

458   John 8:32 (NKJV)

459   Mark 1:26 (NIV)

460   Psalm 91:1 (NKJV)

461   Psalm 91:2 (NIV)

462   John 4:34 (NIV)

463   Mark 16:17 (NIV)

464   Ephesians 5:18 (AMP)

465   Matthew 8:28-34 (NLT)

466   Ephesians 4:16 (NIV)

467   Luke 11:24-26 (NIV) (emphasis added)

468   Acts 2:1-4 (NIV)

469   Luke 4:18 (ESV)

470   Mark 16:17 (NKJV)

471   Mark 6:7 (ESV)

472   Among the books we recommend to our deliverance ministers is Derek Prince's *They Shall Expel Demons: What You Need to Know about Demons - Your Invisible Enemies*, Chosen Books (1998).

473   2 Timothy 4:2 (NIV)

474   Acts 19:15-16 (NIV)

475   Derek Prince's *They Shall Expel Demons: What You Need to Know about Demons - Your Invisible Enemies*, Chosen Books (1998)

476   Mark 16:17 (NKJV)

477   Isaiah 61:3 (ESV)

478   Charlie McCarthy, "Disney Stock at 9-Year Low," Newsmax, https://www.newsmax.com/newsfront/walt-disney-company-woke-stock-price/2023/08/28/id/1132366/, August 28, 2023.

479   Jeffrey A. Tucker, "Why is Corporate America destroying itself?" Zero-Hedge, https://www.zerohedge.com/political/why-corporate-america-destroying-itself, June 5, 2023

480   Hank Berrien, "Targets Share Prices Plummet for Longest Streak in Almost 5 Years," Daily Wire, https://www.dailywire.com/news/targets-share-prices-plunge-for-longest-streak-in-almost-5-years, May 31, 2023

ABOUT THE AUTHOR

Drenda Keesee is an international speaker, life coach, prophetic voice and pastor, businesswoman, television host of *Drenda* and the *Drenda on Guard* channel, and best-selling author of several books, including *Fight Like Heaven! A Cultural Guide to Living on Guard, Nasty Gets Us Nowhere, Shark Proof, The New Vintage Family, Know How Book on Birth: The Miracle of New Life Book* and her latest release, *They Are Coming For Your Children: A Fight We Must Win!* Drenda is passionate about families, freedom, and finances and has made it her mission to fight today's wicked agendas against children, including LGBTQ+, sex-trafficking, depopulation, critical race theory and "climate anxiety."

Drenda has started a movement through *Drenda's Fight Club*, where she exposes the sinister plots, deceptive tactics, and spiritual events being used to assault our children, so that we can all take up our spiritual swords and fight the evil that is attacking our communities, families, and nation.

Drenda and her husband of 41 years, Gary Keesee, founded Faith Life Church ("FLC") in 1995 with campuses in New Albany and Powell, Ohio. As the church rapidly grew, they launched Faith Life Now Ministries ("FLN"), which reaches millions of people across the globe through TV shows, radio, worldwide conferences, online platforms, books, and teachings to spread the good news of the Kingdom. These ministries also distribute Bibles, support churches and ministries in multiple nations, give loving care and a safe place to victims of sex trafficking, provide a stable and nurturing environment for expectant mothers in transition homes, facilitate the translation of FLN's books and courses, and much more.

The Happy Life, a mentorship program that includes video teachings, study guides, curriculum, and The Happy Life Social app—a refreshing Kingdom alternative to Facebook, Instagram, and other social media platforms—where women build community through sharing inspirational messages, Scriptures, godly advice, encouraging words, helpful Happy Life resources, and more.

In addition to her graduate studies at Oral Roberts University, Drenda received a Master's Degree in Christian Counseling from Logos University and an honorary Doctorate of Divinity from CICA International University and Seminary.

The Keesees have five accomplished adult children and many grandchildren.

"LET GOD ARISE, LET HIS ENEMIES BE SCATTERED; LET THEM ALSO THAT HATE HIM FLEE BEFORE HIM.

AS SMOKE IS DRIVEN AWAY, SO DRIVE THEM AWAY: AS WAX MELTETH BEFORE THE FIRE, SO LET THE WICKED PERISH AT THE PRESENCE OF GOD. BUT LET THE RIGHTEOUS BE GLAD; LET THEM EXULT BEFORE GOD: YEA, LET THEM REJOICE WITH GLADNESS."

—Psalm 68:1-3 (ASV)

Printed in Great Britain
by Amazon